THE
EVERYTHING®
BACKYARD FARMING
BOOK

Dear Reader,

I have a confession to make: I've been disappointed with the direction farming has taken in the last century. I've been disappointed by the industrialization of farming, but I've also been disappointed by the "back-to-the-land" movement that sprang up in the 1970s, which was supposed to counter the modern trend.

I grew up on a small farm in the Missouri Ozarks before these opposing forces had become so deeply entrenched. Back then, in that part of the country, farmers didn't buy tractors that cost more than their homes, but they also didn't raise all their animals as pets and depend solely on an outside income to survive. It was about balance. They farmed small acreages successfully with simple ways and small budgets.

That's why I wrote this book. I wanted to recall and promote the sort of farming that was practiced since the discovery of cultivation, until just before the Dust Bowl; a sort of farming that is both humble and rewarding, neither *Progressive Farmer* nor *Mother Earth News*.

I've always enjoyed a rural life, and I had a lot of fun recalling old techniques and ideas and applying them to the modern world. I hope you'll enjoy reading about them as much as I enjoyed writing about them.

Neil Shelton

Welcome to the EVERYTHING® Series!

These handy, accessible books give you all you need to tackle a difficult project, gain a new hobby, comprehend a fascinating topic, prepare for an exam, or even brush up on something you learned back in school but have since forgotten.

You can choose to read an Everything® book from cover to cover or just pick out the information you want from our four useful boxes: e-questions, e-facts, e-alerts, and e-ssentials.

We give you everything you need to know on the subject, but throw in a lot of fun stuff along the way, too.

We now have more than 400 Everything® books in print, spanning such wide-ranging categories as weddings, pregnancy, cooking, music instruction, foreign language, crafts, pets, New Age, and so much more. When you're done reading them all, you can finally say you know Everything®!

QUESTION

Answers to common questions

FACT

Important snippets of information

ALERT

Urgent warnings

ESSENTIAL

Quick handy tips

PUBLISHER Karen Cooper

MANAGING EDITOR, EVERYTHING® SERIES Lisa Laing

COPY CHIEF Casey Ebert

ASSISTANT PRODUCTION EDITOR Alex Guarco

ACQUISITIONS EDITOR Pam Wissman

SENIOR DEVELOPMENT EDITOR Eileen Mullan

EVERYTHING® SERIES COVER DESIGNER Erin Alexander

Visit the entire Everything® series at *www.everything.com*

THE
EVERYTHING®
BACKYARD FARMING BOOK

A guide to self-sufficient living through growing,
harvesting, raising, and preserving your own food

Neil Shelton

Avon, Massachusetts

To my wife, my sister, and my mother.
You have always stood by me.

An Everything® Series Book.
Everything® and everything.com® are registered trademarks of F+W Media, Inc.

Published by Adams Media, a division of F+W Media, Inc.
57 Littlefield Street, Avon, MA 02322 U.S.A.
www.adamsmedia.com

ISBN 10: 1-4405-6601-1
ISBN 13: 978-1-4405-6601-1
eISBN 10: 1-4405-6602-X
eISBN 13: 978-1-4405-6602-8

Printed in the United States of America.

10 9 8 7 6 5 4 3 2 1

This book is available at quantity discounts for bulk purchases.
For information, please call 1-800-289-0963.

Contents

Contents

Acknowledgments

My sincere thanks to Sheri Dixon, Bruce Lewane, Barbara Bamberger-Scott, and Kim Flottum for the knowledge, suggestions, and examples that they shared so freely; to Pam Wissman and Eileen Mullan for leading me, a babe in the woods, through the dark and twisted forest of publishing; and my special nod of appreciation to the memories of J. I. Rodale, Henry Ford, and John Steinbeck for a lifetime of inspiration.

The Top Ten Reasons to
Become a Backyard Farmer

1. To provide a reliable source of healthy and nutritious food

2. To create personal and family income

3. To maintain a connection to the natural world

4. To secure a sustainable lifestyle

5. To protect the environment

6. To protect yourself from financial crisis

7. To protect yourself from hidden allergens in processed foods

8. To teach your children to be less dependent on materialistic goods

9. To adopt a more physically healthy lifestyle

10. To achieve an inner sense of accomplishment and satisfaction

Introduction

At first, the idea of backyard farming may seem like a virtual impossibility. To the twenty-first-century mind, the word "farming" conjures up thoughts of mammoth tractors and endless rows of soybeans, corn, or wheat as far as the eye can see—not the small patch of grass behind the typical home. However, this is a relatively modern concept of farming, quite unlike what the term has meant throughout history.

Traditionally, the goal of the farmer has been to produce an ample supply of food for himself or his family with enough left to trade for the things that he couldn't grow himself, not to fill enormous silos with grain to be sold around the globe. Viewed in this context, the idea of backyard farming is not only possible, it's a traditional, worldwide norm that almost anyone can follow, almost anywhere, and for almost no cost.

There has been a resurgence of backyard farming in modern America in recent years, and like every new trend, a burgeoning crowd of merchants has sprung up to offer the would-be farmer a variety of high-priced products. From complicated plastic compost tumblers to pricey, ready-made chicken coops seemingly designed more for Barbie and Ken than for actual poultry, these manufacturers are trying to convince farmers they need things they don't.

Let there be no mistake: Backyard farming is first and foremost a way to save money, offer a safe, chemical-free diet, and boost the family income. You actually can practice genuine farming in a small amount of space and, because it's not just another silly fad, learning to farm will provide you with a basic sense of security about your financial well-being and a greater understanding of the world you live in, as well as countless indelible lessons about nature.

The intended purpose of this book is to help you become a farmer *right now*, with little or no experience, and with resources that you probably already possess or can easily obtain. Farming, you'll find, is as close to alchemy as you may ever hope to achieve, because the farmer creates the ultimate value of nourishment from the most basic and common elements.

Once you finish this book, you'll feel ready to walk out into your backyard and begin farming right then and there. You may choose to buy a few things along the way, but by and large, you can obtain the basic items you'll need either for free or for next to nothing.

That's not to say that there isn't a good deal of work involved, and you shouldn't get the idea that everything will turn out exactly the way you plan it right from the start. Farming is a discipline that requires constant adjustment as your knowledge increases and conditions change. Some of your crops will fail, while others will astound you with the bounty you can harvest from just a few square feet. Some of your livestock will die or disappoint you, and other animals will seem like pets, even part of the family. Small-scale agriculture requires a healthy amount of physical effort, and while your health and well-being will benefit, you'll pay for these gains, and for your good night's sleep, with sore muscles and sunburned shoulders. However, every farming year will be different.

This book may actually teach you a bit more than you need to know to make a good start, but on the other hand, you'll never learn as much about farming as you'll want to know. You'll see the unkind side of nature and be frustrated by the weather, but you'll beam with joy at the brilliant redness and tangy flavor of your first tomato, and marvel at the wonder of that first egg that appears in the nest-box. In time, you will not only have gained a different definition for the word "farming," but you'll also view the term "prosperity" from a new viewpoint as well.

CHAPTER 1

Backyard-Farming Basics

Farming began about 10,000 years ago, when early man first discovered that crop cultivation was a much more reliable way to feed himself and his family than hunting and gathering. During the early part of the twentieth century as tractors began to replace horses and men, the number of farms, and farmers, began to decline. Today, amid stunning technological advances, many people are seeking a return to the self-sufficiency and independence of the farming lifestyle.

The Origins of Small Farming

Five thousand years before the pyramids were built, some early human noticed that in places where grains had been spilled in the dirt the year before, new shoots of that same grain grew in lush abundance. That discovery, and the subsequent decision to spill some grains on purpose—that is, to plant them—would result in a more bountiful, more independent existence for all of humankind. A millennium or so later, man began to domesticate farm animals, leading to a lifestyle that permitted him to stay and prosper in one place instead of following a nomadic lifestyle that relied more on luck and strength than planning and forethought.

Thus began civilization as these first small farmers enjoyed a greater bounty of crops and sources of protein that they didn't have to fight for. Farmers could not only provide food for themselves and their families, but they could provide an excess that could be traded to neighbors for other goods.

FACT

It is believed that the first farmer was probably a woman, because women were the primary gatherers in ancient hunting-and-gathering societies, and were therefore more attentive to, and familiar with, the growing habits of plants. The first cultivated crops were probably figs.

Modern-Day Farmers

Today, 50 percent of all food is produced on the largest 2 percent of all farms. These "factory" farms have less in common with the farms of your grandparents or great-grandparents than those small independent operations had with the Stone Age cultivators. Many jokes are made about modern children who think that milk comes from a convenience store and dinner comes from a drive-up window, but in fact, the modern food supply is becoming less and less distinguishable from factory-made products every day.

At the same time, the number of farms worldwide continues to shrink as traditional farmers are replaced by giant corporations following the agribusiness mantra from the post–WWII era: "Get big or get out." In a world of large corporations, it seems that if you're not willing or able to go into six- or seven-figure debt for equipment, seed, and chemicals, there's no room in agribusiness for you.

Small and Sensible

You might be wondering, if more small farmers are quitting every day, how you could possibly expect to succeed as a modern-day farmer, especially if you don't have hundreds of acres. The answer is to replace the "get big or get out" attitude with the "small and sensible" philosophy of small farmers from our past and from around the world.

Your ancestors would probably be astounded by the excessive waste of land and resources found in a modern suburban subdivision in America. Virtually all of the outdoor area not taken up by pavement, swimming pools, or patios is covered with a monoculture of grass, which the owners then spend their free time mowing. A visitor from another time would have to wonder: Why spend so much effort to cultivate something that is just chopped down?

A Look Back

In earlier eras, private plots of real estate were used much more efficiently, much as they are in other parts of the world today. Farm sizes were much smaller because they were worked by hand and with draft animals. Food production was much more local because today's vast systems of transportation did not exist. Most Americans in those days were farmers, because farming was the only practical way they could obtain food to survive.

Even though early American farms were usually a great deal larger than your current backyard, much of the land was kept in woodlot, pasture, or simply unused, while the typical family's garden and barn-lot would have fit into a space not much larger than today's suburban backyard. In short, if your great-grandfather was farming the 160 acres that the U.S. Government gave him under the Homestead Act, he was still probably producing 95 percent of his food on less than an acre of his land. In other words, he was probably producing nearly everything his family required on about as much land as you may have at your disposal now. So chances are, all the modern tools and conveniences you have at your disposal won't amount to such a handicap that you couldn't produce nearly everything your family needs on the land you have now.

Small Farming Today

In Eastern Europe and Asia today, private ownership of land is a rarity, and those citizens who are lucky enough to occupy a single home on a small plot of land use every square meter to plant vegetables, fruits, nuts, and berries. A good many of them also maintain livestock in these close quarters. Apartment dwellers in cities can apply for small plots of land, or "dachas," in the countryside that they can farm on weekends.

In several very real ways, these little plots, and the smaller American farms of yesterday, are the true successors of the first farms, as opposed to the thousand-acre monocultures of today. The caretakers of these small cornucopias were, and are, more properly farmers working with the land than are our modern-day agribusiness people, who spend more time working with chemicals, wrenches, and computers than tilling the soil, tending a crop, or minding livestock.

QUESTION

How much can I expect to produce in my backyard?
That depends on a great many things of course, but Jules Dervaes, the driving force behind UrbanHomestead.org, claims to produce up to 6,000 pounds of food per year on a tenth of an acre. Besides maintaining an extensive garden, he raises chickens, ducks, rabbits, goats, fish, and bees in urban Pasadena.

The Farmer's Mentality: Sensible Frugality

The essence of becoming a farmer involves a particular philosophy of conservation. As most anyone who grew up on a traditional farm will tell you, farmers of the past were a frugal, fiscally conservative bunch who hated to part with any dollar, dime, or penny they didn't have to. Keep in mind that all your Stone Age ancestors needed to go from being hunter-gatherers to farmers was a small patch of dirt, some seeds, and perhaps a sharp stick to work the ground. In a very real sense, you don't need much more than that to go from being completely dependent on the modern system to becoming someone who can create much of what you need from nearly nothing.

Just because someone has lots of land and mammoth machinery at her disposal doesn't mean she will be a farming success. The equally mammoth loans required to buy and maintain these things are a constant threat to the farmer's very existence.

You Don't Need Much to Get Started

No matter the size of the farm, successful farming is dependent on the careful conservation of resources. As a backyard farmer, you don't need to compete with agribusiness, so you don't need fantastically expensive equipment or thousands of acres of land. What you need is mostly what you have already: your plot of ground, your free time, and a few very common tools. Unlike the modern big farmer, you don't have to compete in the world-commodities markets. Not only will you not need a $100,000 tractor, you also won't need a lot of the new gadgets and inventions you see advertised in gardening and farming magazines, most of which do a poorer job than the tools that they are supposed to replace.

Your most important market is first, your own household, and second, your own neighborhood, so all you need to do to succeed is create higher-quality food for less money than you're paying at the supermarket. Thanks to today's prices, that's not at all hard to do. Keep in mind that Stone Age people fed themselves and their families without ever stepping foot inside a Walmart or Safeway.

Buy It Used

It's also good to remember that traditional farmers not only didn't buy anything they didn't have to, but when they did need to buy something, they tried to find it used first. A new long-handled shovel costs anywhere from seven to twelve dollars. However, it's not hard to find a perfectly serviceable, used shovel for a dollar or less, perhaps even free, if someone who likes you is cleaning out his or her garage.

Agribusiness uses seeds that are genetically modified to tolerate chemical herbicides, and as a result use 25 percent more herbicide than when they use regular seed. Now this excessive use has resulted in the evolution of herbicide-resistant "superweeds" that can't be killed by the same means, necessitating the use of more dangerous chemicals.

Where Is Your Money Going?

As a consumer, most of the money you currently spend on groceries goes toward things you don't actually need. The price of food from the grocery store includes a small amount for the actual food, and the rest goes toward shipping, packaging, advertising, floor space, store overhead, employee wages, and whatever else it takes to get you to spend money in their store. By contrast, the first garden you create can reward you with more food than you can eat—that is, enough to store or save—and your only costs will be seed, a tool or two, soil amendments, and perhaps a little water, if you have to pay for that. In subsequent years, you can save your own seed, keep last year's tools, make your own compost, and . . . well, maybe you'll still be paying for water if you're still living in a city, although water does fall from the sky, even in incorporated neighborhoods. Needless to say, a tomato that may fetch five dollars per pound at Whole Foods Market can cost you nearly nothing to produce for yourself.

Plants respond best to rainwater. If you have to pay for water, catching as much rain as possible will benefit you, both in enhanced plant health and in actual dollars saved. If your house has gutters, you already have most of your collection system in place.

Boost Your Ready Cash

Of course you can't expect to save 100 percent of your food budget by growing all your own groceries, or if you do, you'll almost certainly be going without some of the things in your diet that you've become accustomed to, like coffee or bananas. While that's true, you shouldn't forget that "doing without" is precisely what farmers did before the Industrial Revolution, when all humankind lived on a considerably more monotonous diet.

Now, perhaps you're thinking that it wouldn't be all that difficult to give up coffee and bananas, and that's great, but your goal should be to enhance your life, not to be constantly searching for more things that you'd like to have but have decided you can live without.

So if you can't grow your own coffee, then you should search for things to grow that you can trade for coffee. If you can't grow bananas in your neighborhood, you need to grow enough of the things you can so as to develop your own balance of trade. Just as people centuries ago had fewer buying choices than you do, they also had fewer sales opportunities or ways to bring income to their farms. Today, there are more cultivars to choose from and more ways to monetize your backyard crops. Depending on how varied your diet needs to be, you should be able to easily cut your food costs by a significant amount, even in your first year.

FACT

In 2011, it was found that of every American dollar spent on food, over 80 percent goes to marketing and only 19.2 percent goes to the commercial farmer. Because of this ever-expanding marketing cost, it becomes increasingly easier for the self-marketing small farmer to be very price-competitive with the corporate food-service industries.

While you can count on the fact that some of your crops may fail, you can also expect others to produce far more than you can use before they spoil. After you've canned, frozen, dried, or otherwise stored all you have, there may still be enough left over to give, sell, or trade to the neighbors. This is especially true in farming communities where it's easy to trade fresh vegetables for eggs or meat, but lots of city dwellers will also happily trade you services or products from their work in return for clean, fresh, organic food.

Moreover, it's rare for a city or town of any size these days to not have a robust farmers' market providing local growers with a ready outlet for their cash crops. Food, after all, is one of the most fundamental needs of mankind, and there is always a ready market for good-quality produce. At farmers' markets and flea markets, you'll not only have an opportunity to sell your goods, but you'll meet new buyers, many of whom may become your regular customers. You'll also meet other producers who'll show you new ways to farm and new ways to make money, such as subscription farming, food co-ops, and selling directly to supply restaurants and other small businesses.

ESSENTIAL

The U.S. Department of Agriculture publishes an annual National Directory of Farmers Markets operating in the United States, which it distributes to consumers. Increasing in size every year since its inception in 1994, the directory listed a total of 7,864 markets in its 2012 edition.

As you become more prolific at backyard farming, you'll find that some of the things you grow are consistently more bountiful than others, and after a while, you may decide that you have a particular knack for producing cucumbers, or strawberries, or eggs. You'll also learn how to extend your growing period, and compact your growing area. You'll be amazed to realize just how much valuable food you can squeeze out of even a very small space.

For example, a four-by-eight-foot patch of ground can easily produce 500 to 600 large cucumbers, and a quarter-acre lot has room for 340 such four-by-eight beds (exclusive of the home). That's not to say that you would want to grow a quarter-acre full of 204,000 cucumbers, but when you see them selling for fifty cents to a dollar apiece, it may give you a few ideas.

It isn't at all unreasonable to think that you can produce a number of valuable cash crops that can be sold to local markets, even if you don't have a large tract of land. Many backyard farmers extend their growing year and the number of items they can sell by adding a greenhouse to their backyard. Once you have one of these, you're ready to produce not just berries, fruits, and vegetables, but other items like bedding plants for an early spring market and hanging flower baskets for later in the year (both of these items will produce more cash for less space per dollar than even those pricey cucumbers).

Save on Health Care, and Save Your Health

Maybe you've noticed how often you see headlines about recalls of food products—even things as simple as lettuce or tomatoes. Actually, it's all quite understandable. Take that head of lettuce sitting innocently on your grocer's shelf, and think about how many people have handled that one lettuce head by the time you chop it into your salad bowl. Ask yourself what you know about the fertilizers and pesticides that have been used to grow it, and the answer, in all likelihood, is nothing. How about the plastic wrapper it comes in? Does that have any manufacturing residue or infectious microbes oozing around on it? In most cases, you don't know any more about that head of lettuce than what color it is, and even that may be distorted by lighting. In fact, you don't know any more than this about most of the raw food you buy at the supermarket. Like everyone else, you're making the assumption that a group of faceless multinational corporations have your best interests in mind and would never let anything bad happen to your family's dinner. That's just the tip of the iceberg.

Packaged Foods

What about all those new products in colorful boxes with ingredient lists that would require a chemist to interpret? Isn't it possible that in the next year you may hear a news story explaining how some food product your family is eating regularly has seriously negative consequences for your health?

ALERT

According to the U.S. Centers for Disease Control and Prevention (CDC), 48,000,000 people, or 1 in 6 Americans, are stricken by food-borne illness each year. Of these, 3,000 will die. Incidences of the most common infection, salmonella, are actually on the increase despite massive efforts to eradicate it.

Food allergies are at an all-time high, food safety is a bigger concern than ever before, and it's no wonder: Today, people are more distanced from their food sources than at any time in history. Food now comes from all over the world in massive shipments that can spread disease and contamination in a matter of days. There's an old idiom that says you wouldn't want to eat sausage if you watched it being made, but these days you have to wonder if you'd eat *anything* if you could see exactly where it came from and what it went through.

You're in Control

As a modern consumer, you don't have much control over the food you put in your family's mouths, but as a backyard farmer, you can have 100 percent control. You don't need to worry about what pesticides are used on your food if you don't use any (which in all likelihood, you will not when you learn alternative methods), or whether you are consuming something you're allergic to if you know what ingredients are in everything you eat. Commercial meat animals are, by necessity, pumped full of antibiotics as pre-emptive protection against disease. If you've ever seen a commercial feedlot stretching across hundreds of acres packed with cattle shoulder to shoulder, or rows of commercial poultry houses filled wall-to-wall with chickens or turkeys, you can imagine the problem that this can represent. In your back-yard, however, you only need to concern yourself with the *actual* diseases, if any, contracted by a few individuals, so you don't have to medicate healthy animals unless they become sick. Not only are fresh, home-grown produce, meat, and eggs healthier and more nutritious than factory-farmed versions of the same products, but spending your afternoon in the garden is better for your mental and physical health than spending the same time in traffic or walking around a crowded mall or supermarket.

The Luxuries of Simple Living

Besides saving you lots of money (and providing you with an avenue to make even more), backyard farming can bring some new luxuries to your life. Obviously, the more money you save on food, the more you have to spend on other things. According to the Bureau of Labor Statistics, the average

American family spends 12.74 percent of their income, about $6,129, every year on food. So if yours is an average family and you saved just 50 percent of your food bill (remembering that in earlier generations, farmers grew *100 percent* of their food) then you'd have about $3,000 more to spend each year.

In addition to that, small farmers have a natural buffer against the bubbles and busts of the national and world economy. You may get laid off at work, but your family is less likely to have to apply for assistance, or go hungry, if you have a sustaining backyard farm and a full larder at your disposal. In fact, you might consider your ability to provide for yourself as the insurance you need to break loose from outside employment altogether, and enjoy the luxury of working for yourself at home, and *that* might allow you the luxury of living somewhere more rural and less expensive where you can have a cleaner, simpler lifestyle.

ALERT

The Internal Revenue Service will expect you to report any small-farm income on your tax return. In order to take deductions for your small-farm expenses, you'll need to show that you have a profit motive. An accepted way of doing this (and there are others) is to show a profit two years out of five.

These days you'll see people spending tens of thousands of dollars on solar panels and wind generators so as to save on a $300 monthly electricity bill, mostly because it makes them feel more independent. That's a noble goal of course, but not nearly as beneficial as the freedom you can develop for yourself by learning to grow both food and income from the soil.

A farming lifestyle offers rewards, both emotional and financial, which don't require any more expense or sacrifice than do many of your neighbors' hobbies.

CHAPTER 2

How to Become a Backyard Farmer

You can become a backyard farmer immediately. You don't have to pay any dues, buy any licenses, pass any tests, or impress anyone but yourself with your ability and intent. What you do have to do is decide that you want to produce as much of your own food as you can, make the most of the resources you have at hand, and create a mutually beneficial relationship with nature.

Farming Is Not a Hobby, It's a Lifestyle

In today's world, you can buy just about anything you want. In fact, if you wanted to, you could completely skip the whole message of this book and hire someone to farm your backyard for you (such companies actually do exist). This highlights the disturbing trend that says every endeavor requires someone else to tell you how to do it properly. You can't exercise without a trainer. You can't invest without a broker. Everything seems to require a guru, a purchase, and perhaps a subscription, but that's not what farming is about. While that sort of "professionals only" attitude is probably very good for the national employment rate, it deprives people of the experience of learning the basics for themselves, which is the only way they'll ever come to genuinely appreciate how much they've accomplished. You can't learn something from the ground up if someone else does all the groundwork.

FACT

During World War II, amid food rationing and labor and transportation shortages, the government asked citizens to do their part by planting "victory gardens" in their backyards, empty lots, and rooftops. Nearly 20 million Americans responded, and eventually came to produce 40 percent of the country's food supply.

The traditional farmer wants to do as much for himself as possible, and to create a relationship with the earth that can make a difference in his life and that of his family. The farmer and the farm family take every opportunity they come across to increase their independence and to learn for themselves rather than just take instruction.

Backyard farming is a very creative endeavor. Just as an artist is not content to simply enjoy the works of others or to paint by numbers, a farmer is not satisfied to buy something that she can create herself from the earth. This is a necessary frugality, but it's a lot more than that. Providing for oneself is more than just a way to save money; it's a route to self-expression and self-esteem.

The backyard farmer's reward is to enjoy better food and a better life, while using less money and preserving other resources. There is a use for everything, and anything without another use becomes part of the compost pile. The traditional farmer is a beneficial part of nature.

FACT

According to *Time* magazine, the number of farms in America has been shrinking for the past seventy years, but the number of small farms (under thirty acres) is growing at the rate of 2 percent per year, now accounting for half of all farms in the country.

Don't Quit Your Job

In times past, it was not always possible for the farmer and his spouse to exist solely on farm income. In this regard, things haven't really changed all that much, as there will probably always be more things needed—or perhaps *desired* would be a more accurate term—than can be produced from the land. That's how the decline of farming began in the first place. People moved into the cities to make more money. However, not all of them left the rural areas. A few found work locally, or found other ways to make money at home other than, or in addition to, growing crops or raising animals.

A hundred years ago, a farm wife might also have been the township tax collector, or she might have worked as a seamstress in her spare time. The farmer might have followed some seasonal employment in the winter months, or maintained a part-time job in town, or offered himself as a hired hand to other farmers to help make ends meet at home.

Becoming More Independent

Today, it's common for all adult members of a household to work outside the home. As a backyard farmer, you probably won't be able to completely sustain yourself with your backyard endeavors, certainly not in the beginning, but you can make yourself much less dependent on any outside source of income. Once you've established that you can produce all or most of the food you need to get by, then you're free to try to take greater control of your life by finding other ways to make money at home, besides farming, that can enhance your income and your family's independence.

This may not particularly appeal to you. The majority of people opt for the security of a "steady" job, and it's certainly easy to see their point, because a large established company is more likely to stay in business than a small start-up enterprise run by an individual—isn't it?

Buffer Yourself Against Hard Times

No job is 100 percent secure. The question is not one of whether a large company survives hard times better than a small one; the question is whether *your job* with a large company will survive. If you were going to lose your job next month, you would most likely be one of the last people in your organization to know about it.

At any rate, there is no disputing that home income and home food production can buffer you against unemployment and hard times. Even if you never attempt to earn an additional cent from your backyard-farming activities, having an abundant supply of high-quality food that costs you next to nothing is always an undeniable benefit. Whatever other troubles you may encounter, your family will always have plenty to eat.

ESSENTIAL

The U.S. Department of Labor reports that there are now more self-employed people, over 14 million, than at any time in history. Home-workers cite increased freedom and independence, closeness to family responsibilities, and a poor job market as motivations to strike out on their own.

Change Your Shopping Habits

Successful farmers tend to be rather shrewd individuals. Not only are they expected to be scientists, inventors, horticulturists, veterinarians, and meteorologists, but they are also some of the most astute and demanding purchasing agents, because theirs is a culture where the waste of any resource is strictly forbidden, especially the waste of money. Taking every opportunity to make the most efficient use of your money tends to make anything you do go more smoothly.

Being a Shopper versus a Buyer

During the last millennium, mankind has created a remarkable collection of devices and novelties designed to cure problems both real and imagined, as well as novel solutions for troubles you never even knew you had. Since the advent of twenty-four-hour television, this fact has been amplified. Now you have an endless flow of perfectly worthless gadgets designed to fill voids that don't really exist. Many American homes have garages, closets, and kitchen drawers filled to capacity with these contraptions. Imagine if you could sell them all back for what you paid for them—what a haul that would be!

Buyers

Most people are able to learn how to avoid buying useless products during childhood, at least to some degree, but many still fall victim to the wily marketers and advertisers. Why will so many people pay more money for an identical product in a colorful and familiar wrapper than in a generic one? If you go to the store and fill your cart with whatever's shiny and brightly packaged, you are simply a buyer. Don't worry, though. It's never too late to change!

Shoppers

Successful farmers are shoppers. When they buy something, they are informed and cautious, and their prime interest is in the value they receive for the dollars they spend. In order for your backyard farm to be successful, you need to emulate this attitude and shop hard for value. That means knowing the difference between a low price and a good deal, or between high quality and wily promotion.

Buying in Bulk

Perhaps you've seen some modern marketing and packaging attempts, such as individual potatoes wrapped in cellophane, or eggs scrambled and repackaged in plastic, that are priced at ten times what their individual components would cost. You can avoid these obvious extravagances as well as many more subtle ones by purchasing as much as you can in bulk. Whether it's food, feed, or other supplies, virtually everything is less expensive when you buy more of it.

You may find that some foods in bulk will be so cheap that you'll choose not to grow your own, but instead devote the space they require to more expensive produce. This is a legitimate argument, albeit one that is becoming less and less appropriate as the price of everything skyrockets. Growing your own can be rewarding and an opportunity to try out odd new varieties, but these may require more labor and garden space than you'd like to devote to them. You might decide that dried beans are an example of something being more trouble than it's worth, given the job of husking the dried beans and how long they need to occupy space in the garden.

So you decide you're going to raise kiwi fruits in place of the beans and you'll take your chances in the dried-bean market, buying what you want for the lowest prices you can find. Typically, a can of beans costs approximately five times what the same amount of dried beans would cost by the pound, and if you find a source to buy larger quantities, the price drops accordingly. Ideally, you pick the best deal you can find on all the beans you can use in a certain amount of time. Storing large quantities of food doesn't have to take up a great deal of space, and after you've used up every nook, cranny, cabinet, closet, or garage-space in your home, there are storage techniques to be discussed later that can utilize some of your outdoor space as well.

Avoiding Processed Foods

One of the strongest arguments in favor of growing your own food or buying it in bulk is that you and your family avoid eating processed food "inventions." For example, potatoes are a starchy food low in fat and high in potassium. They're very nutritious, and rank high among the world's staple foods in terms of having enough nourishment alone to sustain healthy life. There are thousands of very healthful dishes that utilize potatoes, but the vast majority of potatoes grown in America do not go into these healthy dishes—they go into French fries and potato chips, which are considerably less nutritious, loaded with trans-fats and salt, and, depending on the source, preservatives and carcinogens.

ESSENTIAL

Hydrogenation is a chemical process that adds hydrogen to unsaturated oils, converting them into trans-fats, thus increasing their shelf life in processed foods. However, trans-fats tend to increase bad cholesterol in the body and decrease good cholesterol, leading to an increased risk of cardiovascular disease and type 2 diabetes.

Buying in Season

As previously mentioned, it's neither practical nor desirable to try to grow absolutely everything you consume, and since you'll be buying much of what you buy in bulk, it becomes particularly important that you buy items in season in order to get the best quality, the best prices, and the longest-keeping commodities.

Start Saving Your Food

The traditional farmer not only produces food, but he also stockpiles it. Primitive people valued certain foods, not simply because they liked the taste, but because they could be easily kept over the winter until the next growing season. They not only grew foods that could be stored, but also traded for other foods that they could not grow, or had not grown that year. As a backyard farmer, you'll want to do the same, so in addition to space to grow and harvest food, you'll need the means to store your bounty.

Some foods, like root crops, can be stored in protected places outside, others can be dried or canned, and still others will require the modern wonder of refrigeration. Having a deep freezer and an extra refrigerator or two in the garage can be quite handy to the backyard farmer.

Don't forget that nothing keeps forever, so you'll want to keep a record, or some system of rotation, so that you'll know how long you've been storing any given item, and use it before it spoils. Ideally, you'll put away enough to last until the next season's crop is ready to store.

ALERT

Whole grains keep longer than flours, but because they have a greater content of healthy oils, they are more susceptible to damage from heat, air, and moisture. They must be kept in airtight containers in a cool, dry place. If you buy packaged grains, see that the containers are unbroken and note the expiration dates.

Start Food Production Right Now

Daydreaming is a lot of fun, but taking action is more fun, and a great deal more productive. While you obviously can't go out on a December day in New York and plant tomatoes, there are always farm chores to do, and nearly all of them center on your next crop, so as soon as you put this book down, you ought to be able to go out and start farming.

The very first step is to decide what crops and livestock you want to work with. This will change with time and as you gain experience, but it's good to start with a plan in mind.

Your next steps are dependent on the season of the year. Here's what you can do to get started.

WINTER (THE BEST TIME TO BEGIN FARMING)

- Locate the tools you'll need to begin. These are pretty basic. You'll need to work the soil and perhaps do a little basic construction, so get a rake and shovel, garden trowel, hammer, nails, and a saw to start. You'll also need to move materials around, so a wheelbarrow and a couple of 5-gallon buckets will come in handy.
- Scout your neighborhood. Look for sources of soil amendments like sawdust piles, poultry farms, and any place that throws away large quantities of raw materials. All these are well worth cataloging in your mind. If you're an anxious over-achiever, you might even make a map of them.
- Gather tools and materials. Start collecting the things you'll need over the farming year. Auction barns, junkyards, and farm stores are all good sources of tools and equipment.
- Make a calendar of when you should plant each item you intend to grow, and when each item can be expected to ripen. You'll want to start some early plants indoors to get a head start, but be careful you don't start them too soon or they may grow too spindly to plant by the time the last frost has come and gone. The back of the seed package should tell you everything you need to know.
- Winter is a good time to construct housing for poultry or livestock, although it may be too early to drive fence posts into the frozen ground.
- Collect planting containers and building materials for raised beds.

SPRING (WHEN YOUR ENERGY AND ENTHUSIASM ARE HIGHEST)

- Start seeds indoors before the last frost. This is better than buying bedding plants. Plant more than you think you'll need and *never* let them dry out, but don't drown them either. Uniformly moist soil is best. A small heating pad under your plants can improve germination significantly. Peat pellets or mild garden soil make the best mediums; peat pots that you plant along with the seedlings, not so much.
- Prepare your beds and spread soil amendments in planting areas. Boards, ties, blocks, etc. to frame the beds aren't necessary, but they keep things neat, and they can make a handy place to sit while you plant, weed, and harvest.
- Start a compost pile. You may need to rob the family kitchen garbage for the first contributions. If you can find a large supply of a loose material, such as well-rotted sawdust, poultry bedding, or grass clippings, so much the better.
- Build fencing and animal housing. Remember that you not only want to keep your animals in, but snakes, predators, and other critters out.
- Start baby chicks indoors in a cardboard box under a heat lamp. They grow a lot faster than you might imagine, so be sure you'll have a proper hen house soon.
- Begin early planting. Watch the calendar and the weather forecasts, and be prepared to cover your plants during cold snaps.

SUMMER (THE BUSIEST TIME OF YOUR FARMING YEAR)

- Start planting in earnest. By the time summer arrives, you should have most of your plants and seeds planted. If you're just getting started now, make this a priority, and you can still harvest a sizable crop of most plants before the frost.
- Now is the time to create irrigation systems, whether they are complicated automatic layouts or simply a garden hose and sprinkler.
- Summer is a good time to buy and acclimate livestock. If you're buying from an auction, there are fewer diseases going around in summer. Be prepared to learn the weaknesses of your fencing, and when your animals break out, have a way to contain them until you are able

to fix the fence. Remember that a fence isn't just something you build and forget. Fences are subject to constant deterioration from weather, rot, falling trees and limbs, and curious livestock.

- Summer is also the best time to start building your food-storage facilities by collecting canning and freezing equipment, and creating outdoor and indoor dry-storage locations. Consider whether you have room for another refrigerator; they're easier to buy used during this season, when people are moving.

AUTUMN (PLANNING FOR NEXT YEAR)

- Collect mulch and compost materials. (Hint: a lot of good materials are falling from the trees this time of year.) You'll also find a lot of raw materials available as people clean up their lawns for winter.
- Put your storage areas to good use and buy the foods you may grow for yourself next year at your local farmers' markets now.
- Mulch laid down on sod now will result in an area that's much easier to till and break up come spring. If you anticipate putting a bed in a particular corner, covering that area with mulch now will be a good preparation for spring tilling, keeping the soil more moist and loose over the winter.

Advantages of Farming in an Urban Area

It's easy to see some of the problems with farming in an urban area, but there are also a few advantages that you may have over people in more rural locations, and they mostly relate to having more people nearby.

Lots of Organic Materials

Farmers in the country may think that they have lots of sources of organic compounds for composting and mulch, but all told, there are probably more cubic yards of good, free compost and mulch materials available in town where there are so many people throwing away so much stuff.

For example, most cities these days compost the grass clippings, dead leaves, and garden waste that they collect from homeowners. These are then made available to citizens at attractive prices, sometimes already composted, but if that *isn't* going on where you live, ask your neighbors if they'd like you to take away their yard waste for them. You may get a few strange looks, but also lots of leaves, grass clippings, and new friends.

ALERT

Not everything free, loose, and organic makes good mulch. Avoid using sawdust unless it has been very, very thoroughly rotted. Raw sawdust will suck the nitrogen out of your soil, resulting in severe depletion if it mixes with the soil. Rotted sawdust is very dark brown in color.

Grass clippings are loaded with nitrogen and make a reasonable replacement for manure, which may be in shorter supply in the city. Besides being a fertilizer, grass clippings add a great deal to your soil's texture and tilth (condition of the soil).

Cities also have manufacturing companies that may produce sawdust, leather dust, tankage, wool scraps, and the like. Anything that rots fairly quickly and isn't adulterated with chemicals can be put to this use. Cities also tend to attract large farming concerns to their outskirts, such as dairies, stables, meat packing companies, and poultry houses—all good sources of clean organic matter.

Another source of high-nitrogen, which is to say high-potency, compostable materials is your local food pantry. Grocery stores frequently contribute foodstuffs that haven't gone past their expiration dates but will soon to food pantries. On Friday evening, the pantries tend to have excess fruits, especially bananas and strawberries, as well as some vegetables that haven't been given away and will have to be thrown out by the following Monday. They're often happy to find a practical use for them.

Farmers' Markets

Perhaps not surprisingly, farmers' markets in and around populated areas are much more robust and lucrative than those few you find in small towns. Not only can these give you a nearby source of many of the foods you don't grow for yourself, but they're a ready-made market for your excess produce and for other products like hanging baskets or baked goods that you might want to market to make your backyard farm more profitable. As customers for your goods, urban residents are much less likely to be producing their own food than rural folks, and there are so many more of them. They're also more likely to be comparing your prices with what they have to pay at Whole Foods.

FACT

Localharvest.org maintains a database of small organic farms all over America that offer fresh, local food to their community on a subscription basis. That database currently contains over 4,000 entries. If you have a producing farm, you should join this and other free-advertising sites to promote your produce.

Community Supported Agriculture

The CSA, or Community Supported Agriculture movement, was specifically created to bring wholesome fresh foods to urban residents. Foods are sold on a subscription basis where the farmer delivers an agreed-upon order directly to the consumer. You can do this independently, or as a part of a collective. Either way, you have buyers waiting for your produce the minute you pick it, making it much easier to plan ahead and make decisions about what plants to grow. You'll find that working for a subscription, or better yet, for many subscriptions, gives you more direction in your work. It also gives you an idea of what people in your neighborhood most want to buy.

CHAPTER 3

Things You'll Need and Things You Won't Need

When the original hunter-gatherers first developed the technique of planting seeds, it is very likely that they tilled the ground with a sharp stick or a piece of bone. Since then, the tools used for farming have not actually progressed all that much beyond those simple instruments, despite what you see advertised. Today, the basic needs of farming don't really cost a lot of money, at least not if you go about them properly.

Tools versus Gadgets

When choosing the tools or implements you will use in farming, a good rule of thumb is this: if it has a patent number, then Stone Age man probably didn't have one, and if he didn't, then you can probably get by without one as well. That's not to say that all advancements of the last ten millennia were without merit—steel shovels and plows are a nice upgrade from wood, which in turn was an improvement over the shoulder bones of an ox, but even steel tools aren't an absolute necessity.

Since your farming career is just beginning, it's likely that you don't have all the necessary tools that you may need, and you'll need to acquire a few. That in mind, it is strongly recommended that you avoid new redesigns of old tools. If it doesn't look like what you've always considered a rake, a shovel, and an ax to look like, then it is probably inferior to the old standard. There are, of course, a few minor exceptions. For example, some of the ergonomically designed hand tools are easier and more comfortable to use, and fiberglass handles are often superior to wood, even though you have to pay more for them.

Avoid Using Plastic or Steel

It is both a curse and a blessing to live in modern times when so many tools and materials are available to us. In order to ensure that this is more of a blessing than a curse, you need to take a clear look at which new innovations are genuine improvements, and which are simply opportunities for manufacturers to fatten their bottom line by selling you something.

One of the most dramatic ways these innovations have appeared is in the choice of materials used for any given job. For most of history, steel and plastic were completely unknown, but today, they are the most common materials used. There are several good reasons for this from a manufacturer's standpoint, but they don't necessarily translate into good reasons for the small farmer.

Let's start with plastic, the most modern of materials. Plastic definitely has a function in the farming world, particularly because of its resistance to rot. If you need something that won't decompose quickly, then plastic may be the material for your job. It's often a good choice for buckets, tarpaulins, vapor barriers, and other such uses, but you need to remember that its strength is also its weakness; that is, it degrades very, very slowly, and when it does it breaks into flakes that can litter the landscape for years, decades even, after having lost its functional value.

FACT

Traditionally, wooden fence posts have been made from rot-resistant species growing in the vicinity, including Eastern Red Cedar, Osage Orange, Cypress, and Redwood. Some of these, driven directly into the ground without the use of cement footings or wood preservatives, can last a lifetime, even in moist soil.

Steel is about as strong as anything you're likely to encounter on the farm, but it's expensive. It may not be expensive to use in manufactured products: a steel chair may well be less costly than a wooden one; but it's expensive to use in crude situations, such as building fences.

Stone takes this calculation to extremes. As a raw material for fabrication, it can be extremely expensive to cut, smooth, and drill, but as a crude building material, you can have about all you want of it for free.

When money is in short supply, which it always is, it's a good idea to think about how farmers in history managed to cope when they needed to build something. If you do, you'll realize that you don't have to spend a lot of money to accomplish farming goals following the traditional methods.

Assessing Your Farmable Area

The first step in determining what your farm is going to need is to determine what it already has. What are the natural features of your lot or small acreage? The primary considerations are the size and location of your plot, but of course, there isn't a great deal you can do to change this. There are, however, certain other aspects over which you can impose your will . . . to a degree.

Soil

One of the most important things to determine is what sort of soil conditions you have to begin with. As important as this matter is, frankly, there aren't a lot of obvious, concrete answers. You can buy a home soil-test kit, but they aren't very accurate. You can also get the county extension service to test your soil, but they aren't very accurate either, especially in urban/suburban areas where so many things have happened over the years to affect the soil long before your arrival. That's not to say that these soil tests don't give an accurate reading of the nutrient content of the tiny sampling you take, it's just that the tiny sampling frequently doesn't reflect an accurate example of your whole growing area. Perhaps a homeowner generations ago dumped his wood ashes in one corner of what is now your backyard. Later on, someone salted livestock in another area, and perhaps an old log cabin rotted down on another spot. All these things can affect the quality and composition of our soil. Therefore, a soil test may be an interesting learning experience, and it can tell you quite a lot about the six-inch hole where you took the sample, but a single test won't necessarily reflect the content of your whole property accurately.

A better plan is to assume that the soil you start with is only good enough to hold up the plants currently growing in it, and that you'll need to provide all the actual plant nutrients you need on your own. For this and other reasons, you're probably better off *replacing* your soil than trying to improve it. This isn't as difficult as it sounds. In fact, it's the easiest way, but one that is virtually impossible for the agribusiness-type farm to accomplish. Tilling the soil, that is, breaking new ground for planting, is a cliché of agriculture, but if you live in an urban or suburban area, then your soil is likely to have been compacted and contaminated over the decades or centuries, and you'll find all manner of debris from earlier homes and buildings that have been bulldozed to make space for your home. Even if you live in a completely rural location on virgin ground, you're likely to find rocks or hardpan (a subterranean layer of hard, impenetrable soil or clay) that make plowing difficult and unproductive.

So for garden beds, it's a lot less work and much more productive to create raised beds by bringing in lots of loose, loamy soil and compost that's easy to work. For orchard planting, it's better to mix the soil you dig out of planting holes with your own rich and loose mixture.

Sunlight

Most flowering plants, which is to say virtually all plants, that produce fruits or vegetables require a fairly generous supply of sunlight to manufacture their produce. If a location doesn't receive a minimum of six hours of sunlight daily, that spot would be put to better use for storage or livestock/poultry housing. This may mean that you'll want to remove some shade-producing trees, fences, or buildings if that is an option, or you might only need to thin the lower branches of an offending shade tree or two that you want to keep. The latter can be done safely and relatively easily with a pole saw, which is, as you might guess, a saw on the end of a long pole. You can buy one of these cheaply, or if you have a lot of limbs to trim, you can rent a powered version at a tool-rental shop.

ESSENTIAL

While most vegetables require a minimum of six hours of sunlight per day, if your location doesn't quite provide that, you can boost the available lumens by planting next to a light-colored fence or hanging a white sheet in such a way as to reflect light onto your crop.

When you're making this calculation, don't forget that the sun moves about in the sky over the course of the year. A spot that may be in full sun in April can be completely shaded in July. The sun is highest (closest to straight overhead at noon) in the northern hemisphere on the summer solstice, approximately June 20th, and lowest on the winter solstice, approximately December 20th. You can find calculators on the Internet that will give you the precise angle of the sun on these occasions.

To complicate matters further, there are some plants, such as some brassicas like cabbage, broccoli, cauliflower, etc., that may benefit from a bit of artificial shading to keep them cool in warmer months, but this will not necessarily be true of your situation, and it's probably best to determine whether you want to take any action or not through trial and error.

You should also consider the sun and shading when you are building animal housing. A location that is shaded in summer and sunny in winter is ideal. Bees prefer to have the entrance to their hive facing south.

Water

Everyone knows that plants need water, but successful farmers and gardeners also know that plants can get too much water, although that's less likely to become a problem if your crop is growing in full sunlight. An important rule of thumb regarding water is that, unless you live in a very polluted area like Beijing, China, or Gary, Indiana, then natural rainwater is the best water your plants can get. Unfortunately, there are very few locations in the world where rainwater comes in a sufficient supply over your growing period, so absolutely do plan on having some available form of irrigation to supplement nature, and if you can, catch rainwater in buckets, barrels, or tanks to use in your irrigation system. Roughly speaking, it's best for your garden to receive an inch or two of water per week during the growing period. (Note: this doesn't mean that if it rains 4 inches, you don't need to water for a month.)

ALERT

Most plants require good soil drainage to keep their roots from being flooded for long periods of time. This is particularly true for fruit trees. If your lot has a high water table and poor drainage, so that planting holes fill up with water, you can use drain tile from a hardware or farm store to drain the area.

These days, there seems to be a plethora of inexperienced gardeners on the Internet, promoting growing techniques that supposedly allow you to grow in drier climes without irrigation. These tend to rely on methods designed to collect and hold rainwater around the roots as long as possible. This is like drinking several gallons of water on Monday and hoping you won't get thirsty again until the weekend. Plants, like people, need to carry on their natural functions in a steady, recurring process. Not only does the soil need to be watered, but to a certain degree, it also needs to dry out in between watering. Stick your finger into your soil about an inch deep. If it doesn't feel moist there, it's probably time to water; if it does, wait until later.

This is not to say that water-conservation methods, particularly mulching, are not a good idea. Mulching, that is, covering all the soil surface around your plants with a thick layer of organic material so as to slow evaporation, is one of the single best things you can do for your plants, but not to the point that the roots are allowed to remain soggy, or they will start to rot.

Needless to say, the quality of the water you put on your plants matters, although if it's good enough to drink, it's probably good enough to water your plants with.

Too much water can be just as large a problem as too little, because your plants' roots can't breathe underwater any better than you can. A high water table, which creates a full-time saturation of the soil just below the surface, will need to be fixed before plants can thrive, or perhaps even live. The way to do this is with drainage tile, which you can think of as rather like reverse irrigation.

Drainage tiles are perforated pipes, originally made of wood or clay, but most commonly plastic in modern times. They allow water to seep into them through small holes. This water is then free to run out and away because the pipe is installed underground with a slight slope feeding into a creek or canal on a lower elevation. If you've ever seen long coils of flexible, black plastic pipe, 6 inches or more in diameter with small (⅛"–¼") holes—a common item to find around building construction sites where they're used to send water away from building foundations—this is drainage tile.

Installing drainage tile isn't difficult: first you need to dig a trench down into the ground water. This ditch then needs sufficient depth to allow the tile to slope down all the way to an outlet such as a natural stream, a man-made canal, or your local sewage system. If no such outlets are available, and the problem isn't too severe, you may be able to route the water into a small pond, holding tank, or a dry-well, the latter being a deep, wide hole filled with coarse rock.

Air Circulation

Keeping a constant supply of fresh air moving through your plants is more likely to be a problem indoors, such as in a greenhouse, but if your planting area is close and the natural breezes are blocked, this can create a problem anywhere. As your plants go through their natural respiration, they need to receive water, dry out, and receive more. Without adequate air circulation, water tends to stay on the leaves, leading to mildew and disease. Obviously this is a greater problem in humid areas than in dryer ones.

Also, plants need the "exercise" they get moving to and fro in the breeze. Plants that are tightly restrained fail to develop strong stems and are unable to hold themselves up. This may be tolerable for annual plants like tomatoes, but in fruit trees, for example, if the plants are staked so that they can't move with the winds, they'll soon be unable to support themselves without staking.

FACT

Worms are unquestionably a benefit to the garden and you should do all you can to encourage them. Worms loosen, mix, drain, and fertilize garden soil. You can draw more of them to your area by sprinkling corn meal on top of the soil.

Turning Dirt into Garden Soil

It goes without saying that one of the things you're going to need is good soil. However, good soil doesn't occur in nature nearly as often as you might suppose. Native Americans taught the first U.S. settlers to plant corn in mounds with a fish buried with each seed. Even back then, soil amendments were considered a must for heavy feeding plants, like vegetables, which generally require considerably more nutrients for healthy growth than do weeds. If you've just begun your agricultural experience this week, then you'll only have three choices of how to amend your soil, none of which are ideal:

Commercial Chemical Fertilizer

First, you can use a commercial chemical fertilizer. This won't do anything good for your soil, but it will feed your plants (similar to how a doctor feeds a patient intravenously and keeps the patient alive). Don't expect the plants to prosper though. Chemically fertilized vegetables won't have the flavor or the nutrients of organically grown food, and you'll be eating the chemicals you introduced. Since you're doing nothing to build up the soil while taking food from it, eventually the soil will become depleted.

Add Raw Organic Materials

A somewhat better method is to add raw organic materials—like fish—to the soil. Unfortunately, in order for the materials to provide sustenance to your plants, it has to decompose first. Some materials, such as raw manure, will heat up so much during decomposition that they will burn your plants, and you may go out one morning to a garden that looks like it's been sprayed with herbicide. There are other negative factors, such as the smell and the fact that neighborhood animals like to dig up things like dead fish to see if there are any tasty parts left.

Ready-Made Compost

The last solution is to buy ready-made compost at a box store or super-market. This is the best of the "bad" solutions, but besides being expensive when compared to making your own, store-bought compost is usually made from only one ingredient, typically cow manure, and thus offers only a limited amount of different minerals and nutrients.

If you have a bit more time (and if you do it right, it can take as little as two weeks), you can make your own compost out of kitchen scraps, grass clippings, poultry, rabbit droppings, or other things, such as wood ashes or rotted sawdust, that you find lying around. Properly made compost doesn't smell, doesn't attract nearly as many digging animals, and won't burn your tender young plants.

Filling Is Easier Than Digging

After you've secured a bountiful stash of high-quality compost, you'll want to apply it to your plants. You can spread it on the ground, which is known as "top dressing," and eventually it will get to the roots and into the plant's system. In all likelihood though, it won't get there in any great (or even adequate) degree during this growing season. In order to get your plant food to the roots where your plant can enjoy its meal, dig up the ground and mix in the compost. This is a lot of work, even in the sort of loose, deep soil that very few beginners will have to start with, and it's a sweaty, blistering, Herculean task in hard, rocky clay.

FACT

Raised beds can be real back-savers, as they can be constructed in such a way that you can perform most of your planting, weeding, harvesting, and other garden chores from the comfort of a lawn chair, or sitting on the edges of the beds themselves.

You're going to get to do all the digging you want when you plant your orchard; for the garden, a far better choice than digging up sod, for a number of reasons, is what's known as the *intensive bed*. In *intensive gardening*, you build a bed of your best-amended soil above grade level, and plant your specimens more closely together than what is recommended for planting in the ground. For this, you may want to enclose your beds into neat squares with boards, stones, railroad ties, or other materials.

Containing (or Camouflaging) Your Operation

In a perfect world, everyone would realize that backyard farming is a wonderful way to improve both your life and the world around you. Unfortunately, this world is less than perfect, so you shouldn't expect that. If you are living in a populated area, there is a very good possibility that at least one of your neighbors will see you as a kook and a nuisance, out to destroy his insular, urban lifestyle.

For your purposes, it might be helpful to make sure your farming activities don't cause the neighbors undue concern, and if you can keep them from knowing about them at all, so much the better. Having a tall fence or hedge around your backyard can be very beneficial toward this end. Fencing to keep your neighbors out is likely to be a bit more expensive than fencing to keep your animals in, but it may be a necessity. Remember the old farmer's proverb: "Good fences make good neighbors."

ESSENTIAL

Most herbs are less demanding than plants that produce fruits or vegetables and can be used to fill in areas where you may not be able to successfully grow more particular species. Spearmint or peppermint, for example, will thrive in areas too wet for most garden plants, and chives do well in low sunlight.

While virtually every organic gardening book ever written will tell you that properly-made compost does not produce an offensive odor, there is a catch. Most of the ingredients in good compost do give off quite a potent smell capable of wafting throughout the neighborhood if you are lucky to obtain a large quantity of it.

Should you find yourself in this situation, a good recommendation is to deliver it to your compost pile in as inconspicuous a way as possible, and to wet it down generously with the garden hose immediately. After that, cover it with a tarpaulin for a few days until it has settled and the odor has dissipated. If you haven't yet decided where you want to locate your compost pile, do so with this scenario in mind, and place it as far from the neighbors' homes and patios as possible, staying conscious of the direction of the prevailing winds.

Keep in mind (and remind your neighbors) that there are also good sights and smells that go along with your farming. Fruit trees are quite attractive small cultivars with lovely blooms and an alluring fragrance in the spring. In fact, many fruits, such as crab apples, are grown simply for their beauty alone, so it is highly unlikely that anyone would object, even in the most restrictive Property Owners' Association, if you have several fruit trees scattered around your home.

ALERT

When growing in containers, remember that container soil will dry out more quickly than the soil in your beds, and thus will require more frequent watering. Container soil is also colder in winter and warmer in summer and may require protection that in-ground planting does not necessitate.

Additionally, many vegetables look quite fetching growing in containers or even in large hanging baskets. Few folks would object, or even notice, if your hedges were in fact grape vines on trellises, and regular kale is just as attractive as the ornamental kind when used as a low plant beside the front walk. In fact, you may want to consider becoming a *front* yard farmer as well.

In addition to these camouflage efforts, you might choose to share some of your fresh produce with certain neighbors at the end of the season. That sort of good will can go a long way in softening their hearts. Money may not buy you love, but a basket of crookneck squash might get you a little domestic tranquility.

Transportation

While the Stone Age or preindustrial farmer may be a good model for backyard farmers in a number of instances, it's obvious that the ancients didn't enjoy the luxury of motor vehicles. That fact alone is the primary reason that your agricultural efforts can surpass theirs, even if you are a complete novice. Whereas agribusiness relies heavily on big machinery and massive doses of chemicals, small farming relies just as heavily on relatively small machinery to move organic materials and other necessities.

Depending on your transportation options, you may need to make some arrangement that provides for the transport of a number of different things that don't necessarily belong in the passenger area. If you have a car or an SUV, you will need to prepare the trunk or cargo area to haul some of these sorts of things, and if you can lay hands on a small trailer, so much the better. The ideal situation in this case would be if you have a pickup truck. This will allow you to transport building materials, compost materials, and even livestock without damage to your vehicle or insult to your passengers.

Other Modern Conveniences

It isn't uncommon for folks who have decided to live a simpler, less mechanized lifestyle to go off the deep end, so to speak, and try to eliminate everything in their lives that they don't absolutely need. Should this urge grip you, perhaps it's best to think of your backyard farm as a business, because there are a few new-fangled devices that are quite beneficial to business and to farming. Take for example . . .

The Telephone

Telephone rates are, believe it or not, one of the few things that are dropping in price. There are so many advantages to having a telephone that it's hard to imagine a good rationale for not having one. The price of gasoline comes immediately to mind. Most rural residents have known for a long time that it is far more efficient to call the hardware store to see if they have the particular item you need than to drive into town, or even just across town, to ask in person. The telephone also enhances your ability to reserve advertised bargains and to sell your own goods. So don't get rid of it.

The Internet

There's a lot to be learned in going from urbanite to farmer, and the fastest, cheapest way to learn things is by using the Internet. It's also the fastest and cheapest way to advertise your goods, and locate the odd items you'll need to buy at the best prices.

Not only should you have an Internet connection for your education and reference, when you start having enough produce, livestock, or home-made products to sell, you ought to have a website to promote them. Furthermore, turning your job into a home business is monumentally easier if you can present yourself to the entire world for next to nothing.

Credit Cards

Many folks who have trouble paying their bills react by cutting up their credit cards. Don't do this. There is absolutely nothing wrong with having credit. What's wrong is in being irresponsible with it. It should go without saying that you ought never buy anything, whether with credit or cash, that you can't afford and can't justify, but in everyone's life there are times when having available credit can save you money, save an opportunity to make money, or even save your life. Don't trifle with the power good credit can bring you.

Just remember, farmers never pay a dime they don't have to.

CHAPTER 4

Backyard-Farming Obstacles

Just as with all other human endeavors, backyard farming presents its own particular set of hurdles and challenges. There are a number of ways to deal with each of them, some better than others. It's good to contemplate the problems you may encounter ahead of time, and this chapter will cover a few of the conflicts that you can expect to face.

City and/or County Governments

The more developed and populated the area you live in, the more likely that there will be some laws or ordinances that will prove to be a hindrance to your farming interests. Everyone knows that they shouldn't break the law, but a common reaction is to denounce whatever it is as "a stupid law anyway," and to decide that "they" will never find out. This is not a good plan; in fact, it's no plan at all. It's wishful thinking. Seriously, who wants to get busted for an illicit rooster or an inappropriate pig?

Find out the regulations in your area. If you can't find them on the Internet, the County Recorder will be happy to show them to you. Read each rule and consider whether what you want to do violates it, and if so, how you can change or adjust your plans so that you can still accomplish what you want without incurring City Hall's wrath. You may be pleased to learn that most jurisdictions have fairly sensible rules about small livestock, and that compliance will probably be a simple matter. Sometimes though, you may have to decide whether you're willing to do what will be required of you. For example, a permit may be mandatory for something you want to do, and having the permit might put you in a position of reduced competition if you're willing to jump through some hoops that others aren't. This would make compliance good business, or it might just be another expense you don't need. The point is to always look at the benefits as well as the costs, and always obey the rules.

FACT

Even the largest cities (New York City, Chicago, Los Angeles) permit residents to keep poultry and other small livestock, but they make different distinctions about the circumstances under which the animals must be kept and how many are permitted. Be sure to read your local ordinances yourself and don't accept word-of-mouth.

The Bank (or Your Landlord)

Generally speaking, there's nothing wrong with any part of backyard farming as far as a bank is concerned, but when you do something presumed to be a bit out of the ordinary, there can be a number of people who feel that they need to interject themselves into your affairs, including your bank if you hold a mortgage.

Most deeds of trust, or mortgages, have a clause in which you've agreed not to "commit any waste upon the property," or perhaps not engage in "any dangerous, noxious, offensive or unlawful trade or business or for any purpose which will reduce the value of the property."

So what does that mean exactly? Well, ultimately that's for a judge to decide, but who wants to go that far? The purpose of clauses of this sort is to allow the bank to be the *initial* judge, so they can decide if you might be doing something that would cause the property value to drop so dramatically that they couldn't get their money back in the event that you stop making the payments. Then they could try to evict you and resell your home.

Be Aware

None of this is likely to be anything that you need to lose any sleep over, but it is something that you ought to be aware of. The lesson to take away is that you should try your best to see that you don't do anything that might appear offensive to the general public, who don't see much difference between a compost bin and a big box full of manure. In short, don't nix your plans; just be careful to keep the concerns of others in mind.

The Landlord

As an extension of what the mortgage-holder may demand, if you're renting, your landlord will have an interest, and rightly so, in anything that might damage or devalue his property, or put his bank on his case. In either instance, or even if you own your home and land free and clear, there is nothing about raising a garden and a few animals that has to be a detriment to the property. That's not to say that some animals, especially some of the larger ones, can't be pretty destructive, but this isn't going to come as a surprise to anyone, so it should be obvious that you need to provide adequate fencing, housing, and drainage to accommodate whatever sort of livestock you decide to husband before you ever bring the animals onto your property. Good, attractive fencing should be considered an added value to the property. Tenants must remember that since fencing will be permanently installed, it becomes a part of the property and you can't take it with you when you leave.

The Neighbors

If you're going to have any problems with your neighbors over your farming activities, they're almost certain to come as a result of the animals you're keeping on your side of the fence. There are a lot of city and suburban dwellers that just don't understand, and are actually even frightened by, farming activities. For example, people interested enough to learn are aware that bees won't bother you if you don't trap them, sit on them, or bother their hives, but lots of misguided folks think that if you have a few beehives next door to their home, that puts them in danger of being stung to death by killer bees. Educating them would be nice, but there's no reason to suppose that they'll be open to learning much about something they weren't interested in to begin with. You can't expect to hide everything you do, but if you can locate your hives as far from these folks as possible and keep them mostly out of their sight for a few months, then when you bring them a sample of your honey at the end of the year while reminding them that the bees have been there all summer long, things are much more likely to go smoothly.

Raising chickens inside the city limits is getting to be fairly commonplace these days, but problems can arise when the roosters start waking the neighbors up at 5:00 A.M. on Saturday morning. While some folks think that the rooster's crow is a very pleasant way to start their morning, others don't agree, so perhaps it's best to remember that, as magnificent as your rooster may be, the hens don't actually require his presence, or indeed even his existence, in order to lay eggs. That, and their innate deliciousness, is why most roosters wind up on the dinner table.

FACT

Online forums on backyard farming, gardening, and homesteading provide an excellent way to get to know other backyard farmers, learn what's worked for them, and ask them specific questions. You can find real-time help for your issues involving neighbors, marketing, gardening, and animal husbandry, as well as sympathy and understanding from people very much like yourself.

Another critical item you need to keep in mind is that of runoff rainwater flowing from your property to neighboring lots. This may not have been an issue before, but if you start keeping livestock, that means you'll have waste products to control. The best thing to do, of course, is to add the offending substance to the compost pile, but if a hard rain ensues before you can do that, a problem might develop. This is not hard to remedy; just build a shallow berm, or dig a ditch, along the property line so that water doesn't run from your property to theirs.

Another source of ill will is when the neighbors' dogs invade your pens. Once again, a strong fence is the best solution to this and related problems. The dogs may be your neighbors' responsibility, but you will have to repair the damage once it's done. It's better to armor your farming efforts against all possible threats than to worry about who's at fault.

The Spouse and Kids

As mentioned, backyard farming is a lifestyle, and sometimes quite a different one from what you may have been living before. It may surprise you that certain people within your household may not be quite as enthusiastic as you about having their whole lifestyle changed. (If your teenagers are enthusiastic about *anything* you do, you are indeed a rare and blessed individual.)

It would be nice if your family were to change their opinions, and perhaps they will in time, but don't expect lots of free labor from within your family unit. Besides, nothing you can say will have the persuasive power of fresh strawberries warm from the sun. Maintain the peace and move on.

Pollution

If you provide clean soil and water, pollution isn't likely to be a major concern unless you live in a really noxious locale. However, some plants are very sensitive to smoke, even cigarette smoke, and other air-borne pollutants, and this may cause you problems, particularly in low-lying areas with poor circulation.

The biggest threat that you're likely to face from pollution is if your backyard is adjacent to a cultivated field, orchard, or power transmission lines, because all of these locations can be sprayed with herbicides at one time or another by people who have every right to be doing what they're doing, and this puts your garden at risk for drift from the spraying operations. Most farmers will sympathize with your desire to keep herbicide out of your yard, and most power companies will respect the landowner's rights if the landowner will mow the area that was to be sprayed.

Livestock are generally considered to *be* a pollution source rather than to suffer from pollution themselves. Just be sure they have clean water and feed, and you're not likely to have any problems. It's good to remember that grazing livestock can get what's known as Hardware Disease, which is a fancy term for saying that they can get sick from swallowing nails, pop-tops, thumbtacks, and other bits of metal that you allow to fall on the ground in their pasture area. So don't.

Weather

You've surely heard the old joke, "Everyone talks about the weather, but nobody does anything about it." Well, as a backyard farmer, you're going to have to do something about it. Most animals will need some shelter. There are exceptions—in some cases, cattle can come together in a shed in cold weather, where their combined body heat causes them to sweat. When they go out the next morning and their wet bodies are exposed to freezing temperatures, they can get sick. That's why you rarely see any sort of animal shelter on cattle ranches. So consider what would be the most appropriate shelter for the animals you choose to raise, and the best way to determine this will be to visit someone already raising those animals successfully in your locale.

Just as your animals will need protection, so will your plants. If you plant early, you'll need to watch the weather forecast and cover your tender starters if frost is imminent. But don't take the weather forecast too seriously—nobody ever really knows conclusively what tomorrow may bring, and meteorologists are as fallible as anyone else. Further, the predicted temperatures they talk about are for the local weather station, and conditions in your backyard may vary. If you get an extraordinary amount of rain, you need to have situated your garden high enough that water doesn't pool in it—another benefit of raised beds—and if it doesn't rain enough, which often happens, you'll need to have the capability of irrigation.

ESSENTIAL

A good small investment is a recording thermometer. This will show you the current temperature and also the highest and lowest temperatures reached during a given period. They're essential for monitoring such things as minimum garden temperatures at night and the maximum temperatures for your heat lamps brooding baby chicks.

Remember that tall plants like corn and sunflowers may be subject to damage in high winds, so be prepared to stake them or plant them in protected locations. There are some instances where you may want to provide a sunscreen for certain delicate, cool-weather plants: something that limits, but does not completely block out, the sun's rays to avoid sunburn and drying out.

One of the best ways to buffer your garden against the extremes of the weather is with good, thick mulch. Mulch holds in moisture and keeps the soil from becoming parched. Additionally, it provides some frost protection to the roots, and fertilizes and aerates the soil as it decomposes.

If you'll apply your mulch as soon as the plants get tall enough to poke their upper leaves above the mulch material, and add mulch as they grow, you'll be good for the season. After the harvest, you can either work the mulch into the soil, or keep it for next year as permanent mulch. Advocates of permanent mulching promote the practice as an alternative to weeding, which it is, although you shouldn't expect it to be 100 percent effective. Still, it is much easier to pull weeds from well-mulched soil than from hard, dry, unmulched ground.

Finally, don't expect that you'll do a perfect job. Despite your best-laid plans and a watchful eye on the weather forecast, you *will* lose some newly planted starters to the frost. In fact, you may do so every year, so be prepared by having started a lot more seeds than you need, and if all your seedlings get frosted, you can always buy some bedding plants at the farmers' market.

Animals and Insects

It's likely that the biggest threat to your farming enterprise will come from animals, and in some very predictable ways. For example, in fairly rural areas where forage is abundant, the common, ubiquitous squirrels will totally ignore your garden, but in more urban areas, the city squirrel, with a leaner selection of naturally occurring food, will even attack flowerbeds.

Then there are deer, groundhogs, opossums, skunks, and worst of all, the dreaded raccoons. Add to this your local dogs and cats that love to dig and defecate in your moist and friable soil, and it may seem as if you're fighting an army single-handedly. That's how some people see it in fact, and their response is to shoot, trap, and poison the enemy. This is not really a workable response to the problem. The wild creatures are just doing what they do for a living naturally, and shooting or trapping one of them doesn't discourage all the rest; there will always be more. Poison is so indiscriminate that you're likely to wind up killing the neighbor's tame animals. Perhaps they shouldn't be in your yard, but you don't need any unnecessary friction with the folks next door.

Animals

Keeping your plants safe from marauding animals isn't the full extent of your concerns. Your domestic animals also need protection from wild critters, particularly the smarter, more dedicated villains, such as foxes, coyotes, skunks, and raccoons, all of which can be found lurking on the fringes of suburban developments as well as in the countryside, and all of which enjoy a tasty egg or drumstick every bit as much as you do.

ALERT

It isn't a good idea to try trapping predatory or nuisance animals that invade your farm. Even if you use a live trap so as not to harm pets or other domestic animals, there is always the possibility that you'll trap a skunk, a situation that presents a problem all its own.

The only really sensible way to deal with animals is to armor your garden against them with a good fence. Start out with what you think will work and find ways to close the weak spots if and when they become apparent. Simply making it more inconvenient for the varmints to steal from your garden may be sufficient. Wild animals are fewer in more heavily populated areas, but as with the squirrels, urban critters tend to be more brazen, and for these, you may need to make access as close to impossible as you can manage.

Insects

Insects are always a problem. The most important thing to remember is that every single female insect is a veritable bug factory and can procreate incredibly fast. So if you see a particular caterpillar or beetle munching on your melon leaves, take action *right away*, kill the individuals you find, and search your plants for eggs, *right then and there.* If you can get them before they start to hatch, your job will be a tiny fraction of what it can become just a few days, or even hours, later.

When you discover a destructive insect, try to identify it as quickly as you can, and look for the appropriate remedy. Chemical solutions may or may not be the most effective, but you should avoid them if you can. Chemicals tend not to be very selective, and may kill beneficial insects like ladybugs, soldier beetles, or your own bees, as well as the pests you hope to assassinate. Besides, you're planning to feed these veggies to your family, and avoiding pesticides is one of the reasons you want to grow your own. Rather, try some of the several organic solutions, such as diatomaceous earth or insecticidal soaps, and if all else fails, just picking the critters and their eggs off by hand and killing them isn't really all that much trouble.

Snakes

Snakes are also quite fond of eggs, and your hen house should be snake-proof. Since creating a space that a snake can't crawl into can be quite a bit more challenging than you might suppose, it's also strongly recommended that you not gather your eggs at night without a flashlight. Black snakes are the most common predators of hen eggs, and luckily, they are not particularly aggressive, but most folks wouldn't care to reach into a nest box and find that the eggs they're seeking are already inside a coiled reptile. The only upside of this highly memorable experience is that you aren't likely to make this mistake twice!

Veterinary Concerns

When your cat or dog gets sick or has other health issues, you probably take your pet to a veterinarian. Farmers don't do this with livestock unless their animals come down with something beyond their previous experience. It's not a matter of compassion; it's a matter of basic economics and professionalism. When you have a whole flock or herd of animals, hiring a vet for all their ailments moves beyond costly to prohibitively expensive. Moreover, as a farmer you need to be a professional at animal husbandry and that means that it's your responsibility to learn everything you can about all the common ailments and diseases that the livestock you've chosen to raise are likely to suffer from, and how to treat each of them yourself. Of course, when one of your animals is sick and you don't have a clue as to the cause, then you have little choice but to take the patient to a veterinarian. This will be a good time to cultivate a close relationship with the vet so you'll have someone to call when you're unsure of your own diagnoses.

ESSENTIAL

Farm feed stores are your best source of affordable veterinary supplies. There you'll find antibiotics, reusable hypodermic needles, suitable restraints, and all the other items you'll need to keep your animals healthy and comfortable. It's good idea to keep a little penicillin in your refrigerator at all times.

You'll want to know how to give vaccinations, how to assist difficult births, and if such is necessary, learn to do minor surgery, such as dehorning, castration, and caponizing. This isn't for the faint of heart, but you can learn the techniques from an experienced farmer or a veterinarian, and with a little practice you'll get to the point where you can do it without undue trauma to either the animal or yourself.

If you only have a few animals, that is, if they're more like pets than livestock, then you may not want to get this involved, but if their numbers run into the dozens or more, then practicality will dictate that you learn these procedures from as knowledgeable a source as possible, be it a veterinarian or a veteran at animal husbandry. Of course, if you have only a handful of animals, then the simplest, cheapest solution would be to leave them intact and learn instead how to deal with their horns, testes, or other "undesirable" body parts.

It's all just part of being a farmer.

CHAPTER 5

Farming When You Don't Have a Backyard

If the concept of backyard farming sounds difficult to you, the idea of farming from an apartment may seem to border on the bizarre. Just exactly how bizarre it is depends on the nature of your apartment's available light and what other options you may have. If you have ways to extend your availability to sun and soil, you'll be surprised at how much you can accomplish in a small amount of space. It all depends on how much imaginative resourcefulness you can muster.

Minimum Acceptable Light Sources

Unless you live in a greenhouse, the limit to how many plants you can grow in an apartment does not depend on the amount of square footage you have but the amount of sunlight you can get to your plants. A common configuration in modern apartment floor plans is a long, rectangular living space with a glass wall on one end, perhaps with a balcony outside that. If this is the case with your apartment, and the glass wall is facing south, it's probably the best situation you could hope for.

Plants that produce food tend to be the ones requiring the most sunlight, and it would be safe to say that even the least light-hungry food producers like lettuce will require at least four hours of direct sunlight per day. If your largest window faces east or west, you may be able to get that daily for four hours or more, but southern exposure will give you the most light. You can expand the amount of available light with reflective surfaces like mirrors or white sheets, and while there's only so much you can do to improve the situation, it may surprise you what gains you can make with a little bit of creativity.

ESSENTIAL

The best way to tell if your plants are getting enough sunlight is to look for what are known as "leggy" plants. These will have spindly, elongated stems caused by the plant trying to stretch itself forward to get more of the available sunlight.

Some plants will grow in a north-facing window, or in other indirect light, but ferns and ivies are about the only things that will thrive there, and even some of those won't do that well. You'll need more direct light than that if you want to grow food. Don't waste your money on expensive light meters; you either have direct sunlight or you don't, and if you have ways to boost what you have, use them.

What You Can Grow

In places where you have less than six but more than three hours of direct, daily sun, you may be able to grow leafy vegetables and maybe even produce beans or peas. The trailing varieties of legumes are particularly attractive in this case, because their climbing vines can make use of vertical space. While bush varieties will probably do better in limited light, vines are able to climb from the shade into the sunlight. Generally speaking, cool-weather plants get by with less light than others, so these need to occupy your most dimly lit, least-favorable nooks and crannies.

Once you've used up what light you have, or more accurately, once you've put plants in all the spaces that provide as much light as they require, you'll need to find other places close by where you can place additional plants if you want to expand.

Artificial Lighting

Twenty years ago, growing vegetables under artificial light would probably have been just too expensive. Today, it's still not an ideal situation, but advances in electric lighting technology have reduced the cost of operation so that you might consider augmenting the natural light that your plants receive with fluorescent lighting, halogen lights, or LEDs. However, trying to replace the sun with an electric light requires a considerable amount of effort and expense, not to mention some pretty effective lights. It's a good idea to make sure you're taking full advantage of all the natural light you have before you begin buying additional lighting.

Electric Lighting

A simple fluorescent tube can be used with great success in late winter to increase the effective day length, thus encouraging seedlings on your windowsill to sprout and grow during short days when they normally aren't inclined to do so. Other tools, such as those that use full-time electric light, require more effort. When using these applications, you have to take into consideration the color spectrum of your particular light source, as well as how you will cool the area in the presence of a number of high-powered lamps. If you're interested, there is an incredible amount of information available on the Internet (apparently because of the abundance of home marijuana growers). Keep in mind that for the purposes of home farming other plants, artificial light is too expensive, too complicated, and probably not something that you'd be particularly comfortable living with. However, you can assemble a system utilizing natural light supplemented with artificial light, with which you can expect to keep your gardens growing in a natural fashion all year round by simulating the long day-lengths of summer.

Hydroponic Gardening

There is also a growing movement toward hydroponic gardening—that is, the practice of growing vegetables and other plants without soil and under artificial lighting. No one seems to have discovered a hydroponic technique that produces a taste equivalent to plants grown in good soil and sunshine, though. Many, perhaps most, of the hydroponic advocates use chemical fertilizers. Using this method to recreate the produce you find in the grocery store falls short of the goal you've set for yourself, which is to create tasty, natural food superior to what you have now.

ESSENTIAL

Artificial light doesn't emit as much energy from the red and blue spectrums as does sunlight. Plants can be grown entirely under artificial light, but nothing surpasses natural light, which provides an even distribution of all the different color wavelengths of light that plants have evolved to prefer.

SHADE-TOLERANT CULTIVARS

- Root Crops: beets, carrots, potatoes, radishes, rutabagas, and turnips will grow if given four to five hours of sunlight daily, but it will take them longer to mature in this scenario.
- Leafy Greens: arugula, lettuce, mustard greens, and spinach all grow well in limited sunlight and mature early. You can grow them alongside, or in the same containers with, herbs like chives, basil, and thyme.
- Brassicas: broccoli, Brussels sprouts, cabbage, cauliflower, and kale will grow in limited sunlight and appreciate the indoor climate, since they don't respond well to the extreme heat found outdoors in summer.

- Peas and Beans: bush varieties do best in low-light situations, but you may have a situation where you can train pea or bean vines to grow up to better sunlight conditions.

Container Planting

If you have any experience keeping houseplants, know that farming in your apartment isn't much different than that; it's just done on a larger scale. In fact, sometimes it's exactly like keeping houseplants, because you can grow a lot of herbs in regular flowerpots, and many herbs don't require your best, sunniest locations to carry on their natural functions and grow happily indoors.

Types of Containers

For most garden plants, you'll need larger containers than you've become accustomed to providing for your houseplants, and perhaps more sunlight as well.

You can grow a pretty nice tomato plant (or a number of other cultivars) in a 5-gallon bucket, and these are handy to work with, as they aren't too heavy to move around and have handles. You'll need to drill some holes in the bottom to provide drainage (two to four 1-inch holes along the bottom of the walls work nicely), and you'll have to have a large plate underneath, or some other means of catching the water before it goes onto the floor. A quick way to protect the floor is to spread out a sheet of plastic beneath your containers. Put a low berm (a raised barrier) around the edges of the sheet with a frame of 1" × 2" boards under it to keep the water within the plastic. Placing the plants inside a kiddie wading pool is another strategy.

You can also use larger containers, such as the plastic pots that small trees come in at a nursery. Your plants will appreciate the extra room. You might have two or three planted in an 18- to 24-inch tub. Note that these can get pretty heavy if you need to move them around, especially when you've just watered the plants. Invest in cheap plastic containers. They do the best job of holding in moisture, whereas terracotta and other unglazed vessels are more porous, and the plants dry out more quickly.

Drainage

When you care for houseplants, you're supposed to have coarse gravel or potshards in the bottom of your pots to help keep the drainage holes open, and to keep the moisture at the bottom of the pot from growing stale over time as the roots built up. If you use 1-inch or larger holes in the bottom sides of your containers, you shouldn't need anything else. You'll have plenty of drainage, and since nearly all houseplants are annuals, you only have to keep the roots happy until the end of summer, so you can go ahead and fill your containers with planting medium from top to bottom.

FACT

Earthworms increase the fertility and drainage of growing soil and keep it from becoming compacted. They can be very beneficial to plants growing in containers and will not, unless constantly flooded, leave the planting pot. Dig up a few outdoors and add at least one to each of your pots. They multiply rapidly.

Planting in Bags

Other, even cheaper, containers to consider are bags. You can either choose plastic garbage bags filled with soil mix or you can plant directly into plastic bags of commercial potting soil. Bags made from polyester, canvas, or other porous materials are also popular choices. If you use plastic, don't forget to provide drainage holes for water to run out and something to catch the water in. Growing in bags is not easy, though, particularly when growing indoors, where spraying everything with a hose isn't practical. The technique is useful when you have little time or can't find better, more apartment-friendly containers.

Maintaining the bags indoors for a whole season without tipping, bumping, or outright spilling them can take some special attention. When you've finished the growing season with tubs or buckets, you have many mini-gardens that you can till, fertilize, and use again next year; with bags, especially the canvas or polyester ones, reusing them is possible but messy, and keeping the garden in the bag over the winter is more of a challenge. Bags are probably best used as hanging planters, which gives them a new utility and takes advantage of the vertical space in your growing area.

Potting Soil

All plants respond well to good soil, and while it's generally recommended that making your own soil through mixing native soils with compost is best, as an apartment dweller you don't have any native soil, and you probably don't have any place to make an adequate amount of compost. You also can't be shuttling back and forth from the compost pile to your garden with a wheelbarrow, especially if you're not on the ground floor, so it's probably best to use the bagged potting soil and compost you can buy in box stores or nurseries.

If this is what you choose to do, it would be best to have some cheap and convenient way to add fertilizer to the soil as the growing season progresses, and since it rather defeats the purpose of home growing to use chemical fertilizers, you'll need an organic source for your plant nutrition. A simple and reasonably cheap organic fertilizer is fish-oil emulsion, a liquid that you can either pour directly into the soil in your containers or mix with the water you give the plants. Fish-oil emulsion is high in nitrogen and is quickly absorbed by plants.

QUESTION

Is there anything wrong with using bagged, store-bought potting soil?
Not necessarily. There's no strict definition of what potting soil is, and the bag often won't tell you. Good potting soil supplies plant nutrients. It's dense enough to hold water, but porous enough to drain well. It's hard to tell if these qualities are present before you plant.

Another good source of essential elements is "manure tea." You make your own manure tea by collecting an amount of dried manure and placing it in a cloth sack or old pillowcase. Tie the sack closed and suspend it, like a teabag, in a 5-gallon bucket of water overnight. In the morning, take the "teabag" out and pour the infusion on your plants.

Making your own potting soil is easy if you make your own compost. A 50/50 mix of compost and screened topsoil will work nicely. Some gardeners heat homemade compost at 180°F to kill fungi and bacteria, but since this kills good organisms as well as bad, others prefer to use raw materials.

Growing Where It Doesn't Rain

People have been growing plants indoors for about as long as they've been living indoors themselves, and very few of these folks have taken the trouble to collect rainwater for their shut-in plants, so there's no reason to expect that you'll need to do so either. On the other hand, chlorine, fluoride, ozone, and chloramines, all of which may be used in disinfecting city water, are all toxic to plants in large doses. Private well water may be better or worse, as it can contain arsenic, iron, copper, carbonates, or other compounds, depending on the individual well or aquifer. In all likelihood though, your tap water will not be a problem.

Having said that, plants simply adore rainwater, and they'll respond to it if you have the opportunity to put them outside during a rain, or water them with collected rain. Of course under natural conditions, rain falls on the whole plant; you can simulate natural rain by using a mister to spray the plants' leaves occasionally. You can either spray clean water on them or add a liquid fertilizer like fish-oil emulsion. Fertilizing through the leaves is called "foliar feeding." Just be careful not to let water stand on the leaves, as this can lead to new problems with molds and mildews.

Soluble salts from hard water, water softeners, fertilizers, and other sources build up and create an environment that is noxious to your plants. Avoid this by ensuring that your plants have good drainage, so water doesn't stand in the pot. If you see a white crust developing along the edge of the soil, flush the pot out in the bathtub.

The Hazards of Stale Air

Always keep in mind that your plants are constantly transpiring. That means that they're releasing water vapor into the air of the room. It's important that this vapor not be allowed to hang in the air around your plants, because it can foster mildew and disease. Perhaps in the past you've kept one or two plants on a windowsill with no ill effects, but when the number of plants in the room multiplies, so does the problem of air stagnation. Make certain that the air around your plants has some movement, at least part of the time, in order to help them with their transpiration. Gently moving air also moderates temperatures and humidity while discouraging disease and bacteriological infection. If the room you're growing in has a ceiling fan, that does an excellent job of circulating air, but if not, a box fan will do as well.

A Fast, Easy Garden

The best way to start exploring how much food you can create inside your apartment is to put out a salad garden. Salad ingredients mature quickly, aren't particularly finicky cultivars, and, best of all, don't require a lot of space or a lot of sunlight. If you have several pots with the capacity to hold 6 to 10 inches of soil or more, you should be able to grow leaf lettuce, radishes, and chives or green onions. (A head of lettuce is a little more difficult, so it might be best to start with the leafy varieties.) Place the pots so that they get the best sun exposure your home affords. If this is six hours of direct sunlight or better, then you should do well, but if you only get four hours of sun, these items should make a crop for you even if they take a little longer to reach maturity than the time stated on the seed packet.

Water the plants immediately after planting them, and continue watering regularly when the top of the soil gets dry. Stick your finger into the soil, and if you don't feel moisture within an inch, it's time for more water. You may want to add a few drops of fish-oil emulsion to the water when you do.

Plant your salad fixings densely enough that you can thin each crop at least three or four times over the season. Within forty to fifty days or so, you'll be harvesting the first lettuce, and the radishes and onions won't be far behind. Remember when harvesting the lettuce you shouldn't pull the whole plant up by the roots. Just cut off the outer leaves, and leave the rest behind to continue growing. Once you set yourself up with this salad garden, you can plant and replant it, and continue to enjoy greens indefinitely by adjusting the number of plants you keep.

Growing Fungi

Now that you've used up all the available light in your apartment, don't forget that certain tasty, edible things grow without benefit of any light at all—mushrooms. You can grow mushrooms in any dark corner, inside the kitchen cabinets, under the bathroom sink, or better yet, consider all that space going to waste under your bed. Any of these can be ideal locations for mushrooms to grow.

Growing mushrooms is neither complicated nor expensive, but you do need some pretty specific materials. You'll need a growing medium, which may be composted manure, straw, or sawdust. You'll also need mushroom spawn to inoculate (plant) in the growing medium, and you'll need to provide a dark, cool, moist environment. The best way to learn how to grow fungi is to buy a mushroom kit that you can easily find in seed catalogs or online. After you've had the experience of growing your own from the kit, you'll have a better idea about how to create the optimum climate for growing fungi in your apartment, create your own medium, and purchase the spawn in larger quantities, lowering your overall cost. Having a bountiful supply of mushrooms will revolutionize your diet, and if that's not enough, they're in high demand and bring high prices in the markets.

Other Growing Spaces

Without question, the apartment dweller can produce a surprising amount of food in the confines of her home by using every available area. Obviously though, a certain amount of space has to be retained as living area, so there is only so far that you can go before you need to move beyond your apartment walls. There are several obvious choices for places to expand to: the roof of the building, the alley out back, or that vacant lot down the block. In all cases, you'll be using property that belongs to someone else, so whether or not these are viable options depends entirely on whether or not you can get the owner's permission.

Another option might be to make an agreement with a local homeowner, or a few homeowners, to garden in their backyards for an agreed-upon share of the harvest. Should you go in this direction, you'd need to decide whether you want to till up the sod, build raised beds, or use containers. Of the three, using containers is probably the best idea, assuming you wouldn't have the resources to break ground or haul in building materials and soil for raised beds, and it may be easier to persuade folks to allow you to place a few buckets or tubs than to let you tear up their backyard. A few containers in your new partner's backyard can easily be installed and removed as the arrangement warrants.

CHAPTER 6

Backyard Farming on a Small Lot

The typical American building-lot is about a quarter of an acre, and of course, a good part of this is taken up by the home. Done right, this is plenty of room to grow your family's food, keep a few animals, and produce a cash crop. This chapter deals with farming on parcels of one-tenth to one-half of an acre of land, where efficiency is the primary goal, but just about everything agricultural and horticultural is possible if the right techniques are used.

The Front Yard: Landscaping with Food

So your home sits on a small lot, and you want to produce as much food from that lot as possible, while at the same time not incurring the wrath of the community. The good news is that people have been doing this all over the world for centuries. The first order of business is to decide on the areas where you *don't* want to plant. In fact, arranging the planting space should come last.

Arranging Your Garden

Obviously, you want to allow for access to the home above all else, but you probably already have a concrete or other permanent walk going to both front and rear entrances, and in most suburban situations, a driveway and garage. If you're planning on keeping poultry or livestock, you'll need to determine the best location for their housing and exercise areas and then you'll need to design paths to these as well as walkways between the beds that you'll design next.

To get the most bang for your buck, you'll want to plant in both the front and back extensively, but the front—that is, the space between your home and the street—is a better place for permanent plantings than annual vegetable crops. This is a good place to put as many fruit trees, berries, and grape vines as possible, always keeping in mind what their mature sizes and shapes will be (you may not want to block the home's view to the street). There's no reason why fruit and berry plantings can't be as attractive as any other trees and shrubs, so try to arrange them in a layout that's appealing to the eye. Ever-bearing strawberries can make an attractive ground cover and perennial herbs can be used to fill in shady spots along the ground. These don't need to be planted all at once, but you can install each element over time until you've replaced the lawn altogether.

Don't Dig, Fill: Building Raised Beds

The basic idea behind intensive (small-space) gardening is the raised bed. Raised beds are areas of especially rich soil placed above grade, that is, on top of the level of your existing lawn. By filling the raised bed with 8 inches or more of soft, fertile, compost-rich soil, you avoid dealing with the native soil conditions, which may include any combination of rocks, hardpan, construction trash, and poor, hard-packed soil. The additional benefit is that plants growing in this ideal medium can be planted much closer together, eliminating much of the hardest work of conventional gardening—digging, tilling, and weeding. You can work your raised bed while sitting down using a garden trowel instead of a hoe. Yields per square foot increase dramatically, and you spend a lot less effort on the whole.

ALERT

As you design your growing space, pay attention to each bare area, no matter how small, that doesn't have anything planted in it. These nooks and crannies will fill with grass or weeds. You'll need a plan to mow, mulch, or cultivate them so that they can't produce seed to spread to the rest of the garden.

Build a Box to Contain the Bed

There are two parts to building a raised bed. The first is building a box to contain the bed. Where space isn't an issue, this isn't even necessary, but here, where every square foot counts, the box is needed to keep the growing medium from spilling out into the footpaths between the beds.

You'll need some form of low walls to arrange your raised beds. If you enclose your beds with railroad ties or concrete blocks, these provide a place to sit while you work on the beds, but if you build your beds from boards nailed into a box, that will take up less space and may be less costly.

Fill the Box with Rich Soil

The second part of building a raised bed is providing lots of rich soil to fill the boxes. An ideal mixture would be 50 percent to 75 percent topsoil combined with 25 percent to 50 percent compost. This will result in a potent mixture that will be easy to work with, will hold moisture well, and will provide more than adequate fertility while you get your home compost pile producing. How difficult and how expensive it will be to provide this mixture will depend a lot on the resources available in your locale. If you have to buy compost or soil, of course, this will add to the cost of your project. If that's the case, you may find that buying a truckload of compost or topsoil, or both, to be the most efficient way to accomplish your goal. Once you have established the beds, you can maintain them from one year to the next by simply adding a generous top-dressing of your homemade compost.

Arranging Your Beds

In creating your beds, you need to arrange them so as to allow enough room to plant, weed, harvest, and generally maintain them. This means that your beds shouldn't be so wide that you can't reach the center (if there's a walkway on both sides) or half that wide if only one side is accessible. The width of the paths between beds can be determined by your taste or your personal width, but you want to keep them narrow to conserve your overall area. You don't need to use any sort of pavement, but if you don't use some sort of blocks or a boardwalk, then you'll need to do something to control weeds and grass that will grow in the paths.

Determining Growing Space

Probably the question beginners ask more than any other is, "How much garden area do I need to provide food for my family?" Perhaps you've even tried to research this on the Internet. If you have, then you still haven't had your question answered, because the answers are wildly divergent. The truth is that there isn't any good answer because there are so many variables. An experienced gardener in northern Minnesota growing heirloom species in well-developed soil during a particularly cold year will not have the same results as a beginner in California growing hybrids in new ground during a drought. In fact, these two won't even have the same results from one year to the next. That's simply the nature of gardening and its many variables.

Since there's a lot of guesswork involved, a good strategy is to pick a variety of crops you'd like to grow and then plant in all the available space you have, giving approximately the same amount of area to each. That should give you a respectable yield and teach you what does best in your environment. You can then decide what you'd like to have more of, which will make planning a bit easier in your second year.

Other Small-Space Techniques

Intensive planting involves planting your crops as closely together as possible without depriving any of them of sun, water, or nutrients. How do you know how closely that is? Just look on the seed packet, and it will give you a distance to space the plants within the rows, and a distance to space the rows. Take the smaller number and space your plants that far apart in a grid.

Interplanting means planting faster-growing species in the spaces between slower-growing ones. For example, you might plant lettuce and radishes in the space between your tomato plants. You'll be picking the radishes and lettuce long before the tomatoes are full height and ripe, so you don't need to worry about overcrowding. This amounts to free growing space.

Big-farm farmers grow vine plants like tomatoes, squash, and melons and let them trail across the ground, but the backyard farmer can't afford such a waste of space. Always provide these sorts of plants with stakes, trellises, or whatever it takes to keep them off the ground and growing straight up. This is standard practice these days with tomatoes, but you can also grow melons and large squash on trellises, provided your constructions are strong enough and you don't expect the fruits to hang down on their stems. This will work with cucumbers, and you can support those with small hammocks tied to the trellis. Trellising these plants also keeps them much cleaner than letting them grow on the ground.

FACT

The first recorded practice of intensive planting took place in France in the 1890s. Richly fertilized soil was prepared by double digging, a labor-intensive practice that required removing two shovel-depths of soil and replacing it. Later adaptations abandoned double digging in favor of raising the growing bed above grade and adding loose soil.

In order to squeeze the most out of your backyard, you'll also want to squeeze the most out of your growing year. Succession planting is the technique of growing more than one crop in a season, provided your growing season is long enough. Some vegetables that mature quickly can be planted two or three times per season. Others, like broccoli, can produce an early crop, pause (because broccoli hates hot weather), and produce another crop in the fall.

You can fool Mother Nature by starting plants in a cold frame, which is essentially a small greenhouse just large enough to cover the plants and protect them from frost. You can also stretch your growing season as late as possible and throw covers over your producing plants at night in the fall when the first frosts occur.

Making Compost in Close Quarters

Compost is more than a fertilizer. Compost loosens thick clayey soils and builds up loose sandy ones, all while increasing drainage, fertility, friability, and arability. You make compost by combining finely chopped materials that will rot easily with soil in the presence of air and moisture. When combined, the correct materials will heat up internally to as much as 160°F, and the resulting product will have a wondrous effect on your growing plants.

Compost requires materials containing the elements of nitrogen, phosphorus, and potassium. Of these, nitrogen is the most critical to get the composting process underway.

In order to save space, you'll need an enclosure for your compost pile, but because a compost pile needs to be turned with a shovel once or twice during the composting process in order to get oxygen to the inner part of the pile, you need easy access to it, so a three-sided box is probably the best configuration for your purposes. That will allow you plenty of room for turning, while having walls that allow you to build the pile up a couple of feet.

Locate the compost pile as far from the neighbors' homes as possible, and as close to your chickens or rabbits as you can, since they'll be providing some of your best sources of nitrogen.

Animal Husbandry in Close Quarters

When it comes to getting started keeping animals, there are two logical choices that make good beginning subjects: chickens and rabbits. Since chickens produce eggs, they are much more popular. Rabbits produce their fur and a nice white meat that many people compare to the white meat of poultry.

Chickens for Eggs

You can expect a half-dozen laying hens in their prime to produce four or five eggs per day. That's not a hard-and-fast rule, but it's a realistic average to expect. If you have an old shed in your backyard, it will probably be much more economical, and certainly quicker, to convert it into a hen house than to a build new one. If you have to build, don't use new lumber for chickens, which simply don't care about that sort of thing. For six hens, you'll want to provide 4 or 5 square feet of housing per hen, or about 24 to 30 square feet. Inside, you'll want a row of four to six nests, and a few poles hanging parallel to the floor for them to roost on at night. These can be cut from straight sections of a small tree about 2 inches in diameter. Persimmon works well for this, as it holds its bark for a long while.

ESSENTIAL

It is important to remember that poultry and livestock require your attention every day. They will have to be fed regularly and have water at all times; be mindful when it's cold and the water bowls freeze over, or in hot times when they drink three times as much as they normally do. They'll also need protection from the elements, whatever the season.

Your hen house must be snake- and varmint-proof, and have a small door at chicken-level that you can close securely at night. If you use an existing building, you'll have a human-height ceiling so you can go inside to collect the eggs, but if you're building your hen house, you can make it lower, with a panel behind the nest boxes that will allow you to take the eggs out from the outside.

You should also provide an outdoor run for your chickens. This can be constructed as a simple pine frame covered with chicken wire. Ten square feet per hen is a common rule, but this can be altered somewhat to fit the area you have available.

In addition to feeders, your flock will require fresh water at all times, plus a supply of both fine insoluble grit and oyster-shell grit, which they need to digest their food and make strong egg-shells.

FACT

Laying hens need two types of grit: a soluble grit, such as oyster shell, to provide calcium for their bodies to make eggshells, and an insoluble or "flint" grit, which they use to digest their food. The latter may not be necessary if the hens can find grit on the ground of their run.

Fresh chicken eggs are clearly superior to what you buy in the grocery store, but don't be surprised if it costs you more to produce your own than to buy eggs at the store. The higher quality will be well worth the extra expense, if any. You can defray the cost by feeding table scraps, or by keeping a few more hens and selling eggs to the neighbors. Farm-fresh eggs are easy to market to anyone who knows the difference.

As meat producers, chickens are also quite popular. When you buy your baby chicks, or hatch your own, you'll get quite a few roosters, and these typically wind up on the dinner table.

Rabbits for Meat

Rabbits have one major advantage over chickens. Even given how little space raising chickens requires, rabbits require significantly less. As meat producers, rabbits are probably your most practical source because the domesticated rabbit is much calmer in close quarters than chickens that can get rather testy with one another, especially when crowded. (That's where the term "pecking order" came from, after all.) Rabbits need a cage with enough room for them to move around and stand upright on their hind legs. Using three-quarter-inch hardware cloth for the floor will allow the droppings to fall onto the ground below for easy collection. Each cage will need to be around 24 to 36 inches square, and 18 or 20 inches high. A breeding doe and her litter obviously need a bit more room than lone bucks.

Your rabbits will also need to be protected from the extremes of weather. They aren't bothered so much by the cold, so long as their area stays dry, but hot weather will be more of a threat, and they should have plenty of water in either season. Locate the hutches in shade in the summertime and in sun in the winter. In extreme northern climes, you may want to move them into a shed during the coldest months. Anyone with some carpentry skill can build rabbit hutches, but before you try, you ought to check your local farm classifieds or check Craigslist.com for used hutches.

FACT

The manure from both chickens and rabbits will be a definite benefit to your compost pile. Poultry manure is one of the very best manure sources of nitrogen, phosphate, and potash, and rabbit manure is significantly better than that. Some growers say that they raise rabbits more for the manure than the meat.

Goats for Milk

If you have a quarter to a half of an acre, you technically have room for milk goats. However, dairy goats have certain requirements that make their care somewhat more complicated than you might suppose initially. To begin with, you'll need a goat pen, and perhaps another goat. Goats are very adept at getting out of and into things that you'd rather they didn't. You'll want a very secure pen that will be as escape-proof as possible. They are also very sociable animals. Another goat will make things much better, because the extra company will mean that your goat(s) don't spend so much time looking for ways to escape.

Housing Goats

A quick, cheap fence for goats that will work as well as anything can be made of 18-foot hog panels supported by T-posts. These will provide a nearly indestructible fence and the best chance of containing your goats. Make certain that the lower squares of the hog panels you choose are too small for a goat's head to go through and that your corners are well-braced against goats who decide they want to climb.

You will also need some sort of shed that your goat or goats can use to get out of the weather. Finally, you'll need a place to do the milking where you also keep the sweet feed that you'll be feeding them when you milk.

Also remember that in order to keep your goat milking, you'll need to breed her and provide a place for her kids.

Consider Goats Carefully

To repeat, if you have a quarter- to a half-acre, you have room for milk goats. However, it would be a good idea if you didn't make this your first priority. Goats will require a certain amount of your free time. They present a whole new learning curve, so putting them off until you have the garden and other animals under control might be a good decision.

Choosing Your Crops

In planning your planting spaces, there are several things you need to consider beyond how to access them and what sorts of fruits and vegetables you like to eat. If you're systematic, you can get two or three crops from each season, depending on your location. Obviously, the farther south you are, the longer your seasons, but even if you live in the extreme north, you can maximize your growing space by expanding your season. This can be done using the protection of cold frames or greenhouses.

ALERT

Plants grown in containers tend to dry out more quickly and will need to be watered more frequently than plants grown in the ground. For this reason, grow perennial plants in tubs with caution; only the smallest varieties should be used, because those with a large crown of leaves can quickly dehydrate the soil.

When you're dealing with a situation where space is at a premium, you may want to choose bush varieties of plants like squash, beans, and cucumbers. These are available for several species and are not at all uncommon or hard to locate. Besides showing compact growth patterns, bush varieties tend to produce more in a smaller area. On the other hand, they may not be ideal for every situation. You might, for example, have a wall that pole beans could grow up, costing you less of your planting space than bush varieties in beds or tubs would.

Choosing crops that do well in tubs, incidentally, can also be of benefit. Tomatoes and peppers both do well in containers, and containers give you the flexibility to move them about as the exposure to the sun changes over the season.

As you fill up all your planting area gradually, you'll probably use up all the best sunlight areas first, and in the remaining, shadier locations, you can plant more shade-tolerant species, which will include many of your herbs as well as lettuce, spinach, cabbage, cauliflower, broccoli, peas, and beans.

If you have a fence on any outside boundary that faces south, you can place espaliered fruit trees against it. These are regular dwarf varieties that have been trained to grow flat against the wall, thus saving most of the space a normal tree would take up.

Cash Crops That Need Very Little Space

One of the things you'll discover after your first harvest is that some crops will perform a lot better than others. Furthermore, this may vary from one year to the next according to the many variables involved in growing plants. At any rate, you'll come up short of some items and produce far more of others. Those "overachiever" crops will be the ones you can sell at your local farmers' market.

Having said that, there are also certain crops that you can plant heavily and which have the capability of providing you with excess while using very little space.

Strawberries

You can expect 75 to 100 quarts of ever-bearing strawberries for every 100 feet of row, and 50 to 75 quarts of the June-bearing varieties. This may take a bit of calculation to translate into an intensive-bed planting, but suffice it to say that you can get a large yield out of these small, low plants provided you have a little luck and a lot of water during the growing season.

ESSENTIAL

Before you begin selling at a farmers' market, get to know the market itself—they all have their own peculiar personalities. Learn what the customers are buying and what the other farmers are selling and try to make a niche for yourself selling items that other producers don't offer, but consumers in this particular market want to buy.

Cucumbers

Given good, rich soil, a trellising system that allows plenty of exposure to the sun and all the water that they want (and they want a lot), it's not unusual for a 4" × 8" bed to yield 400 to 600 pounds of cucumbers in a single crop. A good trellising method for cucumbers is to hang a wire panel of about the same size as the bed on steel T-posts at each corner so that the panel is horizontal and about 3 to 4 feet above the bed. Plant nine or ten cucumber plants in the bed, and when they start to grow, train the first runners to grow up to and over the panel. You'll have a bed full of fruit below, as well as one covering the panel above.

Leafy Salad Greens

Leaf lettuce, spinach, and kale can provide a bountiful crop from before the last frost of spring to after the first frost of autumn if you harvest them judiciously (cut the dead leaves, don't pull up the roots) and plant successive crops. With a little practice and close attention, you can keep an intensive bed stuffed full of crisp greens all season long.

Herbs

Basil, chives, sage, and others are so easy to grow and so expensive in the stores. Chives, in particular, will grow year-round outdoors if the temperature isn't too low. Planting herbs in 5-gallon buckets or tubs can provide their yield for literally years if you treat them as perennials.

Consistency and Timeliness

The techniques discussed in the previous sections are not new or radical. As the old saying goes, there's nothing new under the sun, and folks have been practicing these methods for centuries with great results. In fact, Mother Nature does most of her planting following the intensive method because she has an infinite number of seeds. The ones that can grow in a particular location grow there, and the others die or take root in more favorable spots. There are very few spots on the earth capable of sustaining life where something isn't growing. Nature also stakes her plants, practices interplanting, and mulches heavily.

Quite frankly, you aren't likely to be as successful at farming as Mother Nature is—certainly not your first year—and the idea of providing all the food you need and having excess to sell may seem impossible after seeing some of your first efforts.

In other words, it's perfectly normal to be discouraged. Just remember that your production will depend, more than anything else, on your consistency and the ability to perform the tasks you need to in a timely fashion. You can't maximize your yields if you don't plant as early as you should (and aren't prepared to protect your young plants from the frost). You'll need to supply water when they need water, and to do any feeding as soon as it's needed. All you need for gardening success is consistent, timely maintenance of a properly planted crop.

CHAPTER 7

Backyard Farming on a Larger Lot

A lot that is a half an acre up to five acres and beyond gives you room to do most anything you should want to do, using only a modicum of restraint. You may have room for a little pasture, or even a small woodlot or a large pond. In fact, on a piece of land this size, you may want to consider a small tractor or loader to help you keep up with the work. As with all farming, you still need to be efficient, but the possibilities are endless.

You May Have All the Land You'll Ever Need— or Not

While success on smaller lots may depend on a number of variables, there's no dispute that you can grow enough produce on half an acre to feed an average family year-round, so any area you have in addition to half an acre can be considered a bonus. An acre of ground is 43,560 square feet, or if square, 208.7 feet on each side, which is really quite a lot if you think about it. It's enough to give you a few options, and that always means new decisions to make. On traditional farms, the acreage may have been larger than we're talking about here as a whole, but more often than not, the base farm—the home, garden, barn, and barnyard—were all clumped together on less than five acres, perhaps much less, and the balance of the property was usually devoted either to livestock pasture, woods, or one single crop.

Tools and Construction

The challenge of a small lot is trying to find a place for everything you want to do; with a larger lot, the challenge is trying to find the time to do everything you need to do. If you want to, you can keep yourself busy all day every day on an intensively planted acre. One to five acres may be more work than you ever counted on. If you do have that much area though, you're going to need certain tools.

Tools

In addition to the regular hand tools you've used before, here are a few things that you probably haven't needed up until now:

- Chainsaw: If you have acreage, you should have a chainsaw. It's as handy for rough carpentry as it is for landscaping chores.
- String Trimmer: You need one of these to keep weeds out of the way. The more fencing you have, the more you'll need to keep brush from growing up in the fence lines.

- Hand Winch: A "come-along" that performs a single job cheaply and can be indispensable at times, it will pull or lift with more strength than five men.
- Fence-Building Tools: If you use wooden posts, you'll need a 13-pound post maul. If you use fence wire, you'll need wire stretchers.

The Barn

When you've gotten all the tools you'll need, you'll find that a barn, or a large utility building, will be a very handy place for keeping feed dry, parking machinery out of the weather, and perhaps housing some of your livestock and a milking parlor for goats or a cow. A chicken coop can be incorporated into the barn if you like, and if you have a small pasture area, that can be accessed from one side of the building. The barn should be connected to a corral that will enable you to move your livestock between two or three pens as well as load them into a truck.

You can accomplish these ends with several smaller buildings, but it would be more efficient to utilize the old tried-and-true design of the two-story, gable-roofed barn. Luckily, this structure doesn't need to be made from the latest materials, and in fact, it doesn't even need to be made from new materials. All it needs is to be strong enough to hold a considerable load in the upper loft, and tight enough to keep the rain and wind out.

As simple as the barn can be, it is still a large building, and constructing one will be a major undertaking. However, barn construction is typically such that you can erect a roofed framework and put that to good use as you complete the partitions and exterior walls over time. Investigate the term "pole barns," which are large, empty shells that can be erected for a very reasonable cost. Once you have the roof on, you can add the rest as time and money permit.

In the simplest terms, you'll find that having a large enclosed area at your disposal will be one of the handiest things you can have for all manner of reasons, so if there's any way possible, plan on building yourself a barn. It really doesn't have to cost that much.

Greenhouse

You can build a small greenhouse very cheaply from plastic sheeting, plastic plumbing pipe, and scrap wood. Once you have a greenhouse, you'll have room to plant all your own bedding plants, plus some to sell. You can start your growing season early by starting plants in tubs inside the greenhouse, or make the season last longer by bringing things inside when it starts to frost in the autumn. A greenhouse can also be used as a place to create potted plants, bedding plants, and hanging baskets for resale.

Room for More Than Just a Food Plot

If you have as much as five acres, you've got room for a sampling of just about any agricultural project you might want to consider. This presents you with the opportunity to experiment and to make some critical decisions. It is a foregone conclusion that some of the pursuits you attempt will meet with greater success than others. When you have the room, you can experiment with different crops, animals, or ways of monetizing the operation. You'll quickly become aware of which work best for your particular situation, and which don't. This opportunity can give you a significant advantage in creating a self-sufficient, profitable backyard farm, as you'll expand on the areas that prove most rewarding and minimize the less successful ones.

Pasture

You may want to devote some of your acreage to larger meat-producing animals than chickens or rabbits, such as sheep, alpacas, small cattle or, if they won't bother your neighbors, maybe even pigs. How much pasture to allow per animal is a complicated question. First of all, if your area has real winters with heavy frost and below-freezing temperatures for extended periods, you'll need to supplement your animals' diet with hay and grains or meal. People manage large dairies just outside cities in the Southwest that don't have any pasture at all, so you can't say that there's any maximum number of animals that any given area will support—it just depends on how much other feed you want to give them.

Beyond that, it depends on how good your pasture is. If you can find a small farming or homesteading forum on the Internet that has members from your local region, you can ask them for their opinions.

Orchard

Sometimes small things are more productive than large ones. For example, it's been proven that you can get more fruit from an orchard of dwarf fruit trees than an orchard of standard-size trees. More than that, you won't need ladders or equipment to pick the fruit. A typical one-acre orchard of standard trees has room for around 100 trees that begin to bear fruit in five or six years, whereas dwarf trees can be planted at 400–600 per acre, or even more, and most will start to bear fruit by the second year. Even large producers have found that dwarf trees are the most efficient way to produce fruit and nuts. In fact, a study done by the University of California at Davis found that dwarf peach trees could be planted as densely as 1,500 trees per acre. They had yields of 13.4 tons per acre the first year, which grew to 30 tons per acre by the sixth year.

Woodlot

While there are some fast-growing species, it probably isn't practical to think about growing your own woodlot from scratch. Trees don't grow that rapidly, and as a general rule, the slowest-growing ones make the best firewood or furniture. On the other hand, if you already have a stand of timber on your property, you can improve your stand for growing efficiency and get free firewood in the process. There are many variables involved if you want to burn firewood to heat your home exclusively. It depends on how large and well-insulated your home is, what part of the country you live in, and what sort of wood burner you're using. Obviously, if you have a drafty five-bedroom home in Maine, you'll need a lot more firewood than if you have a small cottage in south Texas. Then you'll need to consider the differences in growing and burning rates of the various species of trees. To get a reasonable idea of how much land you'd need to grow your own firewood, calculate how much wood you use, and how you use it, and then compare this against the standing timber you have now.

A Pond

Also referred to as a *tank* in the South, this is a body of water smaller than a lake. Digging a pond isn't all that expensive, considering what it's worth, and it will last for the rest of your life. You can have a sizeable pond dug in a day's time (which is to say eight hours or so heavy-equipment hire), but you'll need fairly clay-like soil that will hold water, or you'll have to line it with bentonite clay or plastic. You'll also need enough slope to your land that you can divert rain runoff to keep the pond full. Once your pond fills up with rainwater, it's only a matter of stocking it with a few fish and waiting. If the pond is large enough, you won't need to feed your fish, but they'll grow a lot faster if you do.

ALERT

A shallow valley or depression can make a good place to build a farm pond. You'll need a collection area to get enough rainwater to keep the pond filled, but beware of too large a watershed. A heavy rain can wash your pond bank out in a few minutes if too much water is directed toward the pond.

If raising fish is your desire, you can build a shallow pond with a plastic liner draped over berm walls. This is a better solution than an in-ground pond if you want to raise a lot of fish intensively. It isn't a solution for a livestock watering hole.

Growing Your Own Feed

If you have an acre or more that you might want to devote to field corn, sorghum cane, or other sources of animal feed, then you probably need a small tractor to handle the tilling. Judging exactly how much you can expect to raise during any given year is subject to many variables; some you can control, and others you can't. It might give you a rough idea though, to know that the national averages for field corn production are between 125 to 150 bushels per acre.

As with all the other crops you grow, you'll need some method of storing your homegrown feed. Traditionally, field corn has been kept in whole ears in corncribs, which can be kept in just about any room in an airy barn that is then filled with corn. Smaller grains can be kept in large cans or sacks, or loose in a particularly tight storage room with a cat or two keeping watch for rats and mice. Feed crops like sorghum cane are traditionally made into silage, a fermented, high-moisture fodder. You can make silage on a small scale by packing the silage material into plastic bags and allowing anaerobic fermentation. Silage is a more nutritious meal for your livestock than dried fodder like hay.

Some root crops, such as sugar beets, are also grown as livestock feed. Root crops are easy to store and they hold onto their nutrients well, but getting an acre or two of beets out of the ground at harvest time will require a particularly dedicated effort.

Small Livestock

If you have an acre of good pasture, you can easily keep a milk cow. The better question is whether or not you want, or can use, that much milk. Milk is a favorite food among humans as well as most animals, but selling raw milk legally will often involve more complications from state and local authorities (they will frequently require more licenses, approvals, and inspections than the small operator will find to be cost effective). For that and other reasons, you may want to consider slightly smaller livestock, like a herd of goats, or some of the following:

Miniature Cattle

In recent decades, a number of breeders have developed miniature cattle, some not more than 36 inches tall. These tiny bovines have all the benefits of larger cows, in that they are raised for meat and milk, but they need a lot less pasture area, are much easier to transport, and cheaper to feed. While they go by different names, there are microversions of all the more common cattle breeds, including Hereford, Angus, Jersey, Holstein, and even Brahman and Longhorn. Since these are still an oddity, it would probably be more lucrative to raise and sell the offspring as purebred breeding stock than as meat animals to be butchered. For the home, however, one of these little steers might be just the right amount of beef for your family.

Owners of miniature Holsteins claim they get 2 to 3 gallons of milk a day, so if you prefer cow's milk to goat's milk, miniature cattle might be just what you're looking for.

Alpacas

Like its larger close relative, the llama, the alpaca is related to the camel, which is readily apparent in the shape of the body. Llamas have been used traditionally in South America as beasts of burden, whereas the alpaca is grown for the value of its fiber, which is similar to wool, and highly valued, as it is less itchy than wool and hypoallergenic as well.

There are two breeds of alpaca: the Suri, which has long, straight hair; and the Huacaya, whose hair is wooly and dense like the wool of a sheep. All alpacas use a common dung pile, making the collection for composting easy and leaving pasture areas less of a "minefield" to walk through.

A typical grown alpaca will be a bit over 3 feet tall at the withers and weigh less than 200 pounds, making them ideal for the backyard.

Sheep

Sheep are probably the longest-domesticated farm animal, due in large part to the fact that they produce meat, milk, and especially wool, the most-used animal fiber on earth. Getting started with sheep requires tight fencing in good repair. Traditionally, American farmers have used woven wire, but most of the stone fences in Great Britain and Ireland were built to contain sheep. Ideally you'll have room enough that your sheep can alternate between rotated pastures.

FACT

Sheep are very efficient livestock and the longest domesticated of all farm animals. A beef cow gets 75 percent of her nourishment from forage, whereas a sheep forages for 90 percent of her food if good pasture is provided. Sheep also do not require such strong fencing and expensive equipment.

Sheep need fairly lush pastures and, unlike goats, they aren't prone to eating leaves from taller plants. A mixture of grass, clover, forbs, and other pasture plants suits sheep for pasture; they'll also eat hay, silage, and grains.

Your sheep will need an open-front shed and plenty of clean, fresh water. An old rule of thumb is that you can maintain eight sheep on the land required by one Jersey cow. Each sheep will excrete more than a ton of manure per year. In the compost pile, sheep manure is somewhat hotter (more potent as fertilizer) than that of cattle.

Pigs

Swine are mentioned here because pork is one of the most universally loved meats, and because they can be raised successfully and humanely in very small areas. Having said that, a wise person would only introduce pigs into a suburban neighborhood with extreme caution! You'll find that even the most relaxed and farm-friendly communities, those that will permit just about anything, draw the line at pigs.

Folks advocating for pet pigs like the pot-bellied breed will tell you that pigs are naturally clean animals that do not smell bad. Unfortunately, there is nothing natural about keeping any animal in a small pen, and you will find that pig pens live up to their reputation in terms of both cleanliness and the smell that they produce. It's also said that raising pigs in a pen is unhealthy and that pigs don't like standing in their own filth any more than humans do. However, no one has taken any pig-polls on the matter, and there is much evidence to the contrary, as pigs are raised successfully all over the world in relatively close conditions. If you have a considerably larger area you'd like to devote to raising a pig, this will result in a much more aesthetically pleasing situation. However, don't expect it to be okay with the neighbors.

Helpful Tools

In addition to the smaller tools mentioned earlier, there are a few big-ticket items that can be extremely handy or an absolute necessity, depending on the jobs you decide to do. If you don't have the money for them right now, you can take comfort in the fact that every farm that existed prior to the twentieth century was worked without these conveniences. In the mean-time, you can watch the farm sales, the want ads, and Craigslist for bargains.

Tractor

Although they look alike, there are a lot of differences between a riding lawn mower and a small tractor. It's sort of like the difference between a golf cart and an all-terrain vehicle. A riding lawn mower probably has about three speeds forward and one purpose: mowing the lawn. A small tractor will have four to ten speeds forward, a three-point hitch, hydraulics, and serious, heavy-duty construction that means it won't break easily. Also, when it does break, you can fix it. Small tractors have more implements than you can name, but the more popular ones are bush-hog, mower, plow, loader, grader blade, log splitter and post-hole auger. Tractors are also quite handy when you need to pull a trailer full of things that are too heavy to lift. Tractors make short work of long rows and make it easy to move very heavy items, such as full water tanks or several bales of hay. When you have one, you'll do a lot of jobs that you wouldn't even consider before.

Because tractors are so well built, and because they have so many uses, they aren't cheap. However, like most good equipment, a good used one is the most logical purchase. On a place the size of five acres or less, you'll want the smallest tractor you can get, so this means you'll be choosing one of two types: a small import from India, Japan, Korea, or China; or an old Ford N-Series.

ALERT

Tractors now come from all over the world, but you should try to shop for a common brand name. Some dealers import large quantities of used Chinese and Korean tractors into the United States, which are built by companies that may or may not have parts distributors in this country. Make sure you can get parts for the tractor you buy.

Here are the pros and cons of each kind of tractor: the imports are more modern and come with some features you will find handy, such as very low range transmissions, many forward speeds, four-wheel drive, and modern hydraulics. Some people believe that the imports do a better job and probably won't cost much more than the Fords.

The advantage of the Ford N-Series is that they are extremely simple. If you know the first thing about machinery—or even if you don't—and you have an owner's manual, you can fix everything yourself. Some of the Fords are quite old (they first started making them in 1939), but they've very good, simple designs, and there are still thousands of them available in running condition. They're a little larger and heavier than the imports, but parts are cheap and easy to install, and you can probably get a good one for a little less than you'll pay for an import.

Skid-Steer Loader

Instead of a tractor, you may choose to purchase a small skid loader. As the name implies, the skid loader doesn't steer like a tractor, it pivots by braking one side or the other. A skid loader can turn around in its own length, which is extremely handy in close quarters. Where a tractor is good at pulling mowers, plows, etc., in a straight line, the skid loader excels in working in one spot in a very precise manner. If you need something moved and placed within an inch or so of a certain place, that's a job for a skid-steer loader. Like the tractor, they have lots of available implements, but whereas most of the tractor implements fit on the back of the machine, virtually all skid loader implements fit on the front, and are more devoted to lifting and moving things. Typical implements include buckets, grapples, tree shears, and stump grinders.

ESSENTIAL

Skid loaders are very maneuverable because they skid their tires instead of steering. As a result, they tend to tear up the surface wherever they're operated, so you'll want to be very careful—or avoid—working on lawn turf, although the damage will be shallow and the turf will grow back quickly.

Tractors may be fitted with a loader on the front, but they still don't have quite the ability the loaders do. A loader with a tooth bucket, for example, can dig into the earth and do several light, bulldozer-like jobs; a tractor, not so much. You could dig your own pond with a skid loader, provided you had a few days to do it and the certainty that it wouldn't start raining before you finished.

Loaders are particularly handy around the farm because they can virtually eliminate lifting heavy items. Sacks of feed, hay bales, planting tubs, and building timbers all become infinitely portable when you have a skid loader on the job. If you expect to be farming into your later years, a loader is a worthwhile investment that will make a lot of plain, hard work suddenly easy.

Two-Wheel Tractor

Also known as "walk-behind tractors" or "rear-tine tillers," these little machines can till up even a pretty heavy garden in short order. Not to be confused with a front-tine rototiller, a two-wheel tractor can do this with little input from the operator other than steering. If you've ever used a front-tine tiller in any soil other than the finest, smoothest, and most rock-free, you'll appreciate the difference. Two-wheel tractors can also perform a few other jobs with attachments, such as pulling a cart or blowing snow. If you have ground to till, this is the machine to use, but if all your growing is in containers and beds, you won't have much use for it.

Wood Chipper

In order to make good compost, you need to supply materials to your pile that have been shredded as finely as is possible. If you have a lot of what would be good compost materials, such as heavy weeds, fallen leaves, branches, or anything else of an organic nature that's solid and larger than a half-inch or so in diameter, this is a job for a wood chipper. This is a tool that you can get by without for the rest of your life, but if you have one, you'll use it every time you add to your compost pile.

CHAPTER 8

Compost

Compost is the entire basis of organic gardening, and in a very real way, the basis of all life, because every living thing benefits from compost, and every living thing eventually becomes compost. Understanding how composting works, and how you can make it work for you in your own backyard, will help make all your crops a success.

N-P-K and the Basics of Composting

In the simplest terms, composting is the rotting of materials. Every living thing eventually becomes compost, and every living thing feeds off of compost. What makes composting different from simply letting things rot is that by directing the composting process, you can produce a material that is a cure for most any problem that may arise in plant growth.

Compost is thought of as simply a fertilizer, but it does a great deal more than enrich the soil. Compost can fight the effects of drought by improving your soil's water retention, while at the same time combating root flooding and sour soil by improving drainage. Compost applied as mulch can keep your plants cooler on hot summer days and protect roots against deep frost in the winter. Compost added to hard-packed clay soils will make them looser and more arable, and when added to thin, sandy soils will make them richer and denser.

When you hear all the virtues of compost and then consider that you can make it yourself for next to nothing, you may start to understand why organic gardeners tend to speak of it in such reverent, respectful terms. If you're not yet convinced, and if you're anticipating doing backyard farming, then you need to learn more about how to compost and about what compost can do for you.

ESSENTIAL

Even "finished" compost is only partly decayed. The decomposition continues when the compost is added to your garden soil, which provides food for growing populations of beneficial microorganisms that convert the compost into dark humus through aerobic and anaerobic breakdown of the various organic materials.

Making compost is one of the easiest things in the world. You just lay any organic substance on the ground and wait; sooner or later it will rot and become compost. The catch is that this method takes a long time, and doesn't produce the best compost. In order to speed things up considerably, and to improve the quality of the end product, you'll need to follow certain guidelines.

N-P-K

If you've ever read the wording on a bag of fertilizer, you've seen a series of three numbers, something like 12-10-12. These numbers refer to the analysis of the fertilizer for the three major nutrients plants require—nitrogen, potassium, and phosphorus—by weight. These numbers are always in the same order: N-P-K. So in the example given, a fertilizer with those numbers will contain 12 percent of the weight of the product in nitrogen, 10 percent in potassium, and 12 percent in phosphorus. When you take a soil test of your garden areas, you'll also learn the makeup of these nutrients in your soil. Thus, when you see a deficiency in one or another of them, you'll know that you want to add that element.

Commercial chemical fertilizers provide you with the amount of N-P-K that you want, but add nothing else to the soil, just the chemical. Chemical fertilizers, if applied incorrectly, can burn your plants; even when applied correctly, they do nothing to improve your soil.

When you make compost, the resulting product will also have an N-P-K analysis, but it won't be so constant. The compost will improve your soil in a number of ways other than adding nutrients, and if you've made your compost correctly, you could plant your plants directly into it and they would not burn. By far, the safest and most effective way to improve your garden soil is with composting.

Making a Small Compost Pile

As already mentioned, compost can be made from any once-living thing. However, to make potent compost quickly, you need to concentrate on two things: the physical size of the particles and the nitrogen content of the materials you use. Before you add a material to your compost pile, it needs to be chopped into fine particles of less than a half-inch or so in diameter. If doing this by hand is too tedious, then a wood chipper works superbly. If you don't have a wood chipper, you can get similar results by running a lawn mower over your materials, a bit at a time, until they are ground up.

Grinding or chopping makes the ingredients loose and easy to turn, and it allows oxygen into the depths of the material. Oxygen is necessary for the composting process.

FACT

Building a compost pile is the intensification and optimization of a natural process that goes on everywhere all the time. When a lawn is mowed, when autumn leaves fall to the ground, when insects, animals, and all living things die, these organic substances revert to humus through the composting process.

The materials you use can be anything you have a surplus of, but it's important that you add an abundance of nitrogen-rich compounds to the mix. That's because nitrogen is what will produce heat in the compost pile, and that heat is what speeds up the composting process. Materials commonly used that are "hot" (high in nitrogen) include manures, grass clippings, kitchen waste, and green vegetable matter like weeds.

Once your ingredients are chopped or ground, it's time to place them on the pile. Layering each material is a good way to make certain that the different substances are distributed evenly throughout the pile, and adding a layer of good soil to every third or fourth layer of other materials will introduce new organisms into the batch. Once you've built your pile up to a depth of 3 to 5 feet, sprinkle it thoroughly with the garden hose, and leave it to stand for a few days.

Remember that if your pile is too small, it won't heat up, and thus won't compost. You want it to be 3-to-5-feet deep and at least that much in diameter.

ALERT

Always locate a new compost pile on bare, rock-free ground. If the pile is placed on concrete, worms and beneficial microorganisms can't enter the pile from the soil below. If the soil below the pile is rocky, you're likely to wind up with some of these rocks in the garden.

If it is cold weather when you perform your composting, then you may look out the window on a frosty morning and see steam wafting from your compost pile. This is good, as it shows that the pile is heating up. After a few days, it will be time to turn the pile.

Heating Up

If you have a small pile, shovel it all from one spot to another. As you do this, you should notice that the pile is still steaming slightly and is warm, or even hot, to the touch. There'll be an abundance of gray flecks in the material inside the pile. This is ash, and it shows you that the pile is heating up and speeding decomposition of the various ingredients. If you don't see these gray flecks, check to make certain that the pile is not too wet or too dry (it should be moist but not soggy), that your materials are thoroughly chopped, and that the nitrogen source is evenly distributed throughout the pile in sufficient amounts. After you've turned the pile, it should start to heat up again, but not so much as at first. After a third turning with successful heating, you can be assured you have finished compost.

Once you have a compost pile "cooking," it will initially heat up to over 150°F, which will kill most harmful bacteria and weed seeds, so don't worry about putting it on your garden. You can make compost out of anything, but you want to make certain that your compost is rich in all the essential nutrients. Here are some facts and suggestions about what these nutrients are and how to get them:

- N=Nitrogen

Ideally, you've already supplied a nice base of nitrogen-rich materials to your pile. Besides causing the pile to heat up, nitrogen is extremely important to plant growth because it promotes leaf and stem development, and provides the energy to set fruit and develop seeds. In short, nitrogen is directly responsible for the vegetative growth of plants above ground. When you see a plant with pale green or yellow leaves and lackluster growth, this is a sign of nitrogen deficiency. Too much nitrogen can result in excessive dark-green growth, but nitrogen excess is not commonly a problem, especially if your nitrogen has gone through the composting process; it occurs more routinely when chemical fertilizers are used. Rich nitrogen sources include manure, blood, hair, grass clippings, kitchen waste, and green vegetable matter.

- P=Potassium

Potassium, or potash, increases plants' resistance to disease, heat, and cold. Potassium can even help plants overcome a nitrogen excess. Potash deficiencies result in sickly, purplish plants with weak stems, slow growth, and few blossoms or fruits. You can't see it, of course, but their photosynthesis has slowed down. One of the best and least-expensive sources of potash is wood ash. Ashes from deciduous trees are better than from conifers, but they're both loaded with the stuff, and it's ready for the compost pile as soon as you get it—no preparation is necessary.

- K=Phosphorus

Phosphates are essential to the development of strong, healthy roots. Whenever you see a commercial fertilizer promoted as a "bloom booster" or something of that sort, it is because a high percentage of phosphorus is present. In addition, phosphorus also promotes disease resistance and fruit development. Soils that are low in humus—the dark, organic material in soil produced by decomposition—are also low in phosphorus. If you suspect that your plants aren't getting enough phosphorus, an excellent source is bone meal, but good compost will contain all you need in a typical application. Weak plants that seem to attract insect damage and have thin-skinned fruits suggest a deficiency in phosphorus.

Secondary Nutrients

In addition to N, P, and K, plants need many other nutrients, but usually in such small amounts that enough of them are present in the soil without amendments. Some of these nutrients include calcium, magnesium, and sulfur. If you add lime to your soil to adjust the pH, this lime will contain all the calcium and magnesium you need. Sulfur is found in decomposing organic matter, so your compost pile has plenty already.

FACT

The state of Iowa has lost half of its topsoil in the past century, largely due to conventional agriculture methods that take much from the soil but return little, and loss of topsoil is a worldwide crisis. Composting is the only known way to create new topsoil.

Materials to Avoid

Nearly anything can go into a compost pile, but there are a few things that you should avoid using, or be especially careful when you do. Obviously, you don't want to add anything to the pile that may be poisonous to plants, and some materials, such as newsprint can carry hidden dangers. You also don't want to add materials that, while they might prove to be nutritious to your plants eventually, take too long to break down, perhaps causing deficiencies in the short term. Nor do you want to include matter, which might be dangerous to human health or could draw rodents or carrion-eaters to rummage through the pile.

- **Green Sawdust.** Green sawdust is very slow to decompose, and it can suck the nitrogen out of your pile as it does so. A compost pile can break down green sawdust if there's plenty of nitrogen and not too much sawdust, but you'll spend your efforts better using well-rotted sawdust instead.
- **Newsprint and Coated Paper.** These are sometimes difficult to chop into fine pieces, and some inks are toxic to plants. If you use papers, make certain that they have been cut up as fine as confetti and make certain you use lots of nitrogen.
- **Human or Carnivorous Animal Feces.** As well as used personal products, these present too many health risks. Blood and manure from noncarnivorous animals is excellent, however.
- **Walnut Leaves or Residue.** Alone, walnut products will fertilize a pasture, but don't use them in the compost pile. They contain *jugalone*, a natural compound that is toxic to several plants.
- **Large Lumps of Anything Edible.** While your compost pile will certainly swallow up garbage in time, the bigger the pieces are, the more likelihood that you'll have the neighborhood animals turning the pile for you, and they don't do a very neat or thorough job. They just dig out the goodies that they like, and perhaps spread parts of them on the ground outside the pile as they dine. Many experts will advise you against including anything edible in the compost pile, because it will draw rodents and other pests. However, if the material is finely chopped and mixed into the amalgam, and you can keep the critters at bay, most foodstuffs will produce a potent compost.

Enclosures

Actually, your compost pile doesn't need to be enclosed at all. You'll be more proud of it than ashamed, and it really isn't unattractive, it's just a brown mound in the backyard. However, you may wish to build some sort of enclosure, and having your materials closed in may make it a little easier when it's time to turn them. In any case, if you do build an enclosure, be sure that one whole end, not just a door, opens up to make it easier to access and turn. Building the enclosure out of some perforated or open material, such as picket fencing or chicken wire, will assure that plenty of air can get into the back and sides of the pile. Some folks build two bins side by side, and when it comes time to turn the pile, they shovel the contents of the first bin into the second one.

You also may choose to enclose your compost pile to keep pests out of it, and that may mean putting some sort of lid over it that will let the rain in and keep the varmints out, in addition to enclosing the four sides.

If you build an enclosure that can be easily lifted away when you want to work on the pile, this may present the best of both worlds. If you have a larger pile on a larger lot, you may start using your skid loader or tractor loader to turn the pile or to scoop out a bucketful to take to the garden. If so, you'll want to be able to move any enclosures you've built out of harm's way until the job is finished.

Applying Compost

If your compost is thoroughly chopped and completely finished, you can apply it directly to the garden. It's best to do this right after you've tilled the area so as to loosen the soil, and then apply 3 or 4 inches of compost on top and stir it around to mix it with the loose soil below. Ideally, you will do this a month or so before you plant.

If, for whatever reason, you have some not-yet-finished compost, you can apply this to a section of garden in the late fall, or a few months before you expect to plant, and the decomposition will complete in the ground.

You can fertilize when your plants are already in the ground by placing the compost on top of the soil beside the plants—what's known as "side-dressing"—or better yet, by mixing the compost with some loose topsoil and using the combination as a thick mulch. In this way, you fertilize the plants as the nutrients work their way down to the roots. Meanwhile, your plants will enjoy the benefits of a thick mulch: protection from hard rains and erosion, moderation of soil temperatures, and discouragement of weeds.

Don't worry about applying too much compost. Plants will grow in pure compost, although they need soil to do their best. If you have enough compost to apply 3 to 6 inches a year, your soil and your plants will benefit from it.

Problems You Can Expect

There are a few common problems that folks encounter when building a compost pile. If you follow the instructions here, you aren't likely to encounter any of them, but in case you do, here's a troubleshooter guide.

Pile Too Wet

If you're experiencing a long period of rainy weather, put a tarp over the pile and let it dry out a bit. If you suspect that the problem isn't the weather, perhaps you added some thick, matting material like leaves to the pile without chopping them up. If that's the case, you may need to either pull out the offending material, let it dry, and chop it up, or just wait a long while, and it will compost anaerobically . . . eventually.

ALERT

Covering the pile should only be done on a temporary basis to remedy too much moisture or to control odors in the short term while the pile adjusts itself. All other times, it should be left open to the elements where it can take in rain and oxygen.

Pile Too Dry

It's hard to imagine this happening in any part of the world that has regular rainfall, but if you live in a desert, or are experiencing a long drought, your compost may dry out too much. If that's the case, all you need to do is soak it down with a hose or sprinkler. Compost should be uniformly moist, but not soggy.

Pile Smells Bad

Most likely your pile isn't aerating properly. Perhaps some of the materials are not chopped enough and are bunching up, in which case the solution may be as simple as turning the pile. If that doesn't work, you may need to break down any matted materials. It's also possible that the pile may just be too wet. If it smells like ammonia, that's a sign that you have too much nitrogen-laden material. Try adding something less hot, like rotten sawdust, rice hulls, or even garden soil.

Bugs, Flies, Worms

Follow the instructions for a too-wet pile, and try adding some dryer material, such as chopped hay or straw. If the pile isn't heating, then add nitrogen and turn it again.

ESSENTIAL

Compost can be made in as little as fourteen days, but it doesn't have to be made that quickly. If your compost pile doesn't heat up properly, there are steps you can take, but don't worry, it will compost sooner or later even if you don't do anything more.

Commonly Available Compost Ingredients

Any organic substance will compost, but some of them certainly work better than others. Here's a list of materials that should be fairly easy to find and will work nicely in your pile. A good pile will have twenty-five or thirty times as much carbon as nitrogen. Here are some good, commonly available sources of nitrogen:

- Manure of All Kinds. Rabbit manure is one of the best available, with 2.4 percent nitrogen. Poultry manure, 0.6 percent to 1.1 percent nitrogen, tends to be better than that of larger livestock, which is generally around 0.5 percent to 0.7 percent nitrogen.
- Grass Clippings, around 1 percent to 2 percent nitrogen.
- Cottonseed Meal, 0.7 percent.
- Feathers, 15.3 percent.
- Dried Blood (blood-meal), 10 percent to 14 percent.
- Brewery Waste, 1 percent.

Here are some good, commonly-available sources of carbon:

- Straw
- Rotted Sawdust
- Dried Leaves
- Corn Stalks
- Pine Needles

Composting materials are so varied that you shouldn't need to buy anything to start composting. If you're just getting started, and you have a whole garden to design and plant and nothing much in the way of compost or soil amendments, you may find it is helpful buy yourself a truckload of materials to get started.

As mentioned previously, many cities now compost the spring yard waste they pick up from citizens, and they make this compost available to the public at reasonable rates. However, if that isn't an option in your neighborhood, look around the outlying area for a turkey or chicken farm. These places tend to have huge, long houses filled with poultry, and they keep the floors of these houses covered with loose materials like sawdust, rice hulls, cottonseed hulls and the like, which they refer to as "bedding." They change this bedding with every new crop of birds, and often have a second business selling the used bedding, which is about 50 percent manure. Generally, they'll have a dump truck and will be prepared to deliver a whole truckload of the stuff to your backyard for a very reasonable rate.

When it gets there, it'll be in fine shape: loose, dry, and in reasonably small particles so you can treat it as a ready-made compost pile. Dump it in an appropriate spot, wet it down, and start adding your own kitchen garbage and other compostable finds to it regularly while turning it often. You can use it sparingly as a side dressing (at this stage, it *can* burn your plants if you use too much), or just let the whole thing sit for a few months. Either way, you'll end up with a lot of good compost as easily and quickly as any other method you'll find.

CHAPTER 9

Intensive Planting

Anyone who's ever started with bare sod and turned it into a producing garden knows that gardening can be a lot of work even if you have a small tractor, which most gardeners don't. There are, however, certain techniques in use all over the world that can turn most of the drudgery of gardening into a bit of light exercise in the outdoors. These techniques are referred to as *intensive gardening*, and they'll revolutionize the way you go about growing things.

Intensive Planting in Theory and Practice

Back in the 1890s, a type of gardening was "discovered" that featured double digging the soil and planting plants very close together. This was dubbed "French intensive gardening." Later, the esteemed J. I. Rodale would become a vocal proponent of French intensive and raised-bed gardening. Currently the Internet has brought new promoters claiming to be the inventors of different, but very similar, intensive methods. In addition to "French intensive," there is "biodynamic," "square-foot gardening," and other terms. The essential factor behind all of them is that plants don't get planted in long rows wide enough to accommodate tractor wheels, but in much closer spacing so as to maximize area and minimize weeding and maintenance.

FACT

The idea of planting gardens in long rows originated when horses and mules were used to cultivate crops. Today this practice is still the norm, even though these animals have long since been removed from the gardening process. By contrast, raised beds are meant to be worked by humans.

The close arrangement of plants was a good idea, but French intensive also called for digging a square shovel's depth into the soil, taking that soil out, digging that deep again, replacing the top layer to where the bottom layer was, and vice-versa. This is called "double digging," and you're probably tired already just reading about it, because digging into even the very finest garden soil two spades deep with a square shovel is serious, hard work. Imagine, then, what it would be like if your garden area were tightly packed, rocky clay!

Well, since the majority of gardeners do not have the very finest garden soil, and since the goal of this book is to show you how to become a backyard farmer immediately and simply, double digging will *not* be covered. A better method of achieving loose, fertile soil that works just as well, better in fact, is to lift the planting area up above grade by building raised beds, filling them with rock-free topsoil and compost, and as a companion method to that, growing plants in containers.

Double Digging Pains

Double digging loosens the soil more deeply than traditional plowing did, and by putting the sod layer underground where it would decompose, you add to the fertility of the soil. However, enduring hours of back-breaking labor is a rather high price to pay for these marginal improvements.

If you create a highly fertile, loose, and humus-rich soil mixture and fill your beds and containers with it, you can reap all the benefits of double digging and avoid spending the next day in pain from sore muscles and blistered hands. More than that, unless you were doing this double digging into some mighty fine soil, the soil you create for yourself will be far better, more fertile, and more arable than native soil that's been double dug. In addition to this, there are other techniques, such as companion planting and crop rotation, that you can use to maximize your garden soil space.

Plants Closely Spaced

When doing intensive planting, the ideal result is to space the plants far enough apart to make healthy gains, but close enough that the plants touch one another when they reach mature height. This maximizes the area under cultivation while blocking out the sunlight available to any weeds that may attempt to grow between the plants. In order to assure that the plants aren't crowding one another and competing for resources, it's important to make certain that the soil mixture provides all the nutrients necessary for each plant.

Companion Planting

One of the myriad fascinating lessons of gardening is that certain plants seem to get along well with each other. The American forefathers learned this from Native Americans, who planted corn, squash, and beans together, calling them "the Three Sisters" because of their affinity for one another.

Rest assured there are also plants that seem to positively detest one another. For example, asparagus seems to benefit from being close to tomatoes, and asparagus helps tomatoes, but asparagus dislikes being in the presence of onions or garlic. Marigold and nasturtium tend to discourage insect pests, while sage attracts honeybees and repels cabbage maggots. The list of beneficial and harmful companion plants is beyond the scope of this book, but you'll find long and detailed lists on the subject if you do an Internet search.

You'll find it handy to plant herbs and flowers that deter insects in buckets that can be moved about the garden when you need to place them adjacent to certain plants. This will provide a good many rewards in return for very little effort. Perennial plants like chives, garlic, and walking onions work particularly well for this, because you can overwinter them and have a number of planted buckets on hand each year to place beside your newly planted cultivars. Since they're already planted and ready to go, you don't have to take time away from planting during spring, when there's always a rush to get as many producing plants as possible into the ground.

FACT

Marigolds are the panacea of companion planting, as they produce a pesticide in their roots that inhibits the growth of perennial weeds and nematodes. This substance is so potent that it can last for years in the soil long after the marigold flowers are gone.

Crop Rotation

Another way to squeeze a bit more productivity from your plantings is to plant your crops in different areas each year, based on what has been planted in those spots before. Because some crops take certain nutrients from the soil, while others may actually add nutrients, you can make your decisions based on what might be the ideal location for any given plant in any given year. Corn, for example, is a heavy feeder of nitrogen, and can deplete the soil of nitrogen if planted in the same spot every year. Beans, on the other hand, are legumes, which means that they add nitrogen to the soil (but use a lot of phosphorus), so they would make a good crop to rotate where corn was growing previously. (It's worth noting that corn and beans were two of the "Three Sisters" mentioned earlier.) Crop rotation also benefits the backyard farmer, because he can expect certain insect pests to develop in the soil in reaction to the presence of any given plant, so his response can be to plant something that is unappealing to that insect the following year.

Building the Beds and Containers

After you've built your beds and taken them through a successful growing season, there's no need to make any major changes. Just add a new layer of compost over the winter, and come spring, stir the soil around a bit to mix it in. Then you're ready to plant for the new season with no further preparation. It is best to make your beds and containers from available materials that you can obtain for little or no cost. These will work just as well as items you've paid for, and the less they cost, the more satisfaction you can gain from them.

Raised-Bed Construction

First of all, you don't really need *any* sort of container for your beds; you can just pile up a lot of soil and compost, let the sides of the pile spill over into the paths, and be done with it. However, enclosing the beds saves space, keeps the beds from spreading, and provides a convenient spot for you to sit when planting, cultivating, and weeding. The latter is no small matter when maintaining a large garden.

A popular method of building a raised bed is to use old railroad ties stacked two high. This gives your bed a depth above grade level of about 16 to 18 inches. Ties are about 8 feet long, so if you use full ties for the sides, and ties cut in half for the ends, you'll have a bed of about 4" x 8". Railroad ties work especially well because they're heavy and stable enough that they won't easily get pushed out of place. Not only do they provide a comfortable place to sit while you work, but due to their stability and width, you can stand on them—a position which can be very handy when watering from a can or spreading mulch. Besides railroad ties, other popular materials include concrete blocks stacked without mortar, large and fairly regular stones, or boards nailed together.

Plant flowers and herbs that repel insects, such as garlic, tansy, petunia, nasturtium, and marigold, in small containers that you can set around the garden and move to different spots as the season progresses.

Make your beds narrow enough that you can reach every part of them from a comfortable, seated position. This makes working in the garden so much more enjoyable than squatting down to grade level or crawling on your hands and knees, and because you're going to be dealing with very loose soil under loose mulch, you won't need the leverage to swing a hoe or rake with force that traditional, in-ground gardening sometimes requires. In fact, most of the work you'll do to your beds can be accomplished with a small hand trowel, or even with your bare hands, while sitting down.

When trying to achieve a comfortable working environment, you may be tempted to build your beds higher than a foot or two. This may work well enough, but remember that a raised bed will dry out a bit more quickly than the ground below, and an especially small bed may be somewhat more prone to heat up or cool down to match the air temperature. Also, there's no reason why a bed should only be 8 feet long or square. If you make your beds as long as space will permit and narrow enough to reach across, with a comfortable place to sit along the length, you can work the complete length of the row without ever standing up.

Choosing Containers

Of course you can grow some plants in just about any container, so long as it has enough soil, good drainage, and sufficient water. However, for the most convenient solutions, you want to choose containers that are rugged and cheap, and at least as wide as they are tall. (Tall, thin containers use more soil in proportion to their plantable area and are more likely to be accidentally turned over.) Being easily portable is also a desirable trait for a container, although once you get beyond 18 inches or so in diameter, a container full of soil becomes pretty unwieldy, no matter how handy its shape or how strong its handles are. A 24-inch-diameter container is, despite its full weight of around 200 pounds, still a very convenient size for planting, so be prepared for the fact that you may choose to have at least a few, and perhaps a lot, of containers that are just plain heavy.

How close can I set plants in an intensive bed?
You can use two common methods to space plants. 1) Choose the distance given on the seed packet to space plants in rows, then ignore the row spacing and plant them all at the shorter distance. 2) Plant them close enough that the mature plants will just touch one another.

Five-Gallon Buckets

Five-gallon buckets are also very convenient containers. They have handles and are small enough to move around, yet you can plant about any herb in them, and even grow one respectable tomato vine, or pepper, or broccoli, if you wish. Just make sure you drill a couple of 1-inch-diameter holes in the bottom of the walls just above the floor. The best tool for this is a 1-inch hole-cutter mounted on a power drill. Drilling the holes in the sides of the buckets instead of the bottom makes for good drainage with less material falling out when you move the bucket. You can pay for 5-gallon buckets, but if you're at all resourceful, you ought to be able to find a source where you can get as many as you need for free.

Molasses Tubs

A really excellent planting container is a molasses tub. If you live within a reasonable drive of a farm that raises beef cattle, there's a good chance that they feet their cattle molasses, and molasses comes in heavy tubs about 24 inches in diameter by 20 inches high. Full of molasses, they weigh 200 pounds, and that's about what they'll weigh full of soil, so while they're portable, you probably won't want to move them any more than you have to. They're made from heavy plastic or rubber, and are very tough indeed, since they are meant to be kicked, mauled, and stepped on by 1,000-pound animals. Full of a rich soil mix, they'll easily support two or three tomatoes or a couple of peppers and several companion plants like nasturtium or marigold as well. You'll need to drill holes in the bottom sides of these, too. Four

1-inch holes at 90-degree angles from one another will work very well to provide drainage. If you don't know, or can't find, any cattle farmers, many farm stores that sell the full tubs also sell empty ones for a few dollars.

Recycling Containers

Perhaps the most obviously appropriate containers for planting are those black plastic ones that you bring home when you buy a large plant in a nursery or box store. Your best bet to find them for less than retail is from someone who buys a lot of plants, or from a greenhouse or nursery going out of business. They come in sizes from 1 gallon up to 25 gallons. Once you've built up a collection of all the tubs you need, they're practically indestructible, especially the molasses tubs, and should last you a lifetime.

ESSENTIAL

No matter how good your soil mixture, earthworms can make it better. They improve drainage, soil structure, and fertility. Try to put every earthworm you find in your beds or containers; you can lure them to an area with corn meal. They multiply rapidly in humus-rich soil.

Mulch

Mulch is material spread on the surface of the planting area thick enough (3 to 12 inches) to protect the plants, hold in moisture, moderate soil temperatures, and discourage weed growth. The best mulches are made up of material that can decompose and become part of the soil, but there are times when gardeners may choose plastic mulch or some other inorganic moisture barrier. Generally speaking, these are to be avoided, because they require maintenance to keep them from blowing in the breeze. Since they virtually never rot, if you put down plastic mulch, sooner or later you're going to want to take it up again.

Natural mulches, on the other hand, can be left on the soil indefinitely as "permanent" mulch, or simply tilled in. Adherents of the permanent mulch system never remove the mulch but dig holes into it for planting in successive years, after which they add layers of new mulch as the original lower layers decompose.

FACT

Mulch can moderate the soil temperatures so effectively that the soil under thick mulch can be as much as 10 degrees cooler than unmulched soil. This may vary with the type, depth, and color of mulch used, and the location of the garden in relation to the sun.

Permanent mulching is an easy solution, but stirring last year's mulch into the topsoil and replacing it with a new layer is pretty easy too. Mulch should be made up of fine particles that will decompose readily, and it should be applied thickly. Mulch will not eliminate weeds, but it will certainly lower their number significantly, and the weeds you do have will be much easier to pull out of soft, moist mulched earth than from hard-packed soil. There is little reason to need a hoe in a well-mulched garden.

There's an old idiom that "mulch eats rocks," which of course is foolishness, but the moist, humus-rich soil that you'll find under a good organic mulch after a few years will make you wonder if it isn't true.

Mulches conserve moisture by reducing evaporation and moderate soil temperatures while minimizing erosion and soil compaction. They're a pretty good example of a win-win situation, because they do so much good and create no new problems of their own.

Irrigation

If you try to keep up with all the latest garden-fads-of-the-month on the Internet, you'll get the impression that watering plants is a tedious, unending task without which you'd have a garden that looks like a particularly dry part of the desert. It is not. Not only is watering your garden easy and pleasant, it's one of the few garden chores that can be completely automated, so let it be clear: soil that holds water for unnaturally long periods of time is *not* desirable. Your plants need to dry out after a watering every bit as much as they need the water. This is similar to the way that you need to exhale not so very long after you've inhaled. Plants that aren't allowed to dry up a bit between watering develop root rot, mildew, and other vegetative malfeasance that you don't want.

ALERT

The water in a garden hose lying in the sun can get hot enough to kill or seriously impede the growth of garden plants. If you're not sure, let the water run for a minute or two before you turn it on your delicate cultivars.

As a rough rule, your plants should get the equivalent of an inch or two of rain per week. Unfortunately, Mother Nature is apparently unaware of this fact, so you'll need to be prepared to water your garden at least weekly, and during hot, dry spells, perhaps as much as twice or three times per week.

Watering Devices

There are essentially two sorts of devices to water your garden. The first is the soaker hose that applies water at the base of the plant and soaks the soil, but doesn't get much water on the leaves, which is good in most respects. This can save a lot of water from evaporation in hot, dry areas, and limit mold and mildew in damp, stagnant ones. Where those aspects are of less concern, many gardeners prefer the second type of device—a sprinkler, which can send a fountain of water up and over the entire plant.

Frankly, most sprinklers tend to function poorly in practice, because they spray water through tiny nozzles that invariably get plugged up with use. The best you can hope for is to keep a small screen on the incoming water supply, try to keep your sprinklers out of the dirt, and store them indoors during the off-season.

When watering, your goal is to have the water saturate the soil and then drain off. Using a raised bed helps a great deal in this regard, but try to avoid building your beds in low areas that will tend to leave excess water puddled around the bed. If necessary, you can build up the soil under the bed so as to make it a small hill, thus aiding in good drainage.

Solar Exposure

The very first thing you should determine when laying out a new garden is the location of the sun. More specifically, you should use a compass and make note of where due south is, because all of your gardening design should be based primarily on the location and movement of the sun overhead. That means that you'll need to arrange your tall plants, or those that will become tall, so that they don't shade lower-growing cultivars. If you're planting every square foot of your backyard, you'll need to take note of areas that are in full or partial shade during the growing season. Whereas you'll want to rotate crops among all your sunny beds and containers, the amount of rotating of shade-loving plants that you can do will be limited to rotating them with other shade-lovers, so the type of bed or container you prepare for those areas may be different in design or orientation. You may also choose to use less mulch in shady areas as well. Try taking photos of your growing area in early morning, midday, and late afternoon to see the extent of the sun's travel.

Pests

Just about any animal that really wants to can get into your garden. Having said that, plants in raised beds and containers unquestionably suffer less damage from small animals than those planted in the ground. While a box turtle may be about the only creature that actually can't get into a raised bed, you'll have much less trouble with rabbits, groundhogs, mice, chipmunks, armadillos, garden snakes and the like, who either have less tendency to notice or don't wish to bother with elevated vegetation. This is a benefit to the gardener, if not a panacea. While most of these pests don't tend to climb vertical walls, a hungry animal can be quite persistent and even creative in getting what he needs to survive. You can't expect foraging wildlife to simply ignore a garden just because it's raised up a few inches, and just one small trespasser can wipe out large sections of your garden. A raised bed offers at least a bit more protection than having your produce right at ground level. You may also use the structure of the walls to discourage small climbing animals with such things as electric wire or metal flashing installed along the perimeter.

CHAPTER 10

Growing Vegetables

If you have never grown your own vegetables, then you need to brace yourself for what may be a life-altering experience. You are about to discover that even in your first, awkward attempts, you can grow food for yourself with superior flavor to the commercial products you've been eating all your life. Your produce may not be as flawless in appearance as that in the store, but because it has been allowed to grow naturally and ripen on the vine, you'll be able to appreciate the difference instantly.

Producing Everything You Need to Survive

Modern culture seems to imply that humans have an innate dislike of vegetables. There is some basis behind this, but it is greatly overstated: Studies have shown that the average infant needs to experience a savory taste thirteen times before coming to enjoy it, whereas the same babe needs only to experience sweetness *once*. Unfortunately, due to modern advertising and marketing (working in league, no doubt, with a fair amount of parental innocence of nutrition), many of today's cherubs may have never had the opportunity to taste fresh greens or a sun-ripened tomato for the critical thirteenth time.

The truth, however, is that most folks who have had adequate exposure to good-quality veggies enthusiastically make them a major part of their diet. Not only is this quite appropriate, but even the most dedicated carnivore will have to agree that you can live a healthy life eating vegetables exclusively. In fact, some individual vegetables are so nutritious that they can sustain a reasonably healthy human without any other additional food (not that such a monotonous diet would be desirable).

Having the ability to produce everything your family needs to stay healthy and active may sound like a daunting chore, but it isn't complicated, and even if you do everything wrong, you'll probably produce a sizable crop if you only make the effort. Here are some notes and tips about how to cultivate and care for the most popular garden vegetables.

Tomatoes

Tomatoes are the most popular garden plant. People who have never grown any other plant may have cultivated a few tomatoes in their backyard; they're easy to grow, prolific producers, and attractive to boot. There are literally hundreds of different tomato varieties in a rainbow of colors, including white, yellow, orange, purple, brown, black, and of course, red. There are early and late varieties, low-acid and tangy varieties, slicing and paste varieties, and numerous other sorts. You'll have to determine which of these you like best through trial and error, but at this stage you only need to know about two different variations, and you can grow some of each if you like.

Choosing Your Tomatoes

First, you will choose whether to grow hybrid or heirloom varieties. Hybrids are known to have a robust vigor, and may outproduce the heirloom varieties, but many of them have been developed for traits other than good taste: traits like long shelf-life; smooth, uncracked skin; compact growth habits; disease resistance; uniform shape for packing; and durability in shipping. Heirloom varieties, as the name suggests, are the strains that have been grown and handed down through generations. They may have lower yields and suffer more difficulties from insects or disease, but many people find their taste superior. The important thing is that you can save your heirloom seeds for planting next year, but seeds from your hybrids will not reproduce the same tomato that you grew the year before.

ALERT

If the skin of your tomatoes is cracked, you may not be watering thoroughly enough. Instead of a quick sprinkle, give the soil a good soak once or twice a week so that the water goes deep and provides moisture evenly as the fruits form.

The second important distinction among tomatoes is between what's known as "determinate" and "indeterminate" varieties. Determinate tomatoes tend to bear their entire crop in a short period of time and grow on more manageable, compact vines, whereas the indeterminate varieties bear fruit over a longer period and grow on longer vines that require more staking. Obviously, the determinate varieties were developed more with mass-production in mind, where workers pick the fruit all at once, but the more compact vines are somewhat easier to deal with in intensive planting. Unfortunately, this distinction is rarely noted when you're buying seeds or bedding plants, so you may need to do your own research to find out which you're getting.

Once you've decided which varieties you want to grow, if you're starting early enough, you can germinate your own seeds. If later, you'll have to buy commercial bedding plants, which may limit your choices.

Seeds

To start seeds, set up a seedbed in a sunny south window in February or March, or about two months before the average last frost in your area. You can make your bed from fine, loose soil, or you may wish to start the seeds in peat pellets, which do their job nicely and which don't risk the shock from transplanting that may come from using the soil bed. A cookie sheet with an outside lip of about half an inch works nicely to contain your plants using either method. Tomatoes germinate best at about 70°F.

ESSENTIAL

You can improve seed germination markedly with a small heating pad placed under the growing medium, which will warm the root area ten to twenty degrees above the ambient temperature. You can pick up a germinating pad at a garden supply store, or you can make your own using old rope lighting.

The seeds should begin to sprout within eight to ten days, and should be watered frequently from the bottom. This means you should pour the water into the container (cookie sheet) rather than directly on the seedlings. Let the soil surface remain dry, if possible, while keeping the soil around the seeds moist.

When the seedlings have developed three or four true leaves (not including the two small seed-leaves that form immediately after germination), transplant the sprouts to small containers, such as 8-ounce paper cups. Return them to the window. Check the seedlings daily, and don't let them start to droop from lack of water, but don't water them until they get soggy either.

When the sprouts are seven or eight weeks old, it's time to transplant them into the garden. Treat the starts as gently as you can, taking them out of their containers with as much soil clinging to the roots as possible. Plant them deep, burying them up to the first or second set of leaves, leaving the top shoot sticking out of the soil. Place the seedlings 12 to 18 inches apart.

If you follow these instructions, you'll be doing this around the date of the average last frost date in your area. That means it is very likely that it may frost *after* you've set out your plants, so cover them each night with frost protection, which is anything that amounts to a roof over the plants so that frost doesn't settle on the leaves. You'd need to remove the protection during the day, of course.

Tomatoes do very well grown in large tubs, as well as in raised beds. In either case, however, they will need some support. A wire-mesh cage in a tubular shape works very nicely. You place it over the plant, stake it down, and you're good to go. You can also press a post or stake 5 or 6 feet long into the soil and train the plant to grow upward by tying it to the stake, at intervals, with twist-ties or scraps of cloth.

Peppers

Peppers, both hot and sweet, also come in many shapes and colors. They grow on a bushy, attractive plant and some varieties are grown specifically as ornamental plants, so if you want to place a few alongside the front walk, they'll look very nice. They are grown as annuals, but are actually perennials, so if you have the means to bring some indoors after frost, they will continue to bear fruit for a while.

FACT

Both sweet peppers and chili peppers are excellent sources of vitamin C. In fact, according to *Healthaliciousness.com*, green chili peppers provide more vitamin C than any other food, with 242.5 milligrams per 100-gram serving. That's 404 percent of the vitamin C your body needs each day, from just one serving.

Start your seeds indoors eight to ten weeks before you plan to transplant them to the garden. You can follow the same procedure as with planting tomatoes, but only plant the seedlings as deep as they grow as sprouts. Peppers also do well in containers, and their compact, bushy nature makes them easy to arrange in beds, where you should plant them 18 inches apart. Pepper plants have few natural enemies; the hot varieties have even fewer still. In fact, you can use a puree of the seeds of hot peppers, along with soap, to make an organic insect repellant. If you have a problem with marauding deer, the compact growth habit of pepper plants makes them ideal to fit into cages.

Lettuce

Some of the easiest and earliest gardening you can do is in growing a salad garden of green leafy vegetables. It's recommended that you start with leaf lettuce and expand from there to head lettuce, spinach, chard, and others. Leaf lettuce is among the easiest of all garden plants to cultivate. If you can keep the plants from getting too hot and dry in summer, you can grow successive plantings that will keep you in salad makings from frost to frost.

Sow your lettuce seeds directly into the garden, in fine soil, as early in spring as you can work the ground. Keep the seeds moist, and they should germinate in about a week. Sowing lettuce seeds is rather tricky. They are very small, and it's difficult not to wind up planting them too densely. At any rate, plant them about a quarter-inch deep, and when the sprouts start showing themselves, thin them to about one every 3 or 4 inches. Later, you'll want to thin them again to about ten inches. In all likelihood, this will be the first crop you'll get from your garden, and will be tastier and more tender than what you get at the grocery store. You'll be full of pride.

Like most leafy greens, lettuce is a cool-weather plant, and it doesn't react well to heat. You can have a summer crop and a fall crop, but you may have a bit of trouble keeping the plants from drying out in July or August.

FACT

You can get detailed information on the projected first and last frost dates in your area by looking up the National Climatic Data Center website online at *www.cdo.ncdc.noaa.gov*. They provide frost probability data for spring and fall at every weather station in your state.

Cucumbers

Cucumbers are another vegetable that is extremely easy to grow, and they are very prolific. Cucumbers have been grown in India for over 3,000 years, so their cultivation is commonplace to most gardeners everywhere. They grow rapidly to maturity and can be producing fruit at forty-five days. You can start the seeds indoors, or plant them directly in the ground. If you choose the latter, space the plants every 12 inches. Cucumbers are particularly sensitive to frost, so plant them at least two weeks after the last suspected frost, and be prepared to make a second planting in case the first gets frosted. Like their relatives, melons and squash, cucumbers need a lot of water and will cease production quickly if they get too dry.

You can let the vines trail along the ground, but they will spread far and wide, interfering with adjoining plants and pathways. On the other hand, if you put the vines on a trellis, they are quite easy to control, and you can grow them straight up if you want. A particularly effective configuration is a panel of heavy-gauge wire fence (cattle or hog panel) suspended over the cucumber bed, and about the same size as the bed below. Suspend the fence horizontally and train the first vines to grow up to it. You'll soon have both levels covered with vegetation and cucumbers.

Squash

The squash family consists of a diverse number of varieties, including pumpkin, zucchini, and spaghetti squash. Squash take up a lot of space, and don't produce a lot of fruit in return, especially the winter varieties. However, winter squash keep very well, and there's no denying the appeal of warm, buttered squash on a cold winter day, so provide your plants with a nice *strong* trellis they can grow on, to maximize the amount of fruit you can get in your small space. There are also bush varieties of squash, and this is a particularly rewarding route to take with popular summer varieties like the crooknecks.

Plant your seeds directly in the garden after all chance of frost has passed. Leave two feet between trailing varieties growing on a trellis. Bush varieties can be planted 16 to 24 inches apart, or one to a large container.

ALERT

Squash beetles suck the sap from winter squash and pumpkins in a very destructive manner. If you see a squash beetle, kill it immediately and look for more. Then look for clusters of small, round eggs on the underside of the leaves. Remove the eggs with the sticky side of duct tape and destroy them.

Squash self-prune their flowers. The plants will begin their blooming season by producing several of their typical large flowers, which will then fall off without producing fruit. This isn't a sign of something wrong. The plant generally produces female flowers before it produces any male flowers to pollinate them, so fruiting fails. Later in the year, when the plant has set a number of fruits and is working hard to develop them, it will prune off new fruits before they begin to mature and use up resources.

Potatoes

Potatoes originated high in the Andes of South America, and are a cool-weather plant. Today, there are more potatoes grown than any other vegetable. Potatoes are a crop that benefits greatly from crop rotation, and they should never be planted in the same location in two successive years. Ideally, you'd plant them in an area that previously hosted a legume, and *never* following tomatoes, as they share many diseases. Potatoes require plenty of moisture and an acid soil. They like a fertile soil, but make certain that the plants don't come into contact with fresh manure or lime.

You can plant any potato for seed, but the best advice is that you only use certified seed stock; potatoes from the grocery store can carry disease, and may have been treated to keep them from sprouting, which of course, is what you *want* them to do.

Plant the seed potatoes 5 or 6 inches deep and about a foot apart. Being a cold-climate crop, potatoes like to stay cool, and this can be promoted by using a thick mulch of straw, leaves, or hay. Early varieties can be planted a week or two *before* the last frost of the season.

When the plants begin to make their tiny white flowers, you can dig them up for new potatoes. When the plants begin to wilt, that means that they've grown as large as they're going to get, and they're ready to be dug up.

The Brassicas: Cabbage, Broccoli, Cauliflower, Etc.

While they may look quite dissimilar, cabbage, broccoli, cauliflower, and Brussels sprouts are closely related, and their cultivation is pretty similar as well. They all like cool weather, and you're best advised to get them in the ground as soon as possible. Unfortunately, this means planting started plants as early as you can to avoid frost exposure (although they can withstand light frosts). If it remains cool in your area long enough, you can make successive plantings as the season progresses. While the immature plants are almost identical, cauliflower is the most difficult of the group to grow. For an intensive planting, space the plants about 12 inches apart and sow seeds an inch deep.

You may find out that brassicas do better in your area planted for the fall season.

ESSENTIAL

You can "blanch" plants you want to keep light-colored, like cauliflower, by pulling the leaves over the growing head and tying them there. As a word of caution, this can cause rainwater to bead and set on the head, which may cause rot if you allow an opening in the leaves.

Sweet Corn

Corn is one of the only native American vegetables; it has been grown in North America for over 4,000 years. Corn takes a lot of nitrogen out of the soil, so you should fertilize it heavily with compost. Plant your corn in the same bed with your squash and beans. The beans will provide nitrogen for the corn, the corn will provide stalks for the beans to climb up, and the squash will create living mulch, covering the ground to keep weeds from sprouting.

Plant corn seed about 2 inches deep and thin so that you wind up with a plant about every 12 inches. Corn likes heat and it likes water, two things that seem at odds with one another. Plant corn two weeks after your last frost date, when the soil is at least 60°F. A good strategy is to apply thick mulch, even if you grow the corn with squash, to hold in the moisture. Since the sugar in corn deteriorates rapidly after the ears are picked, many gardeners like to plant corn in successive plantings so that they never have too much at one time. Corn is pollinated by the wind, so plant your corn in blocks rather than in long rows.

Beans and Peas

Beans and peas are legumes, which means that they "fix" nitrogen in the soil. This has little effect when the plants are growing, but after they've died, the soil they leave behind will be richer in nitrogen, a fact you should consider when arranging your rotation-planting schedule.

Peas may be planted very early in the year, four to six weeks before the last frost is expected. Plant the seeds about 1 inch deep, and sprinkle some wood ashes over the soil if you have it available. Peas seem impervious to cold. It isn't at all unusual to see them growing while covered with snow. Peas aren't fond of warm weather (over 70°F), and you're more likely to endanger your crop by putting it in too late than too early. Peas like a humus-rich, well-drained soil.

Beans require warmer weather. Don't try starting bean seeds indoors, as they don't transplant well; wait until after frost and plant the seeds 1 inch deep. Beans come in two varieties: pole and bush beans. Bush beans have a compact, bushy habit that allows them to spread to 2 feet in diameter, but they don't need staking. Pole beans, on the other hand, need stakes or poles to grow up to keep them off the ground. Beans respond well to heavy mulching and regular soil. You can pick beans all summer long if you plant them in two-week succession plantings.

Herbs

Humankind has been using herbs for myriad purposes throughout recorded history, and small wonder, for they are easy to grow, prolific, and have so many uses in the home and on the farm.

Growing herbs in containers is an easy decision to make, because they grow so well in small spaces, and since they grow well in larger spaces too, keeping them contained also protects the rest of the garden from being overrun. On the other hand, since so many herbs are beneficial to so many plants, tucking them into unused corners of your beds can provide insect protection to your other cultivars. In general, basil, borage, marigold, and nasturtium are helpful herbs that you should have scattered around the garden all summer long. Using containers to grow herbs also allows you flexibility that is not available when herbs are grown in the ground. For example, during the summer months when frequently-used kitchen herbs such as fresh basil or chives are in high demand, and at peak production, you may want to move a few of those containers close to the kitchen door for a while, later to be moved back to the garden for over-wintering. Also, beneficial flowers can be propagated in containers in the garden and moved to the front lawn during their blooming period to the benefit of your lawn plants and the enjoyment of your guests.

Of Special Mention: The Sweet Potato

If you were only going to grow one crop in your garden, you'd want to make it the sweet potato. According to the Center for Science in the Public Interest, the sweet potato ranks highest in nutritional value compared to all other major staple foods. In other words, should you find yourself in the situation that you had to live on one food alone, the sweet potato would keep you healthiest of all the staples. There are over 100 varieties of sweet potato, including strains that are red, yellow, pink, white, beige, and purple as well as the more common orange.

The simplest way to produce them is from slips or starts. You can make your own slips by cutting a sweet potato in halves or quarters (or leaving it whole) and burying it in potting soil. Sprinkle a little water on it, and keep it in a warm place for a few days until it sends up shoots. When these shoots get to be 6 or 8 inches long (in five or six weeks), they're ready to be cut off from the larger whole and planted in the ground. (You can also get a sweet potato to sprout by half-submerging it in a glass of water, which is also a way to create a rather attractive house-plant.) Sweet potatoes like a slightly acidic soil, preferring a soil pH between 5.0 and 6.5. Like most plants, they prefer a loose, aerated medium to grow in, and they can't take much frost, so plant the shoots after all danger of frost has passed.

You can plant sweet potatoes intensively by placing the slips 12 to 18 inches apart. Keep in mind that your plants will produce a prodigious amount of vegetation, so much that you may not need to do a lot of weeding or mulching. They start off slow and don't care to be crowded by weeds, so pay special attention to preventing weeds in the beginning; a heavy mulch will take care of this. After that, your plants will respond well to regular watering, but it's a good idea to stop, or reduce, watering a month or so before you expect to harvest. This will result in less splitting of the tubers.

FACT

Sweet potatoes smuggled into China in the sixteenth century broke a famine caused by the Little Ice Age and the lack of moist, fertile land to grow rice. Learning that sweet potatoes would grow on land worthless for growing rice, the government encouraged their planting, and for the next 300 years they were the staple food of China.

CHAPTER 11

Berries and Grapes

Berries are the jewels of the farm or garden, both figuratively and literally. There's nothing more visually appealing than a lush, ripe strawberry bed or vines covered heavily with ripening grapes. At the same time, berries might be the best cash crop for backyard farmers, and will bring a high dollar return and enjoy strong demand in the market. Additionally, properly grown berry plants are prolific producers that can reward you with enough small fruit to sell, and for your family to enjoy, all summer long.

Strawberries

If you want to make money from your backyard farm, raising strawberries is one of the first places you should look. A strawberry bed can be set out quickly and will produce an abundant crop the very next year. How abundant? Well, commercial strawberry producers can sometimes expect to get 20 tons of berries per acre. That works out to nearly a pound per square foot, or about 2 quarts of berries for every 3 square feet you plant.

Of course, you're thinking that you're not a commercial grower, and you don't have the experience or the equipment that they do. Well, that would be partly right, you don't have the experience, but you'll find that strawberries are actually more at home with raised-bed organic cultivation than they are with commercial production. As for the equipment, you already have that, since strawberries are rather manual-labor intensive.

Kinds of Strawberries

Your strawberry bed can be in full production the year after you set it out. When you start shopping the garden catalogs for types of strawberries, you'll find two major categories: June-bearing and ever-bearing strawberries. This is misleading. As June-bearing berries won't always bear in June at your location, and you might not want them to anyway. Also, while ever-bearing varieties produce over a longer period, they don't produce as much.

To maximize your returns, you'll find that you can buy early, midseason, and late varieties of strawberries. You should do this to increase your annual yield, although whether the time of ripening can be predicted accurately depends a great deal on the weather. You can plant some of all three varieties, and if you have a late spring, your berries may wind up all ripening at about the same time anyway.

ALERT

When it comes to berry pests, birds are the worst. You can keep these feathered felons from swooping down and burglarizing your berries by covering your berries with lightweight plastic bird netting the moment the fruit starts ripening. Be sure to stake down the corners of your netting, as it can easily blow away in the wind.

Typically, the ever-bearing strains don't produce as heavily and seem like a poor choice when considering an income-producing crop; however, if you just wanted a few berry plants greeting your visitors by the front walk, this might be your selection.

Maintaining Your Berries

As strawberry plants grow, they produce runners that shoot out from the mother plant and root themselves in the soil. How you handle these runners has an effect on how much work you do, and how high your yields are. There are three schools of thought here:

- The Matted-Row System. This technique calls for the plants to be set about 18 to 24 inches apart, and allows all the plants to send their runners out to make new plants. This is the easiest method and, like most easy methods, is the least productive one.
- The Spaced Matted-Row System. In this method, you place the plants at about 18 inches apart. The mother plants are allowed to send out a few runners, four to six, and the rest are pinched off as they appear.
- The Hill System. This is the method used by most commercial growers. Plants are set every 12 inches and all the runners are pinched off. This does not provide for a crop in the current season, but yields are maximized. Given the goals of the backyard farmer, this seems like the most appropriate method to use.

Before planting your strawberry plants, let them soak in a bucket of water in the shade for twenty or thirty minutes. It's important that the roots not be allowed to dry out during the planting process. When you start planting, dig a hole for each plant, then put a fistful of dirt in the center and arrange the plant's roots over this little pile of dirt so they fan out in all directions and the plant sits upright. When you've finished each hill, make certain that the roots are covered, and the crown (the green part) is above ground.

Now you have a strawberry bed. Your first year's maintenance will consist of plucking off the flower stems that shoot out from the plants. These flowers want to produce fruit, but you want the plant to put that energy into developing strong roots and lush leaves for next year's crop. Soon, the plants will begin sending out runners to make new plants and, unless you've opted for one of the matted-row systems, you'll want to pluck those off too. This is not only a fair amount of work, but it takes a certain mental attitude to pluck off blossoms and runners that would create berries and new plants when the reward for doing so takes another year to happen.

When the crop is growing well, do a little weeding, and before hot weather sets in, mulch your strawberries heavily with straw or pine needles or similar material you can easily find. The mulch will help maintain soil moisture, which is critical. Be sure to keep the bed watered as frequently as you water your vegetables. When winter arrives, cover the plants with a fresh application of mulch.

ALERT

Be sure to learn which Plant Hardiness Zone you live in. These zones are determined by the USDA and are based on average annual extreme temperatures across the country. You can find a map detailing each of the zones on the web at *http://planthardiness.ars.usda.gov/PHZMWeb/*.

If you have a problem with slugs chewing holes in your strawberries just as they begin to ripen, try replacing the organic mulch with plastic. You can install the plastic over the original mulch if you wish. Make sure to stake the ends and sides of the plastic down so the wind doesn't catch a corner.

Come spring, as soon as the plants start to make new growth but not before, pull back the mulch. Do this too soon, and you risk getting your crop frosted; do it too late, and the mulch will inhibit plant growth. The ideal time for this job would be the morning after the last frost of the winter. Of course it's impossible for anyone to say exactly when that will be, so your best bet is to pull back the mulch around the average last frost date, and be prepared to apply some covering, such as an old bed sheet, if frost is predicted after you've exposed the plants. If you don't know your average frost date, do an Internet search on "Average Date of Last Killing Frost."

Once the berries start to ripen, you'll be picking them every day, or every other day, and because you diligently pinched off all of last year's blossoms and runners, you'll be rewarded with more and larger berries than you'd otherwise get.

Blueberries

Long-lived and productive, blueberries present a true triple-threat: the taste is popular with most everyone, the foliage is quite attractive (they are relatives of the azalea and rhododendron), and the health benefits claimed are as attractive as any fruit you can name (they have the highest antioxidant capacity of all fruits). In all likelihood, you will never have eaten fresh blueberries as tasty as the ones you, yourself, will produce in your backyard. This is not because of any inflated sense of pride or accomplishment, although you will be forgiven if you feel either or both, but because blueberries need to stay on the bush until the very last minute, far too late for the commercial growers who've been supplying your blueberry habit up until now. Establishing new blueberry plants isn't especially difficult, and once they are healthy and growing happily, they may outlive you.

In selecting blueberry plants, you'll have several choices to make. There are four types of blueberry plants available for different local climates. The Highbush blueberry does best in Plant Hardiness Zones 4–7, the Southern Highbush blueberry in Zones 7–10, the Lowbush blueberry in Zones 3–6, the Half-High blueberry in Zones 3–7, and the Rabbiteye blueberry in Zones 7–9. If you have any doubts about what types you should grow in your area, check in with your USDA Cooperative Extension System. They'll have an office in your county seat.

Once you've decided on the type of blueberries you want to grow, you'll need to select varieties. Don't just choose one; there should be more than one variety to encourage cross-pollination, which will result in larger fruit in greater abundance.

Maintaining Your Blueberries

Blueberries stand out from other fruits in their soil requirements. They demand an acidic soil pH of 4.09 to 5.0. You can achieve this by mixing well-rotted compost with peat moss at a 50/50 ratio. Aside from the acidity, blueberry soil should be full of humus, well aerated, and moist.

Blueberries need to be planted in full sun. Plant your blueberry bushes at the distance recommended for the type you choose (it can range from 2 to 15 feet) and set the plants just slightly deeper than they were growing in the nursery. When you have them all planted, spread 3 or 4 inches of mulch on the ground to keep the roots cool and hold in moisture. Acidic materials, such as rotted sawdust, make the best mulches for blueberries. When your plants are in the ground and mulched, see that they get an inch or two of water every week—maybe more during hot, dry conditions. This may be more complicated than it appears at first. If you have hard water, you'll need to acidify it. You can do this by adding 2 teaspoons of vinegar per gallon of water.

FACT

If you feel that blueberries need a lot of hard work and preparation, you're not alone, but you need to view the effort you exert in perspective to the potential return. Individual blueberry plants have been known to live as long as sixty years, so the work you expend on your plants can last a lifetime.

As your plants grow, they will require a certain bit of maintenance. You'll want to remove any fruit buds for the first couple of years to allow the plant to thrive, and at three years some pruning will be in order in late winter to remove old wood and poorly placed limbs. You may want to remove some fruit buds to make the remaining ones develop into sweeter, larger berries.

Lowbush varieties should be pruned to the ground every two years. The pruned bushes won't bear the year after pruning, so do half of your bushes one year then the other half the next.

Highbush varieties need to have all the six-year-old wood cut off, and any other pruning needed to alleviate crowding or to eliminate poorly developed stems.

If all this seems like quite a lot of trouble, well, it may sound worse than it really is if you consider the work is spread out over the year. But if you're looking for a somewhat easier and more flexible solution, you might consider some of the Half-High varieties in containers. Don't forget that you'll still need several individuals for pollination, and you should move the containers to a protected, sunny place during Northern winters.

Brambles

Bramble fruits are those growing on thorny canes or vines such as blackberries, red and black raspberries, boysenberries, loganberries, and others. Before considering whether or not you want to raise brambles, you need to ask yourself if you really need to. If you live in a place that would be considered rural, then there may be all the berries you want already growing wild and free. In addition, wild berries are just about equal to the domestic varieties in size and quality, or can be at any rate.

However, if your neighborhood is too urban for wild brambles, or if you can't find any without doing some serious, heavy-duty trespassing, then don't worry, the domesticated varieties aren't much more work to grow than the wild ones, and of course you can grow them right in your own backyard where the ticks and snakes are, presumably, less numerous.

Growing Brambles

There are a large number of different bramble varieties available, and if possible, you should buy your starter plants locally from an established nursery that can advise you as to which grow best in your area.

Blackberries and raspberries will grow well in raised beds; you need to provide them with loose, humus-rich soil and good drainage. They also need full sun, although raspberries, preferring a slightly cooler environment than blackberries, will accept some afternoon shade. You can also grow brambles in containers, but keeping the long canes contained may be more of a problem. Growing your plants alongside a wall, or along the edge of your garden, will work nicely.

In planting your new plants, remember that the new growth won't come from the old canes on the plants, but from inside the root clump. Dig a hole for each plant, and put a ball of soil in the bottom, then fan the roots out around that ball as you would when planting strawberries. You can plant in spring or fall, but spring is preferred. Mulch your plants before hot weather arrives. You may want to weed a couple of times before mulching to eliminate any weed seeds in the ground, but you can mulch immediately after planting if you so desire.

Your plants need regular watering, of course, and as with all newly established perennial plants, this is especially important the first year. Watering brambles with a soaker hose or drip irrigation is best, because it avoids getting the foliage wet and creating an environment for disease to grow.

Brambles require a good deal of pruning, and this is easiest to do if the plants are arranged in rows. You can also grow them in patches, but this method doesn't facilitate maintenance so well, and probably isn't the best choice for cultivation in a limited amount of space.

ESSENTIAL

Set your bramble roots in a bucket full of manure (or compost) tea for twenty minutes before you plant them to keep them from drying out. Dust the wet roots with a sprinkling of bone meal and kelp to give your young plants an extra boost.

Red raspberries and blackberries send out new growth from the roots of old plants. These new canes are green and relatively soft during their first year. In their second year, they become harder, browner, and begin to bear fruit, after which they die. Your job is to keep the dead canes pruned back, and to keep the living canes under control with trellising so that the canes don't sprawl out into your footpaths. You'll also want to prune your new-growth canes so that new blackberry canes occur every foot or so, and raspberries at about half that.

So-called "ever-bearing" raspberries can produce fruit in spring and fall. Many growers simply prune these to the ground, choosing to only harvest the fall crop, which will be more abundant.

When it's time to harvest, wait as long as you can; brambles shouldn't be picked until they are fully ripe, since they won't ripen further after they're picked. Raspberries are ripe when the berries easily separate from the core. Blackberries are ripe when they easily separate from their stems.

As you've probably already guessed, brambleberries don't keep very well. That's part of why raspberries cost so much in the store. Probably the best way to store your crop is to freeze them on a cookie sheet and then transfer the frozen berries into plastic containers for the long term.

Gooseberries (and Currants)

They grow like weeds and look like ornamental shrubs. As with brambles, you may discover that gooseberries are so common growing wild in your area that you choose not to bother growing your own, although most folks aren't so aware of wild gooseberries as they are of wild raspberries or blackberries. Wild gooseberries are perhaps more of a delight for farm kids who grew up on those great green gooseberry pies. At any rate, gooseberries, and to a lesser extent, currants, grow on well-behaved, attractive bushes that would double as ornamental shrubs or hedges. Also, as with anything that grows wild, they aren't hard to cultivate.

Gooseberries and currants aren't too particular about their soil, and they like to have thick mulch placed around them. They'll grow in raised beds and containers, but make certain that they're fairly large containers, and pay close attention that the plants don't dry out between generous watering sessions. Unlike nearly everything else that produces fruit, gooseberry bushes can tolerate some shade.

FACT

No one is sure where the name "gooseberry" originated, but one plausible suggestion is that it is a corruption of the French word *groseille*, or red currant. This might be a bit of a stretch, as the words don't sound too similar, but the currant is a relative of the gooseberry.

Wild *ribes,* as gooseberries or currants are called in biological terms, grow like weeds and produce berries for years on end without any maintenance whatsoever, but most growers of domestic bushes prune out canes over three years old. Pruning to manage space isn't really necessary, because these bushes tend to spread slowly and have a nice, compact growth habit. Just throw a little compost around the base of the plant every spring and give them enough water to keep them from wilting, and they'll reward you appropriately.

The Home Vineyard

There's no doubt that grapes are the most valuable fruit crop worldwide, or that grape growing is the world's largest food industry. Grapes have been cultivated (and made into wine) for the last 7,000 years or so. There are more than sixty species and 8,000 varieties, so it's understandable if you're having a little trouble deciding which ones to grow. Grapes can be grown for use as fresh treats, as raisins, in wine, in juice, or in preserves.

Select a spot in your backyard with plenty of sun and southern exposure. Like so many plants, grapes like a lot of sunshine. If you're planting a small vineyard, raised beds may not be the best plan because the plants can live for many years and rock-free rich soil is not one of their particular needs due to very deep rooting. In this instance, you may want to forego raised-bed planting for the simplicity of planting directly into the ground. Plant the rooted vines six or eight feet apart. If you plant them in rows, the rows need to be that far apart. You can decide whether you want to keep the weeds down with mulch or by mowing. If you choose the latter, your rows might need to be a bit wider, depending on the machinery you plan to use.

Dig holes for each plant wide enough that you'll have room to spread the roots out, and deep enough that you can plant the vine at about the same depth it was in the nursery. Do not let the roots dry out during planting, and don't add any fertilizer to the holes; grapes produce well on surprisingly poor ground. Just fill the holes up with good topsoil and press it down so as to create a slight depression to hold rainwater. Make sure to check the plants in the early weeks to make certain that they get enough rain, an inch or so a week, and water them when they don't, but be careful. You need enough moisture for the plant to establish itself, but grapes need good drainage above all else, so make certain that your soil is at least three feet deep above any rock strata, hardpan (a hard or nearly impermeable layer a short distance beneath the grade level of the soil), or anything else that could stop water from draining down into the subsoil.

And that's about all . . . for the first year, at least. As that year comes to a close, however, you need to have posts set in the ground about every fifteen feet along the rows, so that you can run two horizontal #10 wires between them to support the vines. This configuration, by the way, is the most common among home growers, and is referred to as the four-cane or four-arm Kniffin system.

FACT

Apparently, North America has always been a productive place to grow grapes. When the Norwegian explorer Leif Ericson arrived at the northern tip of Newfoundland in A.D. 1001, he was so impressed by the abundance of grapevines that he named the place Vinland.

Pruning is one of the many arts you can expect to learn in growing grapes. If you prune too much, you'll get lots of vine growth and poor yield, although the clusters and the grapes will be large. If you prune too little, you'll have little vine growth and lots of fruit in small clusters of small berries of low quality. As a general rule, you want to leave no more than sixty fruit buds on a mature vine, but at least forty. These buds will be where this year's growth develops, and that new growth will be where this year's fruit will grow.

The best of this year's new growth will come from one-year-old wood. These vines will have a smooth skin, or bark, and later will develop the rough bark of older vines. If you let the vine have its way, that is, allow it to grow unpruned, eventually the fruiting buds will grow farther and farther from the roots until they don't produce at all. In order to keep fruit production going reasonably close to the main trunk, cut off that which produced the fruiting vines last year and allow newer one-year arms to grow off the main trunk, or off the base of the old arm near the main trunk. You'll also need a vine to save for fruiting next year, so you leave a short arm near the base of the arm you've chosen to fruit this year. Thus you ensure production this year and the next. On the branch you leave for this year's production, there will be smaller vines branching off from each node. Cut these back to two or three buds.

Obviously, this is just one way to train a grape vine, and this method will provide a good basis for as large a vineyard as you want to grow. If you only want a few plants, you can grow them on a trellis or trellises, or on an old-fashioned grape arbor, so long as you prune them with this two-year growth plan in mind.

If you decide to grow grapes on an arbor, plant one vine for every 50 to 100 feet of area under the arbor, depending on the nature of the soil. Fifty square feet would be the minimum needed for a healthy plant on marginal soil, and vigorous plants on deep, rich soil should have 75 to 100 square feet.

While grapes will benefit from good soil, they don't demand it, and grape roots can grow as deep as 15 feet, so heavy watering isn't needed either. Mild mulch, not too full of high-nitrogen materials, will suit grapes well, and green manure crops plowed (carefully) in between the rows will also add an appropriately gentle amount of fertility. Don't try to rush your plant growth with strong boosts of fertilizer; grape culture is more sophisticated than that.

CHAPTER 12

The Backyard Orchard

The first cultivated fruit tree was probably the fig, which fossil evidence indicates was domesticated in the Middle East over eleven centuries ago. That makes it arguably the earliest recorded cultivar, which in turn makes the orchard an even older concept than the garden. That's proof that mankind loves fruit above all foods, and today some new techniques mean that you can produce more of man's favorite food in a small area than ever before in history.

Standard versus Dwarf and Semi-Dwarf Trees

A frugivore is not someone who eats very cheaply, but someone who primarily eats fruit. These days, it would be easy to mistake one for another, because home fruit production will allow you and your clan to eat very cheaply—once you've got the orchard installed, that is. Like so many other parts of farming, there's definitely some work involved in setting out an orchard, and like most work, the most important part of it is the planning.

Plan Your Orchard

When planning your orchard, the first thing you have to decide is what size trees you want to grow. Fruit trees come in three sizes: standard, semi-dwarf, and dwarf. That sounds simple enough, but it gets a bit more complicated. Standard trees are, of course, the largest, being typically 18 to 25 feet tall and wide—except when they aren't. A standard-size peach or nectarine tree is only 12 to 15 feet in height and width, which is the size of some semi-dwarf trees.

Standard trees take longer to bear fruit than dwarf and semi-dwarf varieties, and they produce more fruit per tree. However, they are planted much less intensely (typically 100 to 110 trees per acre) and as a result, they produce far less in terms of their yield per acre than the smaller trees.

Dwarf trees, on the other hand, can be planted very densely and will produce some amazing results in terms of productivity. For example, in studies done by the University of California at Davis, dwarf peach trees were planted at 500, 1,000, 1,500, 2,000, and 3,000 trees per acre. According to their findings, 1,000 to 1,500 trees per acre was the optimum planting distance. In their tests, dwarf trees planted at 1,500 per acre yielded 30 tons per acre the third year after planting, compared to 15 tons per acre for standard-size trees planted at 108 trees per acre in their sixth year. In other words, dwarf trees produced twice the fruit in half the time. It's hard to argue with numbers like that.

Add to this the matter of convenience. Dwarf trees can be picked standing on the ground, where-as standard trees can be as much as 25 feet tall, and even semi-dwarves will reach 12 to 15 feet in height. In short, with standard-size trees, you'll be picking from a ladder, and even then, you'll be leaving some fruit on the tree at the highest points. So dwarf trees are not only more productive and more efficient, but because they don't require a ladder, they're even safer!

QUESTION

Can I revitalize my long-neglected older fruit trees with pruning?
Yes. You may be able to reinvigorate a neglected tree with heavy, educated, and thoughtful pruning, although some trees are too far gone, and if this is the case, you're better off cutting the old trees down and planting new ones in their place.

In terms of yield and convenience, dwarf trees would appear to be a simple choice of more versus less, easier versus harder. However, it isn't quite that much of a no-brainer. Putting 15,000 dwarf fruit trees on a single acre of ground is pretty intense and a great deal of work by anyone's standards, even with heavy equipment, which you would surely want to have. That gives you an average of 5 feet, 4½ inches between the trees, so obviously, you're not going to be doing any maintenance with the help of a tractor after planting.

ESSENTIAL

Grafting is accomplished by taking cuttings from a single tree known for the desirable traits you want to encourage (such as good taste, large fruit, or winter hardiness) and joining each cutting to a root system and trunk base (rootstock) of another tree also known for its desirable qualities.

Not only that, but 30 tons of fruit per acre is quite a bit of food all happening at once, so depending on how much you plant and how well you maintain the trees, you may have a lot of produce on your hands in a short amount of time. To complicate things further, 1,500 dwarf trees present a whole lot more work for the orchardist than do 108 standard trees. Digging 108 holes to plant fruit trees is plenty of work in itself, but consider digging 1,500 of them. Additionally, whereas orchards of standard-size fruit trees are clearly a collection of freestanding trees, modern dwarf orchards, the way the professionals grow them, look more like vineyards because of the way they're supported on trellises. These days, dwarf trees are planted either with a single stake supporting the main trunk of the tree, or on a trellis system similar to the trellises on which grapes are grown. As for the fruit itself, the fruit on dwarf trees is at least as big as that on standard trees, and the quality of fruit on the dwarf is usually equal to, or better than, the standard.

Planning and Planting

Fruit trees can live from fifteen years to a lifetime, another reason why it's important to plan your orchard thoughtfully. As a general rule, you can expect that the more intensely your dwarf stock is planted, the more effort will be required. If you're looking for the most crops you can produce on your land, then you'll opt for the most intensive planting, and you'll need to be prepared to do the most extensive maintenance.

In selecting a good site for an orchard, you'll either have what it takes or you won't. First of all, a good site is one that has good water drainage and air drainage. If you live in a valley with a high water table, or if your planting area has a depression or depressions that trap water, this is not a good location because of poor water drainage. If you live in a valley with hills all around, then you probably don't have very good air drainage. That is, as the sun goes down, the cooling air flows downhill the way water would, and it then settles in the valley and stays there. Locations like this are often called "frost pockets," and you'll find that the last average frost here can be some days behind that of the hillsides or hilltops in your area. Of the two, poor water drainage is the bigger problem, because fruit trees cannot live with their roots in standing water. It is possible to grow fruit in bottomland valleys; it's just better to do it at a higher elevation, if possible. Hilltops and southern slopes are preferred over northern slopes and low areas.

ALERT

All newly planted trees need water critically, but not too much. Thoroughly wet the ground around new plantings and keep the soil evenly moist for the first summer, but not saturated. Overly wet soils displace air in the soil with water, which can kill the trees.

As for the actual planting, the timeworn rule says to dig a hole as deep as the root ball and twice as wide as the spread of the tree's roots. Fruit trees do not require a great deal of fertilization, so you shouldn't fertilize the planting soil, but they do like a nice, deep topsoil to grow in, preferably up to 3 feet deep, although as little as a foot will do. At this point, you need to decide if you want to keep the soil you have as it is, perhaps cleaning out any rocks or adding very well-rotted compost to it, or replace all the existing soil with good-quality topsoil. This is critical, because fruit trees very much want to be able to send out roots easily, so they need a loose medium in which to expand in all directions. If your soil is hard-packed or extremely rocky, or if it has an impenetrable hardpan below, these situations need to be remedied before you plant.

If you're setting out a micro-orchard of just a handful of trees, then, planting directly into the ground is probably the best route. But if your soil is severely rocky, or if you have a hardpan underground, you might want to plant your trees in a raised bed.

ALERT

You should never fertilize the planting hole of a fruit tree with anything but well-rotted compost. Chemicals or organic materials that are only partially decomposed may prove toxic to the roots. Well-rotted compost, on the other hand, will be beneficial to the tree if thoroughly mixed into the soil.

Digging the proper planting holes for an orchard full of fruit trees of any size is no small undertaking, and if the number of holes you have to dig is too many to do in an acceptable amount of time, you should consider renting a powered hole auger. If you have very loose, workable soil and a friend to help, you can get a hand-held, two-man, gas-powered auger, but in all likelihood, you'll need a little more muscle (and stability) than that, so a skid loader or farm tractor with a larger-diameter auger attachment will make relatively short work of this big job.

When planting the trees in the holes, you need to keep the grafts (the round knot at the base of the stem where new roots were grafted onto this plant) an inch or two above the soil. If you have to dig deeper than the root ball to break up hardpan, remove rocks, or eliminate other compaction, you should make certain that the soil doesn't settle back into the hole in such a manner that the graft is beneath or touching the soil grade level. If that happens, the top portion (or scion of the graft) will grow roots and negate the effect of the grafted root system. Make sure that your trees are exposed to the sun for as long as possible each day. If you're planting in rows, arrange them to run north and south. The soil pH should be between 6.5 and 7.0, and you'll want to add quite a bit of organic matter before you plant. The latter point is very important, because you don't have much control over the soil conditions after the tree has been planted.

Organic Orchards

Maintaining an organic orchard is more difficult than keeping an organic garden. In less arid areas where deciduous trees make up the majority of the forest, you may need to spray for insects several times per year if a problem develops. Doing this organically will result in lower expenses for the spraying, but also in fruit with more insect damage. If growing organic fruit is your goal, you'll want to fertilize with compost instead of chemical fertilizers, of course, but there are a few other tips of note. For example, if you see fruit developing with blemishes or worm damage, don't hesitate—pull it off. If you keep the distance between fruits on the limb at 6 or 8 inches apart, it will result in less disease and larger apples. New tree varieties are being developed constantly, so stay tuned-in to local growers' groups and Internet forums for the latest developments of disease- and insect-resistant strains.

Pruning Fruit Trees

Fruit trees need to be properly pruned and trained in order for them to yield more and higher-quality fruit faster than if they had not been trained for correct shape and form. Trained trees will also live longer. The goals of pruning are to remove dead or diseased limbs, and to develop a strong tree whose branches will not break or split under the heavy load of a bountiful crop. Pruning also opens up the tree canopy to the sun, which in turn permits the movement of air through the canopy, discouraging disease.

Pruning tools should always be kept sharp and clean. Dull shears require more effort on your part, and since they don't make such clean cuts, the tree doesn't heal as quickly and is subject to more risk of disease or insect attack. Wipe the blades of your shears with rubbing alcohol after pruning each tree to avoid spreading disease from one tree to the whole orchard.

Espalier

Suppose you only want a few fruit trees in your intensely planted backyard farm. In that instance, you'll probably be looking for space-saving ways to provide for the most harvestable fruit in the smallest amount of space amidst all your other garden plantings. In that case, you'll want to familiarize yourself with the ancient technique of *espalier* growing, in which trees are trained to grow in a two-dimensional single plane, such as against a building or wall. Espalier was originated by the ancient Romans; however, the practice was expanded in seventeenth-century Europe as an attractive way to buffer against cool, wet climates and maximize growing spaces in courtyards and formal gardens.

ESSENTIAL

If you live in a climate that may be marginal for growing fruit trees, you can extend your growing season by espalier-training your trees along a warm, south-facing wall that will reflect more sunlight, warm the soil, and protect the tree from those cold north winds.

Espalier can be very decorative, but it also has a practical side. There are several typical patterns that espalier can take, with descriptive names like "candelabra," "fan," and "palmette," but the idea remains the same: to train the branches into a single plane so that they grow out horizontally to a desired distance, at which point the spurs are encouraged to grow vertically. Apples and pears are most commonly used in espalier training, but most any woody-stemmed plants will work as well. Espaliers are not always trained against walls but can also be freestanding, to create a low hedge full of fruit.

Citrus

Oranges, grapefruits, lemons, and tangerines are exotica for those north of Planting Zone 8, and if you're going to be growing them there, it can only be in a container that can be moved indoors in winter; but if you're in Zone 8 or south of it, then you're in business.

Citrus is different from the other fruits in more ways than its climactic requirements. For example, container-grown citrus trees transplanted into the ground are very slow to send their roots out into the soil of the new location. You can speed this process up by using a garden hose to wash off the top half-inch or so from the root ball just before putting the tree in the ground. This will leave the tips of the tree's roots in contact with the new soil and hasten the adoption of the new location.

Citrus trees require excellent drainage, as they don't care to have their roots in standing water any more than any other fruit tree—probably less. They want a soil pH of 6 to 8, and the soil should be as salt-free as possible. For these reasons, you might want to consider growing them in raised beds, using imported soil. You'll need a planting hole equal to what you'd use with any fruit tree, and it's important that it be planted a little high—the top of the root ball should be about an inch higher than grade—so that rainwater runs away from the trunk. It isn't recommended that you mulch your citrus trees, or if you do, that you keep the mulch a good distance—a foot or two—from the tree itself.

Nut Trees

Not all orchards are full of fruit. A managed planting of nut trees is also called an orchard. However, growing nut trees is generally quite a bit different from cultivating fruit trees, perhaps especially so for the backyard farmer. To begin with, most nut trees are hardwoods, which is to say that they grow very slowly. They are, in fact, among the slowest-growing plants on earth. When it comes to planting new trees, how long it will take your saplings to bear nuts may well be your major criterion. Here's a list of nut trees, their heights, and bearing-year information:

▼ **DOMESTICATED NUT-TREE ESSENTIALS**

Tree	Mature Height	First Bearing	Harvest	Hardiness Zones
Butternut	40–50 feet	2–3 years	September	4–7
Almond	12–15 feet	3–4 years	September	5–9
Chestnut	25–30 feet	3–5 years	September	4–8
English Walnut	30–40 feet	4–5 years	October	5–9
Black Walnut	40–60 feet	4–7 years	October	4–9
Pecan	75–100 feet	7–10 years	October	5–9
Hazelnut	15–18 feet	7–10 years	August	5–8

If you decide you want to plant your own nut trees, the best advice is to plant domesticated varieties. They will reward you with a harvest in much less time than the wild varieties of the same species, and they also may contain improved genetics that will manifest themselves in bigger nuts with thinner shells, disease resistance, and/or taller, straighter growth. Since so much time and a large amount of space are being invested in each nut tree, take advantage of the best seed stock of which you can avail yourself. Most states have forestry departments that run nurseries that make bundles of bare-root seedling trees, including nut trees, available to residents of the state for extremely low prices. Place your order the year before and they will supply the trees to you in early spring.

▼ **WILD NUT-TREE ESSENTIALS**

Tree	Mature Height	First Bearing	Distribution
Butternut	40–50 feet	5–6 years	Midwest-Northeast
Hickory	80–100 feet	5–10 years	Midwest
Black Walnut	70–100 feet	10 years	Eastern United States

Planting Nuts

On the other hand, if you just want a large tree that happens to bear nuts, and time has little meaning to you, then you can simply plant a few nuts in the ground and wait. Nut trees tend not to be especially particular about soil conditions, and if you collect your seeds from local trees, you're assured that the seedlings will do well in your climate.

Nut trees in general do not lend themselves well to the smaller backyard farm. In addition to their slow growth and their late bearing age, they take up a lot of space vertically, laterally, and underground, as the roots often mirror the size of the tree above ground. However, you can control the ultimate size of the tree by pruning and by purchasing smaller cultivars, so if you really want your own nut orchard, having it is within your grasp. If you already have a mature nut tree bearing nuts in your backyard, you should definitely keep it, but if not, you can probably put the space to better use.

Pruning Nut Trees

There are two schools of thought regarding pruning nut trees. If nut production is your prime or only interest, then the trees should be pruned in much the same way as fruit trees, seeking to form an open crown that exposes the inner branches to sun and air. If timber production is part of the equation, the central trunk of the tree must remain intact, although pruning of the branches to remove dead wood and open the canopy is acceptable.

While it may seem more frugal to grow trees for the double purpose of nuts and timber, you should keep in mind that the tree you plant today won't be providing you with lumber in your lifetime. Many people decide to enjoy the nuts during the seven or eight decades they have, and let their children and grandchildren worry about the lumber when the time comes.

Selling Black Walnuts

If you already have a black walnut tree, or you know someone who does, you may want to look into selling walnuts. While not highly lucrative, if you have an abundant source of walnuts, you can make a few dollars in a weekend or two. The Hammons Products Company of Stockton, Missouri, has walnut-buying stations set up each summer in sixteen of the eastern United

States. You bring them your harvested walnuts, and they'll husk them, weigh them, and pay you accordingly. Don't expect to get rich at this enterprise— prices paid generally run from twelve to fifteen cents per pound which, when you take everything into consideration, will net you about as much money for the time invested as will a minimum-wage job. It's not something that you'll give up your day job to pursue. A bushel of walnuts, by the time they've been hulled, will yield about nine pounds of nuts. On the other hand, if you weren't doing anything with the time anyway, you'll be a few bucks ahead. Besides, if you do have a large walnut tree that's produced a bumper crop, you'll need to be picking the nuts up off the lawn anyway, or you'll be stepping on them every time you walk through the grass. Not to mention they make some awful noises when you hit them with a lawnmower.

CHAPTER 13

Poultry

The backyard farmer is usually somewhat conflicted about raising poultry. While he recognizes that farm-raised eggs are unquestionably superior to the ones for sale in the store, he questions the financial viability of small-scale egg- and meat-production. These days, to the amazement of many, raising chickens in the urban or suburban backyard is one of the latest major fads, which is leading some folks to some very un-farmer-like purchases.

The Pros of Keeping a Few Chickens

Some organic producers claim that whatever they're producing is superior to what's available in the stores. For the most part, this is true, but occasionally you'll come face to face with some products, such as potatoes, where the homegrown version doesn't seem appreciably different from the store-bought spud. If that's how you feel, and if you've never experienced a farm-raised egg, then you may find it most convenient to remain innocent in this regard, because once you've savored the taste of a "real" egg, you will never want a store-bought egg again.

Eggs

There's a common misconception that the farm-fresh egg is fresher than the "factory-fresh" egg, and that this lack of freshness is what makes the difference. This is far from true; a farm egg will never turn into the same egg that the factory egg is, even in ten years.

FACT

Chickens begin the natural process of molting, in which they shed all or some of their feathers, at about eighteen months. They'll cease laying eggs during this time, which can last from two to four months, and will begin laying again afterward, though perhaps not as prolifically as before.

So-called "farm-fresh" eggs are not superior because they are fresher; they're superior to store-bought eggs even when the store eggs are fresher. That's because on a farm, chickens have a very varied diet, where they get to browse over a natural, grass-covered terrain. There they ingest bugs, grass, small rocks, and even table scraps if you make them available, which you should. The factory bird, on the other hand, sits in a cage all day eating nothing but chicken pellets. You'll sometimes see commercially produced eggs that claim to be "free range" or "cage-free." While this may be technically true, in many cases it is a come-on, because the "range" that these chickens browse on is shared with hundreds of other birds on ground that hasn't seen a blade of grass or an insect since the company was started.

While information on the egg carton will not tell you everything you want to know, the product will give you the full story. Farm-raised eggs have dark, orange yolks that stand up perkily above a clear egg white. The shell is a little harder to break, and the taste is infinitely superior. Factory-egg yolks, which are about the color of butter, lay flat, nearly flush with the whites, and the whites are actually a translucent yellowish color. The flavor isn't bad, it's just that there isn't much of it when compared to the flavor in farm eggs.

Meat

The eggs are enough of a reason to raise a few chickens in your backyard, but you'll also be rewarded with an everlasting supply of fresh meat, as the roosters you get aren't required for egg production. Also, your chickens will supply you with some of the finest-quality manure to go into your compost pile. Then there are the intangibles, such as the charming cock's crow at daybreak (note: some neighbors may not find this so charming), or the opportunity to teach your children firsthand about how poultry is kept, how to raise chicks, and perhaps even how to incubate your own eggs.

The Cons of Keeping a Few Chickens

Unfortunately, it *is* pretty easy to put a price on eggs, and when you do, you may find what you learn to be a bit discouraging. It is very difficult to compete with supermarket egg prices when raising your own hens. This is especially true if you only want to produce enough eggs for your own household, and you'd like to pay less than what you pay for eggs at the store. The fact is, you probably can't do it. Even though chicken pellets alone aren't all that your hens will want to eat, they'll still eat more of them than anything else, and this cost may exceed your monthly egg-money allotment.

ALERT

When your order of baby chicks arrives, they will be thirsty. Provide a gallon of water for each fifty chicks and dip each of their beaks in the water right away. Each chick needs to learn to drink and where the water is. You should never let your birds run out of water.

Whether this is true will depend a little on where you live. In the Midwest, farm eggs sell at competitive prices to store eggs, but on the coasts, they may run you twice as much. So if you're buying farm eggs in California or New York, you may find it easier to produce your own eggs for those prices than if you were living in farm country where more folks have their own hen houses. A solution to this cost-to-egg problem might be to increase your efficiency by raising more birds and selling some of your eggs to the neighbors, but before you launch into this business, do a careful estimation of your expected income and outcome.

ESSENTIAL

Chickens need poultry grit in order to digest their food and oyster-shell grit in order to produce strong eggshells. Free-ranging chickens get all the grit they need for digestion off of the ground, but in confinement, they need to have it made available to them.

To further complicate the financial aspect of raising poultry, you'll need a hen house and chicken run for your chickens. If you're a true farmer, then this won't be of much concern; you'll simply build what you need from used lumber and metal roofing and you're good to go. You can buy a premade chicken house, but these can cost upwards of $1,500, and as a rule they are smaller and more cramped than what you would build yourself. Suffice it to say that it becomes even more difficult to break-even on eggs when the chickens' house costs more per square foot than your own house did.

You might also encounter neighbor or zoning problems, although most municipalities these days will permit you to keep at least a few hens, and if you can keep your rooster quiet, your neighbors aren't likely to have anything to complain about.

Finally, as with any other animals, you will have to take care of your chickens. If you have other livestock, taking care of a few hens won't add appreciably to your chores, but if these are your only animals, then you can't be away from the farm for long without finding someone to feed and water them. You'll be responsible for making certain that they go in at night; you'll have to be the one to clean out the hen house regularly; and it will be your responsibility to keep their house and run predator-proof.

The Hen House and Chicken Run

Here are the basics that your chickens will need for living space: first, they'll need a hen house. This doesn't need to be any larger than what is required for the chickens to fit in, but if you have an old shed or can build one that you can walk into to gather eggs as well as fill the feeders and waterers, you might find this quite a bit more convenient. Then you'll need a fenced, outdoor area where your hens can browse and scratch. The amount of area this requires will be dependent on how many chickens you have, of course, but it should be enough that they don't wear the grass away down to the dirt, as this defeats part of the purpose. You can find lots of advice on the Internet about how many square feet a hen needs in the house and how many in the run. These are generally pretty small numbers: as little as 2 to 3 square feet per bird in the hen house and 4 or 5 square feet of run per adult. These numbers may get you by if you absolutely don't have any more space, but the more crowded a hen house is, the more problems you'll have with overly aggressive individuals, and respiratory problems from ammonia build up. The more room you can give them, the better. Smaller, more docile birds in cleaner quarters do better than do larger, more aggressive ones where manure is allowed to collect. It's also hard to say with precision how many square feet of run each bird will need, but if you want to keep grass growing on the run, you'll want it to be considerably larger than 4 or 5 square feet per bird. How much larger that needs to be is dependent on how quickly the grass in your yard will grow, which depends on your soil and weather. In both cases, it's best to provide all the room you can spare.

FACT

Most hens will start laying eggs at between five and seven months of age, and they'll lay most prolifically at one to two years. Pullets lay small eggs at first and larger eggs as they mature. Younger hens will lay an egg every three or four days, whereas a thirty-week-old hen can lay two eggs every three days.

When growing vegetables, you might grow them shoulder-to-shoulder. This isn't the right way to raise chickens. The hen house needs enough room for the chickens themselves, plus nest boxes for them to lay eggs in (not more than five chickens should share a box) and horizontal poles for them to roost (sleep) on, at least 4 inches per bird on roost poles 6 inches apart

Nesting boxes should be placed 18 to 24 inches above the floor, and be about 14" × 14" × 12". In the run, you need enough area that the grass doesn't get worn away. A good way to ensure that this doesn't happen is to make a chicken tractor, which is a movable caged run. When the grass starts to get thin, you just roll the tractor to a new location. The hen house can be built into the tractor and move with it, or you can roll the tractor back to the hen house every evening when it's time for the birds to go to roost.

You'll also want to provide feed, water, and grit for your birds, and it's best to have these inside the house if possible so that the chickens aren't waiting for you to let them out in the morning before they can have breakfast.

Remember that everyone likes eggs, and not just everyone in your family, but also snakes, opossums, skunks, raccoons, dogs, and even chickens on occasion. The housing you provide needs to be sufficiently secure to keep all of these animals out, except the chickens, of course.

Starting Baby Chicks

When your chicks first arrive, you'll need to prepare a special place for them in the hen house. Depending on how many chicks you have, this can be a large cardboard box or a set of boards to partition the hen house floor. Cover the floor with least 1 inch of wood shavings, rice hulls, sand, or straw. Don't use cedar shavings, fine sawdust, or treated wood chips. Cover the floor with newspapers the first day so the chicks will eat the feed and not the litter.

ESSENTIAL

Chickens of all ages may peck on one another or on a single individual. This can be because of crowding, lack of feeder or water space, too much heat, or just to establish dominance. Instead of having your birds debeaked (partial removal of the beak), try spreading fresh grass clippings, weeds, or lettuce on the ground.

At first, the chicks will need about half a square foot per bird. Inside this area, you'll want to hang a brooder lamp with a 250-watt bulb that will provide heat and light for the chicks. The bulb should have a shade or shield to create an umbrella of warmth that the birds can get under. They will tend to clump together under this light. If the chicks appear to be spreading out from the light, it is too hot, in which case you can raise it a little. You can stop drafts by placing a circle of cardboard 12 inches high around the birds, but make certain that they have enough room to get out of the heat if they so desire. Some people use a plastic kiddie pool for this.

In the beginning, the chicks will need commercial chick starter in feeders and water in a waterer. Allow 4 feet of feeders and a 1-gallon waterer per 50 chicks. Don't let water pool on the floor. On the third day, sprinkle some chick grit on the feed very sparingly. At four months, you should increase the available floor area by 50 percent, increase the number of feeders to give 3 inches per bird, and the number of watering founts to 1 gallon per 20 birds. Also make sure that they get the proper-size grit for their age.

Turkeys

Turkeys are raised in much the same way as chickens. However, they're larger, of course, and require more of all resources, particularly water. Lots of raisers opt for automatic watering founts that you attach to a garden hose. Most turkeys are raised for meat, and in small operations, they are allowed to range for at least a part of their food. You can use almost any pasture grass that will provide plant and insect feed for your turkeys as your range, although fescue should be avoided. If you plan to plant the range your birds will be eating, they'll do well on clover, alfalfa, orchard grass, or bluegrass. They also like acorns and other nuts, forbs, tubers, bulbs, berries, and other wild mast. Farmers with large fields of crops have long used turkeys to clean up the fields of wasted grains after the harvest. Others use turkeys to catch insects in the garden, but this needs to be done with some caution, because as much as turkeys love to eat insects, and they do this with an admirable gusto, they may also enjoy many of your garden's products.

Young turkeys (poults) need supplemental heat to keep their body temperatures up until they are six to eight weeks old. Weather permitting, they can be introduced to their range anytime after six weeks. You'll need a fence around the range area that will keep the poults in, and the predators out, and you should have a movable roost for the birds to climb up on. Turkeys like to perch on the highest thing in their immediate area, and manure tends to collect rapidly below. This is why you need a movable roost, and why it's a bad idea to have any trees within the range area.

Turkeys feel more secure and at ease when they have a place to perch at night, excepting older, heavier toms. Roost poles for turkeys need to be larger than the poles for chickens, from 15 to 30 inches above the ground and about 24 inches apart. Each bird should have 10 to 15 inches of perch space.

ALERT

Most turkeys can fly rather well from six weeks of age (the larger, heavier toms, not so much), so you'll need to be prepared for this by clipping the primary feathers from one wing, which will cause an imbalance that prevents them from escaping their pen.

How densely turkeys can be placed on a given pasture is dependent on the weather, the soil, and the plants that make up the pasture. Twelve birds per quarter-acre would be a fairly modest stocking rate, so start there and add more turkeys as your range can support them.

Other Poultry

Once you've raised a few chickens and perhaps some turkeys, you may want to try a few other species. They all have their own characteristics, of course, and their own particular uses for the backyard farmer.

Geese

Geese are large, relatively intelligent birds that have definite personalities. They produce some of the best meat in all of poultry. Geese are frequently used in commercial farms as weeders of strawberry, cotton, onion, and garlic crops, among others, because they graze so closely and so completely. However, if you use them at home, you need to be warned that they will also graze your lettuce and cabbage.

Geese are excellent mothers, and the best way to get started with them is to buy a couple of geese and a gander and let them raise their own, or if you can get hold of a clutch of fertilized eggs, you can brood them under a broody hen or goose. Geese don't require any housing in warm weather, but they need protection from the cold, from severe storms, and from predators.

Ducks

Ducks are also easiest raised when allowed to produce their own offspring. Start with a trio and stop when you've got all the ducks you can handle; they reproduce abundantly. Ducks don't need to have a creek, pond, or pool, but they're very happy when they have water that they can swim in. If that isn't a feature of your backyard farm, then they'll be content with enough water to drink and to wash in.

Ducks will make their own nests if you supply them with bedding material, and they'll hatch out twelve or fifteen ducklings as often as twice a year. These little ducks will imprint on you as the first human they see, so treat them nicely, because they'll be judging all of humankind based on how you behave. Ducks just need a basic shelter, a roof over their heads in bad weather, and of course, they'll need protection from predators, such as a tight fence around their range area. Most small farmers raise ducks for meat and eggs.

Guinea Fowl

Guineas have several uses. They are voracious consumers of all sorts of insect pests; they make a good substitute for recipes calling for wild game such as wild grouse, partridge, or quail; and many people keep them around for use as feathered "watchdogs."

ALERT

Chinese geese and guinea hens are both recommended as good "watch dogs" because they are prone to making much noise when an intruder appears. Be cautious of raising them both together, because they will also react to each other, and the combined racket that results may be more than you bargained for.

Guineas were never quite domesticated; most people who have a flock just let them run loose. They'll roost in the trees at night and generally take care of themselves, getting all the food they need from free ranging. However, you can keep them from wandering off into the jaws of predators if you supply them with a regular source of chicken pellets at the same place every day. Buy a few adult guineas and you'll have a lifetime supply of them.

Peafowl

Peacocks and peahen chicks can be brooded much like chickens, but supply them with game-bird feed instead of chicken pellets. This is readily available at most feed stores. The best way to obtain a flock is to buy chicks. Many of the hatcheries that sell chickens also sell peafowl. Before ordering peafowl, you may want to take notice of the fact that they have a very distinctive call: a blood-curdling scream. It is up to you to decide how your neighbors are likely to react to this. Like guinea fowl, peafowl can live a quasi-wild life roosting in trees and taking care of themselves if you provide them with a steady supply of feed, which will keep them close to home.

Quail and Partridge

These game birds are generally raised for their meat and eggs, but there is also a market for hunters who use them to train bird dogs. Quail don't require a lot of space and are generally raised in cages inside an outbuilding. An old rabbit hutch can make a good cage to raise quail in. Six to eight of them only require one square foot.

Start them out on chick starter, and later they can graduate to game-bird feed. Professionals recommend different feeds for quail that are intended for meat, egg production, or brooding. You may not be able to find this selection locally; if not, you can order the type you need.

Pet Birds

One of the most likely ways to actually make money raising birds on the farm is in selling pet birds such as parakeets, cockatiels, or lovebirds. The first step is to line up a pet shop or pet shops that will agree to buy your birds and then just keep your market happy.

Parakeets require two flight cages of perhaps four feet in each direction—one for males and one for females—and smaller, one-square-foot breeding cages with nesting boxes for breeding pairs. The birds breed for two clutches, that is, two batches of eggs they've laid in the breeding cages, and rest for three months in the flight cages before being set up again. They lay an egg every day, and start sitting on the eggs to hatch them immediately, unlike chickens, which wait for the entire clutch to be laid before setting. This means your youngest baby parakeet will be a fraction of the size of the oldest, which may only be two weeks older. The parakeet parents will both care for the babies until they're about five weeks old and then they'll need to be placed into a baby cage for a week to be sure they're healthy. After that, they're off to the pet store. A parakeet can hatch four or five clutches of babies a year at four to six babies per clutch, so depending on the deal you're able to make, this can be fairly profitable. Parakeets require a good seed mix and something fresh every day—they love sprouts and corn, but some will also eat apples and citrus.

Raising cockatiels and lovebirds is very similar, but the cages need to be larger, and you'll need to remove the babies from the parents at about a week and then hand-feed them four times per day until they're ready to sell. For this and other reasons, they bring a higher price than parakeets. Experts recommend that you start with good breeding stock in order to maximize your own profits.

CHAPTER 14

Small Livestock

In agribusiness, cultivators of plants are generally referred to as "farmers" and breeders of animals are called "ranchers," but the traditional farmer manages both crops and livestock. This is appropriate, because the two go hand in hand. However, sometimes duplicating what happens in nature isn't the easiest decision to make when financial concerns are at the forefront. Your crops will nurture your livestock, and your livestock will nurture your crops, but you have the challenge of getting the process started on budget.

Your Goals and the Market

It should be noted that it is difficult to make money raising livestock of any sort. Unlike plants, whose food is nearly free if you make your own compost, animals need to be fed regularly with commodities like corn, wheat, and alfalfa, which, unless you have the capability of growing your own, can expand your cost of operations and deflate your budget in short order. In addition to that, many laws regulate the sale of milk and meat, which may make selling those items impractical for the small farmer. Then there are the veterinary bills if anything goes wrong.

From the standpoint of the backyard farmer, it is probably better to raise livestock because you want a source of meat of a higher quality than you can buy in the store, and you have the willingness to pay a little extra for the assurance and satisfaction of raising it yourself—at least in the beginning. As your experience and capabilities grow, you're likely to find more ways to cut costs, increase profits, and put a value on the manure you're getting, but you should expect to fall short of break-even as a beginner.

Miniature Cattle

Tiny cattle are relatively new animals on the scene. As of this book's publication, the International Miniature Cattle Breeders Society and Registry lists twenty-six breeds of compact cattle, most of which you would recognize as smaller versions of common cattle breeds, from Angus to Zebu.

FACT

Most cows require more effort to milk than goats, and most miniature milk cows' udders are too close to the ground for comfortable milking. This can be remedied by building a platform for the miniature cow to stand on, raising her udders for milking.

The mini-cattle business is still in its infancy. Like all new breeds, most of the examples you'll find for sale are quite expensive, and their owners treat them more like pets than livestock. The best way to make money in miniature cattle, at this time at least, is to breed them for sale as registered purebreds. They are quite acceptable as beef or dairy animals, but until the prices begin to drop, these little animals will make for some very expensive beef and/or milk. So if it's food you're looking for, you might be better off with goats or sheep, but if you can afford the initial price, you stand to make more money raising miniature cattle for resale.

▼ **MINIATURE CATTLE BREEDS**

Breed	Full-Size Counterpart
Dexter	N/A
Lowline	Aberdeen Angus
Miniature Hereford	Hereford
Miniature Jersey	Jersey
Miniature Zebu	Zebu
Panda	N/A
American Beltie	Belted Galloway
Red Kentshire	Dexter/Hereford cross
Miniature Highlander	Scottish Highlander

Miniature Cattle Housing and Fencing

If you have any experience with full-size cattle, then you only need to downsize from that to get the mini-cattle equivalent. A three-sided loafing shed is plenty of shelter, and your tiny cattle will use about one-third the pasture area you'd need for standard cattle.

ALERT

When planning to keep livestock, remember that your animals will need your attention every day. You must make certain that they are fed, watered, and that their living quarters are clean and dry. If you take frequent spur-of-the-moment vacations, you'll need to find someone to care for your animals while you're gone.

Miniature cattle range in size from around 36 to 46 inches at the shoulder, so the barbed-wire fence that you'd use for large cattle will work fine and can be a foot or so lower in height. This brings up one of the most practical aspects of raising miniature cattle. If you've ever had to load a 1,500-pound steer into a truck or catch and restrain him for veterinary work, you'll immediately appreciate the convenience of dealing with animals that top out at around half that weight. Not only are you less likely to suffer pain and injury to your person, but mini-cows put less stress on the facilities as well, and fences, pastures, and equipment don't require so much upkeep as they do when you're raising full-sized bovines.

Horned or Polled?

Most miniature cattle are polled, that is, they are born without horns. If you have a herd of cattle, some with horns and some without, the ones with the horns will get much more to eat unless you feed them all individually, and it can be moderately dangerous to walk through a herd of horned cattle. Having said all that, it doesn't make a lot of sense to raise purebred miniature longhorns and then cut the horns off. Also, if you're not accustomed to lots of blood and much commotion, then you don't want to be around when dehorning is performed, especially during the period between the first horn coming off and the second one being removed, when the animal has just learned what's going on.

QUESTION

Doesn't goat's milk have a funny sort of "goaty" taste?
It can, but shouldn't. Milk from a lactating doe kept in close proximity to a buck or one fed on certain plants (brassicas and alliums) near milking time can have an unpleasant flavor, but these situations are easily avoided.

If you have any reservations about raising animals for slaughter, then miniatures may appeal to you in this way also; by some estimates, over 70 percent of all miniature cattle are raised as pets. Home milk production also factors highly in the typical uses, as does raising animals to show. For those who do raise their animals for the beef they produce, minis have been bred with an emphasis on grass-rearing and are said to thrive on a leaner, less grain-oriented diet.

Alpacas

Alpacas are related to llamas, vicunas, and camels. They originated in South America, where they have been domesticated for millennia for their fiber and meat. Alpacas have been imported to the United States since 1983, and registered animals tend to command a high price, even today, largely because the Alpaca Registry Inc. only permits registration of the offspring of currently registered animals, thus eliminating competition from animals imported from Peru or Bolivia. Full-grown adults are about 3 feet tall at the withers and weigh around 150 pounds. A baby alpaca is called a "cria." Adults usually produce one cria per year. Alpacas have a gentle, even disposition, but have been known to kick and spit, mostly at other alpacas, but occasionally at humans.

Raising these micro-llamas doesn't have any complex requirements. Housing and fencing that work for sheep will work as well for alpacas (they're also ruminants), and sheep pasture plus some low-protein grass hay will provide their diet. It is claimed that alpacas eat far less than most animals of their size.

As mentioned previously, there are two basic types of alpaca: Huacaya and Suri. Huacaya have more compact bodies and fiber similar to sheep's wool, whereas the Suri exhibit longer necks and legs, are generally lankier, and the fiber is more similar to that of lustrous hair.

Frankly, alpacas are initially quite expensive, and the backyard farmer who wants to raise them needs to either raise and breed them for show, and thus, for the sale of equally expensive offspring, or get cheap pet-quality individuals for home use. If you're only casually interested in these animals, you'd do better to look at more common livestock unless you are willing to become deeply committed financially.

Sheep

Sheep have been domesticated longer than any other animal except the dog—over 110 centuries—so it's no surprise that there are so many breeds and so many uses for sheep. Sheep are raised for meat, wool, milk, leather, and in recent years, as ecofriendly lawnmowers. Sheep differ from goats in a number of ways, but of most importance to the inexperienced farmer is how they differ in diet and temperament. Goats will eat leaves, brush, shrubs, and vines, whereas sheep prefer a pasture of soft forbs and grasses, and sheep are easier to keep behind a fence than the more gregarious goats.

As a farmer on extremely small acreage, you may have some difficulty in finding a financial rationalization for adding the term "shepherd" to your resume. As with any other meat animal, it's hard to match the price of lamb or mutton in the store by raising your own. Of course in addition to the meat, sheep can give you wool, but unless you do some creative marketing, what the commercial market will pay for wool doesn't make it worth your effort.

FACT

Sheep are known for their flocking behavior even to their own detriment. This instinct is so strong that in 2006, in eastern Turkey, 400 sheep plunged to their deaths after trying to follow one of their flock that had tried unsuccessfully to cross a 15-meter-deep ravine.

Even though people have been milking sheep for millennia, virtually no one consumes sheep's milk in its fresh state. Instead, this milk goes into some of the finest cheeses in the world. Owing in part to how long sheep have been domesticated, there are hundreds of individual breeds of sheep, and each of them has particular uses. A few of these are as follows:

▼ **A SAMPLING OF SHEEP BREEDS BY USE**

Meat	Wool	Milk
Dorset	Rambouillet	Lacaune
Dorper	Romney	East Friesian
Coolalee	Bond	British Milk
Llanwenog	Lleyn	Latxa
Polled Dorset	Navajo-Churro	Sardinian

Of course there are also numerous breeds that claim to be good for more than one use.

Sheep Housing and Fencing

The sort of housing you'll need for your flock depends a lot on the usual variables: your climate and your available cash. Assuming you have a reasonably moderate climate, and not a lot of available cash, you can probably serve your charges well with a three-sided shed with an open side facing south. About 10 square feet per sheep will be about the right size, but of course more is always better.

There are two popular fencing solutions to keep sheep in and predators out. The traditional fence is 48-inch-high woven wire with a strand of barbed wire or electric wire above it. Woven wire is quite expensive. The modern, cheaper solution is an electric fence made up of six or seven strands of electric wire with decreasing space between the strands the lower they are installed on the fence. A good pasture for sheep will consist of cool-season grasses and legumes.

Goats

Goats and sheep have their similarities, of course, but their personalities are very different. Goats are one of the mainstays of the small farm today. They're more popular than sheep, possibly because they are seen more as milk animals than meat providers, although they are, of course, both. Goats also are noted producers of marketable hair, called cashmere in this case, which is a fine, downy undercoat of hair that grows as the autumn days grow shorter in length.

ESSENTIAL

Breeding goats is a simple matter if you have a buck, but keeping bucks has its downside in that they have a distinctive, unpleasant odor that they transfer to the milk of any female goats in their vicinity. They are also quite destructive and often have profoundly unpleasant personalities.

Milking goats should be fed high-quality hay, either grass or legume, and a grain ration that will support their health and milk production. Lactating does should have all the hay they will eat, plus a pound of grain for each three pounds of milk they produce. Sweet feed for milk cows will serve goats as well.

If you've ever seen a mountain goat scrambling across the rocky face of a precipice, then you can imagine how their domesticated cousins may be a bit difficult to keep behind a fence. You can lessen this problem a bit by providing your goat with company, as goats are quite outgoing and enjoy the presence of other goats.

▼ A SAMPLING OF GOAT BREEDS BY USE

Meat	Fiber	Milk	Dual purpose
Auckland Island	Australian Cashmere	Anglo-Nubian	Pyrenean
Rove	Pygora	British Alpine	Sahelian
Barbari	Canindé	American Lamancha	Chamoisee

Goat Housing and Fencing

Goats do not like getting wet one little bit. As with sheep, a three-sided shed with the open side facing south will make a good shelter, except in extremely cold climates. Unlike sheep, you may need to consider that the roof must withstand goat traffic, because if they can climb on it, they will. Goats are also more curious and adventuresome than sheep, which is not necessarily a good thing if you're the one responsible for keeping them penned in. There is no goat-proof fence, but a reasonable attempt at goat fencing would be five-foot-high woven wire, with fairly close openings, such as a 2" × 4" mesh. Be sure you use woven wire rather than welded wire. The emphasis is usually on fencing the goats into their pasture, but if you live in the country, or even close to it, you may have the greater concern of fencing out predators. If so, you'll discover that it takes a pretty good fence to keep a coyote away from a flock of tasty goats or sheep, so a good additional measure you can take is to acquire a good guard dog. Livestock Guardian Dogs (LGD) are usually bonded to the herd as puppies and they function as members of the flock. They may blend in with the ruminants, as many are white like "their" sheep or goats. These breeds have an instinctual desire to guard the flock and their mere presence is usually enough to keep predators at a respectful distance.

Rabbits

It is unlikely that the backyard farmer can find a cheaper, easier, more efficient way to produce meat than raising rabbits. Their requirements are so minimal that almost anyone can raise them and get started right away. Rabbits are raised commercially for meat and fur, and more than a few gardeners raise bunnies exclusively to get the benefits of their manure, which is a boon to any compost pile.

ESSENTIAL

The most popular rabbit meat breeds are of medium size (8 to 12 pounds in maturity). The larger varieties, such as the Flemish Giant, have a much higher percentage of bone to meat, and actually require more feed to produce an equal amount of meat to the smaller breeds.

Rabbits are typically raised for two purposes: for meat and as show animals. It is worth noting that while rabbits are easy, fun, and reasonably inexpensive to raise, they are not particularly profitable from a financial standpoint. Rabbits can provide you with a source of high-quality meat with a very low cholesterol content and high digestibility, but there isn't a large market for the meat.

ALERT

Only farm work dogs such as the herding and guardian breeds, like Border Collies or Great Pyrenees, should be allowed near rabbits, because only in these breeds has the instinct to kill small animals been (mostly) bred out of them.

The two most popular breeds being raised for meat are the Californian and the New Zealand White. A good starting point for the novice would be to purchase a young buck and three or four young does. This gives them the time to acclimate themselves to their surroundings before they begin breeding.

Rabbit Housing

While some breeders raise rabbits on rotating pasture, rabbits appear to be perfectly happy living out their lives in very small cages. An individual cage, or hutch, can be 24" × 30" and tall enough for the largest of them to stand up, with a little more room given to does with litters. Because the bunnies will tolerate such close quarters, giving them just the right environment is a very easy thing to do. They are most sensitive to heat (high temperatures can prove fatal), so the hutch should be kept in a cool, shady, and well-ventilated place—ideally on the north side of a building or fence—in the summer months; in winter, they can be moved either to the south side of the building or taken inside a barn or shed.

Your rabbits will require plenty of water and will do very well on commercial rabbit pellets, which you may wish to augment with grass, clover, alfalfa, and other forages.

Beekeeping

It is unlikely that you will find smaller livestock than honeybees, and pound-for-pound (or gram-for-gram) you'll also have trouble finding more profitable creatures for your farm. A working bee operation can take advantage of your farm location, and when you fill all the allotted space you have, you can expand by placing a few hives at other locations. In fact, large commercial honey producers make part of their money by renting out hives to farmers where they can pollinate large farm crops.

Getting into beekeeping is easy and relatively inexpensive. You'll need hives, of course, which will consist of not just the boxes, but frames filled with wax foundation for the bees to build into honeycomb.

Buying Hives

It is very tempting to buy used hives, but if you do so, do this in the presence of an experienced beekeeper, because used equipment can carry with it contamination of American Foulbrood (AFB). AFB is a bacterial contamination of beehives that quickly destroys the entire brood. Bee larvae ingest the spore-forming bacteria, and these bacteria then germinate in the entrails of the larvae, killing them as they release up to one hundred million spores per individual. These spores can survive for more than forty years in honey and beekeeping equipment. The accepted and reliable way to eradicate AFB is by gamma irradiation. If you're just starting out, it's much simpler to start with new boxes and equipment.

Filling Your Hives

Filling your hives presents a couple of options and a few challenges. Obviously, the cheapest way to get bees is to capture a wild swarm. This really isn't that difficult if you're properly equipped, but a larger problem might be finding a swarm. When you locate a swarm, you'll want protective clothing, a bee smoker, and an empty hive to put the swarm in. Swarming bees are generally very docile since they have no hive to protect, and can be gently shaken or brushed off of the limb, building, or whatever they've settled on and into the waiting hive.

FACT

While there are other species of insects that pollinate plants, bees are the only ones that can be moved from place to place and generally manipulated by humans to pollinate crops when and where they choose. That's why many domesticated crops rely solely on the honeybee.

Most beginning apiarists buy their first colony or colonies. Most commonly, the bees will arrive in a package that contains worker bees, and a queen inside a smaller cage that is plugged shut with a candy substance that the bees eat, freeing the queen to take over her duties in the hive.

Experienced apiarists will advise newcomers to start with a couple of hives of Italian bees. (A couple so you can compare the two, and Italian bees because they are the standard of the industry.) Don't experiment until you know enough to know why you're experimenting. In other words, stick with the tried-and-true methods while you're getting started, and don't buy anything unless you know what it's used for. There are lots of things you can buy that you don't absolutely need, so stick with the very basics at first, and if you see a particular need arise, you can purchase the solution if you so desire.

Locating Your Hives

You can locate your hives almost anywhere. There are very few places where humans live that bees can't forage enough nectar to support a single hive, but the more humans there are in an area, the more folks you'll encounter who are afraid of bees.

Just for the record, bees will not attack humans unless they feel that they need to protect their hive. A bee will sting you if you try to harm her, but her major concern is her hive and keeping it from harm.

Unfortunately, if you have any neighbors who are afraid of bees (*apiphobic*), this argument won't be likely to faze them. Remember, however, that people keep bees even in the largest cities, and there are solutions to the problem of neighbors. Keeping your hives behind a high wall not only obscures them from sight, it also forces the bees to fly higher overhead, and above the heads of people in the area. Bees can be a nuisance around swimming pools and other sources of water because bees use quite a lot of water themselves. This problem can be remedied by providing a plentiful supply of water near the hive. A good apiary site will be hidden, yet exposed to full sunlight with water close by, and be in close proximity to as many flowering plants as possible.

Finally, don't be surprised if you don't have a honey crop the first year. It's more important that your hive or hives be allowed to put away honey for winter and maintain a strong, vibrant colony. There's always next year.

CHAPTER 15

Pests and Pestilence

Just as the backyard farmer will struggle to feed himself and his family, thousands of other critters are also bent on feeding themselves, and their broods are working against him. Call it a war, or simply a challenge, but the farmer needs to win in order for everyone to survive. This fight can be waged violently or passively, depending on what works best; but there will never be a truce, because for every tomato you plant, or every chick you hatch, or every lamb you foster, there's something else out there that wants the fruits of your labors every bit as much as you do.

Rodents

Four in every ten mammals are rodents. Rodents are characterized by having two large incisors on both their upper and lower jaws. These teeth, unlike our own, are continuously growing, and their owners keep them at workable lengths by gnawing on things. This gnawing is the signature characteristic of squirrels, groundhogs, mice, rats, and others and is a formidable weapon that can be destructive to your buildings, your fences, and even your electrical circuitry.

ESSENTIAL

Rodents have a strong aversion to peppermint. If you have a rodent problem, try soaking a few small rags or cotton balls in pure peppermint oil, which you can find in any health food store. Scatter these about wherever you suspect rodent activity.

Fencing is the best way to stop larger rodents, but it is of little value against the smaller ones like rats and mice. Poisons can be effective, but are indiscriminate, so they are best avoided if at all possible. You don't want to inadvertently poison livestock or a family pet. You will probably always have some issue with rodents, but here are a few ideas about how to hold your own against the onslaught.

Groundhogs

Groundhogs (also known as woodchucks) are relatively easy to fence out of the garden, as they don't climb very well, and a 2" × 4" wire mesh will probably present more trouble than they'll want to get into your cabbage. However, they are very accomplished diggers, and if your broccoli is the only attractive food in the area, they can get under a fence easily. Even worse, and more likely, is if they decide to make your yard their home, which they will probably do by digging a burrow under a building or some other obstacle that will complicate your plans to evict them. If this has happened to you, the problem may be more difficult to cure than you might suppose at first. Many peoples' first reaction is to try to shoot the offending chucks, but this is actually not such a good choice for a number of reasons:

If you live in a populated area, it may be illegal; in the country—especially so in the country—if you manage to kill the groundhog, relatives will likely remain behind in the burrow, or move into it on the original tenant's demise, so it comes down to a contest to see whether the groundhog has more relatives than you have cabbages.

ALERT

If you encounter a skunk face-to-face, he will give you a warning. If he sees you as a threat, he'll run directly toward you, stop, stomp the ground, hiss, and assume a high-tail position. If you're still in the area while he's doing this, walk away slowly and quietly (but deliberately).

The very best way to relieve yourself of groundhogs is to make your yard unattractive to them. Of course, one of the things that attracts them the most is your garden, especially the brassicas like cabbage, cauliflower, and broccoli, but you're going to fence off your tasty plants with wire mesh. One of the other things that groundhogs (and lots of other pests) appreciate in a home is cover. Tall grass and brush allows them to come and go easily without drawing the attention of dogs or landowners, so if the burrow you're trying to evacuate is hidden in brush or weeds, the obvious solution is to clean the area out and keep it mowed regularly. If that fails, or if the cover that the groundhogs have burrowed into is your garden, then you can try some of the smoke bombs manufactured to kills moles, gophers, groundhogs, and other burrowing animals. If you take this approach, you'll want to bear in mind that groundhogs, like most burrowing animals, always build their tunnel-dens with two openings, so even as you're pumping smoke down one hole, they may be watching safely from a distance.

Smoke bombs, however, are far from foolproof, and if you use up your supply before you eliminate the groundhogs, you might try placing used kitty litter or droppings from some other carnivore in their dens. Filling up the holes with rocks is a waste of time, as the groundhogs will just dig around your handiwork.

Squirrels

If you have a squirrel problem, the appropriate fencing solution is to build a frame that can be set over your plants, and then you should cover this frame on all four sides and the top with chicken wire. Those who think they can shoot every squirrel giving them trouble are naïve about the reproductive capabilities of squirrels.

If you live in the country, the squirrels can probably find enough nut trees that your garden won't interest them, but in the urban areas, squirrel forage is more limited and squirrels will be more aggressive, perhaps to the point of even tearing up flower beds.

FACT

If you've ever wondered about their "squirrelly" activity on the highway, it's because startled or frightened squirrels dodge back and forth to confuse predators and give the squirrels time to escape. Obviously, this unusual strategy works better against cats and dogs than it does against automobiles.

If you're in an urban or suburban situation, the squirrels are likely to be living either in your attic or walls, in the attic or walls of a neighbor, or in a nest, which will usually be located high—like 40 or 50 feet high—in a tree. Obviously, you can't do much about your neighbor's attic, but you can make yours inaccessible by covering all possible openings to the attic with half-inch wire mesh or chicken wire. This isn't a complete solution though, unless you're willing to extend the mesh to cover every area of wood that a squirrel can conceivably gnaw through. If you see a squirrel's nest in a tree, you can do what you can to remove it, but you have no guarantee that this is the nest of the squirrels that are giving you trouble, or even whether the nest is occupied at all. It's entirely likely that the squirrels destroying your garden live in or on someone else's property.

The best way to get rid of squirrels, and keep them away, is to have a cat or two patrolling your farm. There is some argument that active breeds such as Abyssinians, Bengals, or Siamese are the best mousers, but any active and dedicated cat will chase and terrorize squirrels, and get rid of lots of other pests as well.

Mice, Voles, Rats, and Others

The first thing you need to concentrate on when you want to rid your farm of pests is to eliminate the things that attract them to your property in the first place. Unfortunately, on a farm, there are so many things that attract rats and mice that you wouldn't be farming if you got rid of them all. Stock feeders, compost bins, stored feed, and garden produce all attract these little critters, and while you may be able to design a mouse-proof fence (make sure it's buried a few inches under the soil), trying to fence even a backyard-sized farm against mice is too much effort.

FACT

If you see a mouse, you can bet that his nest is close by, because mice only forage close to home, usually not more than 10 to 25 feet from the nest. They may make twenty to thirty trips to different food sites each night.

Traps and predators are the best solutions, as they don't just eliminate a few individuals but stay around for as long as they're needed. Poisons are less desirable, because they leave behind dead bodies to decompose between walls and in attics and crawlspaces, and most of all because they can kill predators that eat poisoned rats or mice.

If you don't have cats or other predators, or even if you do, you can encourage screech owls by building or buying a screech owl box and placing it 8 to 15 feet up in a tree. (*Audubon* magazine offers plans for screech owl boxes on their website, *http://mag.audubon.org.*) Owls are ferocious predators of small rodents as well as insects.

Larger Animals

Tight fencing best controls deer, raccoons, opossums, skunks, coyotes, and the neighbors' dogs. Of these, the raccoons are the greatest threat, as they are smart, strong, and determined. Also, they are notoriously omnivorous, and being nocturnal, they do their worst while you're asleep.

It is easier to fence these pests out of the garden than to protect your livestock, as their hunger for fresh vegetables is not nearly so urgent as their desire for fresh meat, and they will do everything within their power to steal eggs or kill chickens. If fencing proves inadequate in protecting your livestock, then you might want to consider investing in a guard dog.

Birds

There are those who try to control birds in the garden with guns or poisons. These methods are neither safe nor effective. The very best way to control bird damage in your garden or orchard is with plastic bird netting, which is cheap and effective. Be sure that when you cover a plant or tree with netting, you tie it down at the base or stalk so that it doesn't blow away.

Additionally, you can try using scarecrows. These can be dummy humans (this is where the term originates), plastic snakes or owls, foil pie pans or old CDs hung on strings to catch the sunlight, or dark-colored cloths placed in the limbs of trees to simulate cats waiting for a bird to land.

Insects

If you have a garden, you *will* have an insect problem. Scientists estimate that there are 900,000 known species of insects, representing ten quintillion individual bugs. Since there are so many insects that love fresh fruits and vegetables, it is wise to have a reference book, or website, with photographs or drawings so you can look up each new insect that comes to ruin your day and your garden. You'll find specific information about what to do to eliminate the little vandals, but for now you'll benefit from learning a few general techniques of insect control.

Prevention

As with other problems, the best solution is to take care of the source of the problem before it happens. There are several things you can do to keep insects out of your crops in the first place:

- Fertile, Healthy Soil: Studies have shown that strong, healthy plants are less likely to be attacked by insects than weak, marginal ones. Build up your soil with compost, mulch, and natural fertilizers.
- Get Rid of Weak Plants: These not only are most susceptible to insect invasion, they may invite it. Don't harbor plants that are clearly diseased or weak; they won't get any better, and they can endanger the rest of the garden.
- Rotate Crops: It's not good to grow the same thing in the same place each year. Pests can overwinter in the soil, giving them a head start.
- Practice Companion Planting: The roots, leaves, and flowers of many herbs and vegetables attract beneficial insects or repel harmful ones, usually by their scent. Learn all the best companions for the plants you grow, and then provide them with the company they prefer.
- Eliminate Bug Habitat: Clean up all the unnecessary weeds and debris that can harbor insect breeding grounds.
- Avoid Standing Moisture: Water the garden early in the day so that the moisture on the leaves will have time to dry out. Consider using soaker hoses or drip irrigation to keep your plants drier, which in turn will discourage insect and fungus growth.

Insecticidal Soap

Neophyte gardeners and frustrated veterans are sometimes tempted to use chemical insecticides. While this is understandable, it isn't a good idea. Chemical insecticides are dangerous to human and animal health, dangerous to the environment, dangerous to the variety of plants found in the typical garden, and as if all that weren't enough, they are generally expensive. Insecticidal sprays and compounds that kill harmful insects will kill beneficial ones as well, so be cautious and conservative in their use. Only treat the infected plants and areas, and inspect the plants after the first treatment to guard against plant damage from the pesticide.

Grubs can be easily controlled in the garden or lawn by sprinkling milky spore bacteria, which you can purchase at nurseries or garden stores. Milky spore not only kills grubs one year, but it reproduces itself, so one treatment can last for generations in the soil.

Instead, you can use organic insecticidal soap that is quite effective against soft-bodied insect pests such as aphids, earwigs, lace bugs, mealy bugs, spider mites, thrips, soft brown scales, psyllids, rose slugs, pear slugs, sawfly larvae, and whiteflies. You can buy insecticidal soap, or you can make your own using this recipe:

- 1 Tablespoon Murphy's Oil Soap, Castile or any all-natural, fat-based soap; **not** a detergent
- 3 Tablespoons cayenne pepper
- 1 Tablespoon vegetable oil
- 1 Quart warm water

Apply the soap with a clean spray bottle, making certain that you get the insects you're spraying wet. It kills them by dissolving their protective covering and attacking their inner cells. If this mixture damages or burns your plant leaves, cut the amount of soap in half.

Diatomaceous Earth

Diatomaceous earth is referred to as a "mechanical pesticide" because it kills insects from the outside by either dehydrating their bodies if they are arthropods (animals that have an external skeleton, like spiders), or in gastropods (commonly known as slugs), by slicing them up as they move across it, like broken glass might for larger creatures. It is a white powder similar in appearance to talcum made of soft, siliceous sedimentary rock. Diatomaceous earth has a number of uses, including as an abrasive in toothpaste and facial scrubs, so it is very safe to use, although it is recommended that you avoid breathing the dust. Many people take it internally for health reasons.

Diatomaceous earth, or D.E., is pretty handy stuff to have around the farm, because it can be used effectively against spiders, roaches, silverfish, ants, fire ants, carpenter ants, bedbugs, lice, mites, earwigs, flies, fleas, box elder bugs, hair lice, scorpions, crickets, millipedes, centipedes, slugs, and snails, among many others, but will not harm earthworms or other beneficial soil micro-organisms. One of the other advantages of diatomaceous earth over chemicals is that insects cannot build up an immunity to it.

Apply D.E. with a shaker made from an old coffee can or some other container. Sprinkle it on the plants you want to protect, and reapply after a rain.

Hand Picking

Sometimes, when you find that you have an infestation of particularly destructive insects, such as tomato worms or squash beetles, it's best to kill all the individuals you can find by hand. You should also look under and upon the leaves for eggs, and destroy those as well. Then keep things under control by applying insecticidal soap and/or diatomaceous earth.

Beneficial Insects

You can attract or purchase beneficial insects that prey on destructive insects and their larvae. Here are a few of the most noteworthy:

- Ladybugs: Eat aphids, mites, scales, and whiteflies. You can purchase them or attract them with asters, daisies, sunflowers, tansy, and yarrow.
- Praying Mantises: Eats most garden pests. Buy eggs through mail-order or online and set them out to hatch in the garden.

- Brachonid, Chalcid, and Ichneumon Wasps: Eat leaf-eating caterpillars and can be lured into the garden by planting carrots, celery, parsley, caraway, or Queen Anne's Lace.
- Bumblebees: Surpass even honeybees as prolific pollinators.
- Lacewings: Eat aphids and are attracted by the same plants as ladybugs, or you can buy them through mail-order or online.
- Fly Parasites: The natural enemy of nuisance flies—including the common housefly. The female seeks out a host, drills through its cocoon, and lays her eggs inside. The resulting parasitoids eat the pupa.
- Mealybug Destroyers: Attack aphids and soft-scale insects as well as mealybugs.
- Nematodes: Destroy cutworms, beetles, and root weevils. Their microscopic eggs can be purchased, and are applied to the soil.

Plant Diseases

Like all living things, plants are subject to an immense number of maladies. The good news is, your plants almost certainly will not encounter more than a few of them at once, so you only need to learn to combat those diseases that are plaguing your patch at any given time. You may have a reliable old volume of text that deals with such things in detail, such as *The Encyclopedia of Organic Gardening*, by J. I. Rodale, but a faster method would be to list the symptoms your plants are displaying in a brief form, such as "cracks in fruit" to get several possible diagnoses. Also, the University of Minnesota has a well-designed diagnosis tool entitled *What's wrong with my plant?* at *http://www.extension.umn.edu/gardeninfo/diagnostics/index.html*, which you may find helpful.

- Fungal Diseases I. There are, of course, hundreds of plant diseases, including blights, cankers, galls, mildews, rots, rusts, and wilts. Nearly all of these are fungal in nature, and many can be cured by regular applications of a mixture of 2 tablespoons of baking soda mixed into a quart of water and sprayed on the infected areas every few days until gone.

- Fungal Diseases II. Combine 1 tablespoon of cooking oil with 2 table-spoons of baking soda and a few drops of Ivory soap in a quart of water and spray on the affected plants every few days until the problem ceases to exist.
- Anthracnose. Infected plants display dark, water-soaked lesions on stems, leaves, or fruit. Their centers will become covered with pink globules. The disease most often occurs during moist, warm conditions. Do not compost infected plants or save their seeds. Sulfur or copper powders or sprays can be applied weekly to infected plants throughout the growing season, but they will not kill the disease, only prevent the spores from germinating.
- Blossom End Rot. Manifests itself as large black or brown spots on the lower (blossom) end of otherwise normal fruit. Common on cucumber, eggplant, pepper, and tomato, this is a problem caused by low levels of calcium during the formation of fruit. Too much fertilizer, high salt levels, low soil moisture, or uneven soil moisture often cause it. To avoid, add bone meal or some other calcium source to the soil when planting; reduce nitrogen fertilizer use. To remedy existing rot, try spraying with a kelp or calcium solution. Mulch helps.
- Brown Rot. A common fungal disease affecting the blossoms and fruit of almonds, apricots, cherries, peaches, and plums. It first infects blossoms in spring and grows back into the small branches, causing cankers that kill the stems. The fruits develop brown spots that spread rapidly. Quick removal and destruction of infected areas along with sulfur and/or copper sprays may control the disease.
- Damping Off. A soil-borne fungal disease affecting new seedlings that germinate normally, but fall over and die a few days later. There is no cure, but damping off can be avoided by providing good air circulation and only planting seeds in sterile soil.
- Fusarium Wilt. A fungal disease that attacks eggplant, pepper, potato, and tomato plants, causing foliage to wilt and turn yellow. The lower, older leaves are usually affected first; then it spreads and kills the whole plant. Fusarium wilt is caused by a fungus living in the soil, which can survive for many years. It is spread by water, insects, and garden equipment. See Fungal Diseases mentioned earlier, or try Mycostop Biofungicide. There are many varieties of each cultivar that

are resistant to Fusarium wilt, and these should be planted if this is a recurring problem.

- Mosaic Virus. The virus overwinters on perennial weeds and is spread by aphids, leafhoppers, whiteflies, and cucumber beetles that feed on these weeds. Symptoms are yellow or light-green spots or stripes on weeds, similar in appearance to symptoms of nutrient deficiencies. Treat with insecticidal soap and diatomaceous earth.
- Powdery Mildew. A fungal disease that starts on young leaves as raised, blister-like areas that cause leaves to curl, exposing the lower leaf surface, and eventually developing a white, powdery growth. A half-and-half mixture of milk and water sprayed on plants afflicted with powdery mildew has proven effective if treated weekly until gone.
- Verticillium Wilt. A persistent fungal disease that causes new growth to die during the summer months. Commonly, leaves at the ends of branches turn yellow, wilt, and fall before the entire limb or branch dies. The disease is soil-borne and can live for up to a decade in the soil, even without a host plant. There is no cure, but sulfur applied weekly to the soil may be of some benefit. Choose resistant varieties and avoid high-nitrogen chemical fertilizers.

Weather

Weather is the perennial foe and friend of the farmer, and as the weather becomes more severe and erratic, learning to cope with what nature throws at you becomes increasingly important. Some weather events like large hail, floods, and tornadoes are obviously more than anyone can be expected to contend with, but if you are serious about harvesting a crop, you should be prepared to cover your plants each evening when frost is forecasted, and also have sun shades and mulch available for when the late winter turns to an early summer, bypassing spring and drying out your plants with blistering heat. You'll also need to protect young fruit trees, garden trellises and tall, staked plants from high winds and ice storms.

Do scarecrows actually work to deter birds in the garden?
Yes, scarecrows do work to deter birds, to a limited degree. Scientific studies have shown that certain devices like the Bird-X Scare-Eye balloons (*www.bird-x.com*) have reduced crop damage. Other scarecrows that look like people or predators are thought to be effective for a time, which can be extended by moving them around the garden.

Needless to say, every garden should have access to plenty of water at all times during the growing season, and no garden should be planted where there is no running water unless that basic necessity is simply not available, in which case you may want to consider not planting at all. Techniques that claim to lessen the need for regular watering are simply not the best for garden plants, which need a continuous cycle of watering followed by a period of time for the soil to dry out a bit.

CHAPTER 16

Fencing

Fencing is the most important construction on the farm—more important to the farm's existence than even the farmer's house. That's because everything that makes a farm a farm is dependent on strong, effective fencing to keep the livestock in and the predators out. Fencing can be extremely expensive, but it doesn't need to be, as some of the oldest methods still work effectively even today, and these days, fencing also serves the additional function of keeping the farmer out of court.

The Most Important Construction on Any Farm

It would be safe to say that nearly everything about farming is easier in modern times, with an impressive array of tools, products, and supply chains. However, in one regard, farming was a lot easier one century ago and before: In times past, most livestock were raised as "free range," meaning that animals were permitted to run freely, and the farmer's responsibility was to fence the garden simply to keep the neighbors' stock from doing damage. This practice quickly fell from favor in the first half of the twentieth century, when automobiles and the broad network of highways that sprung up in their path made it very impractical for free ranging to continue as it had before. Where it had once been the case that motorists were liable for any harm done by their automobiles to errant livestock, when the laws changed, and as speeds increased, it became the farmer's responsibility to keep his cattle or other livestock off the highway. If he failed, the resulting lawsuits could ruin him financially. A couple of generations ago, if a horseless carriage struck one of your cattle, that could have been a harm to the animal, which the motorist was responsible for avoiding. Today, a large animal on the highway can cause the complete destruction of a vehicle, and even serious harm or the death of the driver, and avoiding such mayhem with good fencing is the legal responsibility of the farmer.

FACT

Mortared walls have a shorter life than unmortared "dry stone" walls do. Rain and snow creep into the cracks and seams of mortared walls, freezing and pushing the stones apart, but in dry stone walls, the water simply drains away without doing any damage to the structure.

Fencing has also gained legal importance as not just a marker of boundaries. On some occasions, fencing can become the legal definition of the boundary, even in opposition to actual surveys. In cases of what the legal profession calls "adverse possession," judges can find that a fence long assumed to be the boundary between two properties holds precedence over the actual surveyed property lines showing that fence as having been built in error.

Pre-Industrial Fencing

It is, of course, impossible to say how long humankind has been using fences. Sheep have been domesticated for over 11,000 years, but the earliest shepherds were nomadic and did not necessarily fence in their livestock. By the time of Julius Caesar about 2,000 years ago, however, fences were in common usage both marking property and containing animals. Many of the techniques used by the farmers in the past still work quite well today. And erecting a fence from humble materials is the most inexpensive way to keep your farm safe.

Stone

Visitors to the United Kingdom will immediately notice that much of the rural land is divided by a latticework of stone walls and fences, some of them dating back thousands of years. These ancient fences have been in place since the earliest times, when Hadrian built his famous stone wall across England to keep out the barbarian Scots of the north, but when you spend some time on one of these traditional farms, the stone fence comes into clearer perspective as a dynamic, changing presence that moves about over time.

When a British farmer needs to pass between two fields, rather than having a gate in the fence, he simply takes down a section of the wall as wide as he needs for the opening and then stacks it back up when he's done. In this way, a fence that may be hundreds of years old actually moves and morphs over time, while remaining in about the same location as always.

Stone fencing

Stone fencing is quite flexible. "Dry-laid" stone fences, that is, fences built without mortar, offer this flexibility and were quite popular in America prior to the 1900s and the advent of barbed wire. Most stone fences were built without any sort of foundation, as their loose construction was flexible enough to withstand frost-heaving, so all the farmer needed was plenty of stones—a feature of many small farms—and time to build the fence. Since the stones can come from the pasture that is surrounded by the fence, building a fence is a win-win situation for the farmer. Stone fences can be used to contain all sorts of larger livestock from lambs to horses. Generally, they are built about 4 feet high, but of course this varies depending on how they are being used. Stone makes an excellent fencing material today, especially for cross-fencing between small pastures.

Wattle

Wattle fencing is another ancient method that can be adapted very well to modern times. Wattle dates back to Neolithic times, but is most associated with Great Britain today. It is the reinforcing basis for the construction technique called "wattle and daub" in which a mud-and-straw mortar is "daubed" on woven sticks.

Essentially, wattle is wooden fencing made with basket-weaving techniques. First, upright posts are driven into the ground. Then smaller, lighter sticks or saplings are woven in and out between the uprights to form a solid fence tight enough to turn back smaller animals, such as rabbits, that you might want to keep out of your garden. Wattle fencing will only cost you for your labor, and done properly, it will make a very effective barrier that will last for several years. Using the same basket-weave technique, you can make a quick gate or screen using lighter uprights that aren't driven into the ground and are lightweight enough to make a portable unit to be set in place where needed.

Split Rail

The third preindustrial fence still valuable today is the split rail, a collection of fence rails, long quarter-round beams split lengthwise out of the trunks of trees (rails). You've seen plenty of split-rail fences scattered around the countryside. They're the ones that consist of split rails laid in a zigzag pattern, at least four or five courses high. They're simple to build and easy to reconfigure once you've done the hard work of splitting the rails. If you're going to be splitting rails for yourself, you'll find that some species of trees, such as white oak, split cleaner and easier than others, and while most of the drawings you'll see of Abe Lincoln splitting rails show him doing it with only an ax, the biggest part of the job is done with a steel wedge driven into the rail with a splitting maul. This, incidentally, is not easy work, but once you have the rails split, they can be used and reused for decades.

ALERT

When building a gate fence, remember that the hanging gate creates a constant load for the fence post it is hinged to. This will eventually bring down the post, but you can extend its life considerably by placing an "H" brace in the fence, using the post that the gate is hinged on as one side of the "H."

Split-rail fencing

Most of the split-rail fences you see today have been made purely for the sake of appearance. If you are building a split-rail fence to contain livestock, you want to do things a little bit differently. First of all, whereas cosmetic fences are usually built lying directly on the ground, farmers who plan for the fence to remain in place for quite some time set the bottom course on flat rocks placed at each bend, so that wood never touches earth, which keeps rot to a minimum.

Second, most functional split-rail fences are taller than the decorative ones, since they're meant to hold larger animals in place. In fact, the split rail can be one of the most effective hog fences you're likely to find, especially considering the low cost compared to modern hog fencing.

Modern Fencing for Security

If your backyard is in a very rural location, then the traditional fencing that has been used for centuries may be all you'll need, but if you're in a more urban setting, fencing becomes even more important than just a matter of keeping the livestock in and the predators out. There are situations in which your fencing may, in fact, be a matter of life or death, such as when your backyard adjoins a busy highway. For this sort of application, you want the most secure fencing that you can provide. If you have a situation in which your animals absolutely, positively must not breech their fencing, you'll want to use some of the following techniques.

Corner Bracing

In order for the modern fence to remain strong and rigid, it must be braced at the corners. Corner braces consist of either diagonal or horizontal braces fitted between upright posts as shown.

A welded-steel fence corner utilizing two types of bracing. Bracing of this sort can withstand the forces of tightly stretched wire, whether single strands or woven wire, and can be made of welded-steel posts or wood.

Wire

Cattle and horses have the strength and body weight to go through lesser fences easily, and they frequently penetrate even well-built fences when sufficiently frightened, hungry, or exposed to sexual opportunities. Cattle are generally contained by barbed-wire fencing with 3 to 6 lines of wire. Three wires used to be the standard, but as keeping your cattle contained becomes more important, 5 and 6 strands have become the norm; sheep and goats are sometimes kept within 7 to 10 strands of barbed wire.

FACT

Poultry netting (chicken wire) makes a cheap and effective barrier for the garden fence on level ground, but as with any woven wire, when the terrain is rolling, the netting tends to bind so severely that it can't be attached to the posts without folding or cutting.

More often though, sheep, goats, and hogs are kept in by woven-wire fences of about 48 inches in height with 1 or 2 strands of barbed or electric wire on top. In either case, the fence wire needs to be stretched very tight in order to be most effective.

Steel T-posts like this are easy to drive and long-lasting.

Posts

Fence posts can also be wood. Wooden posts can be simply split, sharpened rails of oak, hickory, or any reasonably straight wood. They can be treated with wood preservative, or they can be made of naturally rot-resistant woods, such as eastern red cedar, locust, or cyprus. Of all of these choices, red cedar posts will last the longest in the ground, and many people regard this species as a "weed tree," so they're easy to obtain.

Steel T-posts are rapidly replacing wood in many installations. They're easier to drive into the ground, last the longest, and if you compare them to the price of purchasing wooden posts as opposed to making your own, they're competitively priced. Posts have also been made of concrete, and even quarried rock, but these materials are not commonly used in agricultural applications.

Gates

Steel-pipe gates are the best and most common gates. Wire gaps—sections of wire fencing that can be taken down briefly and reclosed—are not secure enough to be used in high-liability situations like highway frontage.

Stock guards, parallel bars flush with the ground that vehicular traffic can cross but cattle will not, can be effective at containing cattle, but they cannot be relied upon to keep other animals in.

Electric Fence

Electric fencing can be a godsend when you need an effective fence in a hurry. The posts can be either existing fence posts, short rebar, or plastic posts driven or pushed into the ground. Then the fencing material—smooth steel wire, electric poly tape, or electric sheep netting—can be installed on insulators affixed to the posts. Steel wire is the cheapest, but the poly solutions are much easier to work with, don't require such tight stretching, and need less maintenance.

ALERT

Be careful of placing an electric fence too close to an old wire fence. Many people do this when the old fence no longer works and they need a quick replacement, but it's all too easy for the old fence to come into contact with the new electric fence, shorting the connection and rendering the electric fence worthless.

Electric fencing is also very easy to move about, and you often see it employed in intensive pasture rotation plans. That's not to say that it isn't without its drawbacks, not the least of which is that it's difficult or painful to test if it's turned on and working properly. If you don't fancy grabbing the fence yourself, and you can't get anyone else to do it, you can always carry a pocket voltage tester. However, if you have no experience at all with electric fence and worry that it may have a negative effect on your animals, you should test the wire yourself by touching it. If you keep the wire up all summer, you're very likely to receive a shock or two anyway. The electricity is sent through the fence in pulses. If you touch it during a pulse, you'll receive a small shock that won't be extremely painful, but you won't want to do it again. That is the desired effect.

Living Fence

A particularly inexpensive and attractive method of fencing, if you can make it work for your farm, is the hedge. You are probably familiar with hedges as a part of the urban and suburban landscape, but perhaps not with those planted specifically to keep livestock in. Farmers have been employing hedges for centuries; about as long as they have been building fences. In keeping with the purpose of a hedge to contain livestock, most hedge species produce thorns, such as hawthorn, blackthorn, and Osage orange. Hedges not only provide containment for livestock, but can also protect animals and crops from high winds. In the United States in the 1920s, many agricultural hedges were burned or bulldozed to make more room for planting. This contributed to the Dust Bowl, since drought and winds were prevalent and windbreaks were a rarity.

You can create a hedge fence for yourself fairly easily: just plant a band of thorny species close together and wait for them to grow. A traditional way of making the hedge more livestock-proof was called "laying hedge," in which the hedge was allowed to grow to about 8 feet tall, then the individual trees were bent over to about 45 degrees, and the stems were cut most of the way through. Posts were then driven at regular intervals, and the trees of the hedge were tied and woven between these posts rather like the wattle in wattle fencing. Thus prepared, the hedge would go on to grow thicker, and where the stems were cut, much bushier growth would come forth at the base of the plants. This resulted in a very dense mass of vegetation. Some of these living fences are now thousands of years old and still in use.

Fencing to Keep Peace with the Neighbors

In addition to keeping her livestock in place, keeping the animals out of the garden, and keeping predators out of the hen house, the backyard farmer must also consider relations with the neighbors. The old saying "Good fences make good neighbors" may be a cliché, but it makes a point. Besides keeping what belongs to you separate from what belongs to the folks next door, a proper fence can completely close in your backyard so that your beehives or compost pile will be invisible to those living next to you.

There are a lot of ways you can accomplish this. First, and most obvious, is with a 6-foot full-screen fence of 1" × 12" boards. A less-expensive, lighter, easier version would be 6-foot posts interwoven with thin boards or even plastic webbing, or you could try growing your own hedge, which, if you use the right species, can be 6 to 8 feet tall in just a few seasons.

FACT

Fencing out deer is always a problem, and the common solution is a fence 6 feet or taller, but some farmers use a double fence, one that is about a yard inside the other, or fence leaning toward the deer at a 45-degree angle. The deer won't try to jump a barrier that they think they might not clear.

Any tree or shrub can be planted into a hedge, but when it comes to keeping animals out, you want something that will grow to at least 6 feet tall, preferably a fast-growing species. The thorned species mentioned earlier tend to be hardwoods and fairly slow growing. Also, you may not wish to give the folks next door the idea that you're being particularly antisocial, so a dense hedge full of thorns might not be the best for fostering good neighborly relations. Instead consider willow, which is a fast-growing species frequently used for privacy hedges; or lilac, a mainstay shrub that grows not quite so fast as willow, but quickly, while producing beautiful, fragrant flowers in spring, which might tend to be seen as an attractive benefit to those on both sides of the fence.

Tools for Building a Fence

Building your own fence isn't difficult, but like so many things, you need to have the proper tools to do it the right way. It's just as much work to build a fence that sags and leans as it is to build one that doesn't, but if you do things the correct way, your fencing will hold any animal you place in it and last for years to come.

Wire Stretchers

Old-time cowboys make fences by stretching barbed wire with just a claw hammer around a post. If you're not an old-time cowboy, then you're going to need a set of wire stretchers, or perhaps a come–along tool can be used as an acceptable substitute. You can tell a novice's fence easily, because the wire will be limp. If animals can create a large enough opening to slip through just by pushing on the wire of the fence, well, that's not really much of a fence at all.

ESSENTIAL

Nailing fence wire to a tree makes for a strong connection, but is a very poor idea for the long term. As the tree grows, it will "swallow" the fence wire, making it very difficult if you ever want to cut the tree down in the future.

Wire stretchers require a little practice and getting accustomed to, but when you get the hang of them, you can build as tight a fence as anyone. If you don't have wire stretchers, you can do the same job by pulling the fence wire supertight with a hand winch or a high lift jack, but you'll need to stretch only one end at a time, and anchor the jack or winch to the ground.

13-Pound Post Maul

If you're going to be driving wooden posts, you're going to need a post maul. Even a large hammer isn't going to give you nearly enough force to do the job right, so make sure you get something that packs a little momentum. Be sure, however, that you never use your maul to drive metal posts, as that will result in splitting the cast iron maul head clean in two, probably before the first post is fully driven. If you don't have a maul, the mechanized way of driving wooden posts is to use a hydraulic post driver on the back of a tractor, or if the ground isn't too hard, you can press them in with a front loader.

T-Post Driver

The only easy way to drive a T-post without mechanization is with the tool made for the job. A T-post driver is a heavy metal tube with one end closed, and two handles on the sides. You put it over the top of the post and then slam it up and down until the post is as deep in the ground as you want it. It's a lot of very good exercise, but not nearly as much as using some other tool would be. Don't try to drive metal posts with a hammer; it does a poor job and will probably wind up damaging the post, the hammer, and perhaps your hand.

Staple Pullers

You'll see these listed as "fence pliers and staple pullers" so they don't get confused with the little office product that pulls staples out of paper. If you're driving staples into wooden posts, or repairing that sort of fence, these are invaluable, but they also come in handy as wire cutters strong enough to cut through barbed wire, and that curved horn on one side is handy for prying out lots of things besides embedded staples.

Clam-Shell Post-Hole Digger

This is the poor man's auger. Yes, they're slow and tedious, but compared to a tractor and Power Take-off (PTO) auger, they're very cheap. However, you can make the job easier, or even eliminate it altogether in some cases, with the next item.

Long Pry Bar

Wooden posts require that you dig a hole before trying to drive them into the ground with a maul. For large corner posts, this definitely requires a clam-shell digger, but for smaller line posts of 6 inches or less in diameter, you can make a quick hole in the shape of an inverted cone to start your posts in with a 5- or 6-foot-long heavy steel bar with one end sharpened to a dull point. Just thrust it into the ground and roll it around until the hole is the right shape, and it's ready to take your post and hold it upright while you drive it in.

Fencing is an art as well as a science, and the best fences combine both: they are pleasing to the eye because of simple, strong and tight construction, which you can learn by studying the techniques of others and practicing by building fencing for yourself. Like many farm constructions, building good a fence requires contemplation of the future. You can assume that your fence rows will attract weeds which will turn into brush, that your animals will put every stress on your fence that they can devise, and that the weather will constantly provide good conditions for rot along with wind and ice storms that will try to bring your fence to the ground. Keeping your fence functional, once it has been built, is a never-ending job that's easiest if you stay on top of it.

CHAPTER 17

Equipment

If you are young, healthy, strong, and farming a very small lot, then nearly every task that arises is one you should be able to accomplish with your bare hands and perhaps a few hand tools. However, if you have a larger acreage, or if you're getting older, or your health isn't so good, or all of the above, you can still keep up your farming chores if you have the right equipment. This chapter discusses some of the choices you'll find available.

Small Tractors: Better Than a Hired Hand

Tractors aren't just for plowing fields. In fact, owing to the vast array of implements available, a tractor can be outfitted to automate just about any heavy job you'll encounter on the farm. Unfortunately, machinery always comes with a few of its own inherent costs, from the original purchase price to the costs of maintenance and repair, and then of course, you need a place to store your machinery when it's not in use.

How large a tractor do you need for a half-acre? A tractor with a Category 0 three-point hitch (0 to 20 hp) should do. It's hard to imagine a need for a tractor larger than Category 1 on any farm less than 20 acres. On a very small acreage, the maneuverability of the machine is probably more important than the power.

Initial Cost

It is assumed here that if you're going to be in the market for a small tractor, then it's going to be a used one. Even when money is not a great concern, the difference in price between a new and a used farm machine definitely favors buying used as the most sensible solution. Of course one can make the argument that buying used equipment can be full of pitfalls, just like buying a used car can be, but a machine with only a few hours on it can still save you as much as a few thousand dollars, and while any nightmare is possible, the likelihood is that if you are a careful and diligent buyer, you'll enjoy substantial savings and have no regrets. If you can afford a newer-model tractor, then you will unquestionably get longer service and more work done easier than with an older model. But if you can't afford a later model, there's a tractor in a price range that will fit almost anyone's budget, and there can still be a lot of work left in a tractor that's as old as you are, or perhaps older than your father.

You can buy a tractor from a private party, an equipment dealer, or at an auction, but in order to feel confident in your purchase, you need to have a reasonable knowledge of what similar machines are selling for, and you can acquire that confidence simply by shopping around—a lot. Fortunately, you can now accomplish a lot of shopping pretty quickly on the Internet. Probably the best place to start is at *www.tractorhouse.com*, where you'll find thousands of tractors and an equal bounty of implements for sale all over the United States, and to a lesser degree, all over the world.

A good way to get an idea of what you can expect to find for the amount of money you want to spend is to do a search on their database. Choose the "Less than 40 HP" option and sort by price. You'll see that you can find a large number of small tractors in running condition for less than $2,000.

ALERT

New tractor tires can be quite expensive, and size is a big factor in the price. If you have a particular model of tractor in mind, find out what a new set of tires costs, because the condition of the tires may make up for the difference in price between two similarly-priced machines.

If you were to visit *www.tractorhouse.com* to shop for the venerable Ford 8N tractor, you might find seventy-nine of them for sale, ranging in price from $1,295 for a rusty, dented example with pretty good tires and a free rear blade in Rogersville, Missouri, to $7,250 for a perfectly restored 1951 model with brand-new tires in Fremont, Ohio.

Now, of course, you can't tell from photographs what sort of mechanical ills either of these machines might be suffering from, but you can get a fair idea of what the inside might be like from looking at the outside, and knowing the price range of seventy-nine examples should give you an idea of what Ford 8Ns are selling for.

Another point you ought to keep in mind is that a sizable market for "classic" tractors has developed, and you can often get a more generic imported tractor that is capable of more work than a similarly priced classic. This is not to say that one is superior to or a better buy than the other. If you maintain your tractor conscientiously, the generic import will retain much of its resale value, and the classic may even gain in value while you own it.

Operating Expenses

Luckily, most tractors don't use a lot of fuel. Gas-powered models are fairly frugal, while some of the diesels may cause you to wonder if the fuel gauge is broken. In all likelihood, you probably won't put enough time on your tractor to need to change the oil and filters more than once a year. That's good, but there are expenses beyond this.

For example, keep in mind that you'll need parts from time to time. This is one of the very distinct differences between used cars and used tractors: both require parts on occasion, but tractors require parts *frequently*. It's not as if their components fail all that often, or are poorly made, but in the course of doing work, you'll put stresses on parts that cars and trucks don't even *have*, such as the loader and the hydraulics. You'll also lose lots of pieces due to vibration—predominately the removable lynch pins that hold the implements to the three-point hitch. These are small and, if you manage to keep them for any time at all, they're rusty, so when one comes loose and falls in the grass somewhere, it's a lot better to have a stockpile of them on hand than to spend the afternoon on your hands and knees, looking for a seventy-five-cent part.

Also, if you have a tractor and don't live next to the dealership, you're probably going to need a trailer capable of hauling your machine. This is a good thing to keep in mind even before you buy the tractor, because due to the supply and demand for compact, affordable tractors, you can often get a larger machine, maybe larger than you need, for about the same price as a smaller one. Tractors contain a lot more metal-per-foot than cars do, and even a small tractor can weigh a ton or more. To do jobs at a distance from home, you'll want to be able to haul the tractor with at least one implement attached, so a double-axle trailer is probably the minimum you can get by with.

Repairs

If you have any skill as a mechanic, you can probably do most of the repair work to your machine yourself. Tractors, especially older ones, tend to be fairly simple, without many of the modern electronics and sophisticated hydraulic systems that you find on later models and highway vehicles. Tractors are much easier to work on than automobiles, mostly because they're a great deal simpler. The parts tend to be larger, less tedious to work on, and they usually do not involve computers of any sort. Get yourself a factory shop manual for your make and model of tractor, and if you have a box full of the most common mechanic's tools, you're all set to go.

If, on the other hand, you're not particularly adept at fixing things that break down, or if you don't have the time, or if you've broken something deep inside the machine, experience suggests that you find a long-time tractor mechanic working in his own shop.

FACT

The first chainsaw was invented in the 1830s as a surgical tool designed to cut bone and tissue. The first chainsaw for logging came about 100 years later. It weighed several hundred pounds and required a crane to maneuver it. It was not a commercial success.

In the olden days, you'd simply take the machine to a dealer, but that can be a financially risky practice these days as older dealerships sell out to new owners. When you see all the tractor dealerships of a certain make in your region being consolidated into the ownership of one large company, you can rest assured that the prices of both parts and labor will be significantly higher than they were under the former management. There's nothing wrong with this per se; these folks have a right to charge as much as they want, and since there are so many suburbanites who tend to think of John Deere the same way they think of BMW, the modern dealers can justify their higher rates by the fact that they have plenty of naïve doctors and lawyers willing to pay them. However, there's also nothing wrong in your wanting to get the best deal you can find as well, and the best deal in the twenty-first century is usually found in small, poorly lit twentieth-century garages.

Basic Capabilities

When shopping for a tractor, you may encounter specimens that are either too old to have three-point hydraulics, or that are in fact only glorified lawn mowers. The three-point hitch is to the farm tractor what the opposable thumb is to primates. Don't buy anything that doesn't have one.

In dealing with heavy equipment like tractors, the overall weight of the machine has a lot to do with its effectiveness in any given working situation. While weight alone is no indication of quality construction, a heavy machine exerts more momentum in any job it performs, and traction is greatly improved in most field conditions.

Also of great value, but not so universally available, is a front loader. While most new tractors are equipped with these, and while they are extremely handy, especially if you have a lot of lifting to do, they aren't all that common on older tractors. If you find one on an older model, such as the aforementioned Ford 8N, the hydraulic system may not really be up to the task of powering a loader, at least not fast enough to make it seem worth having. You shouldn't buy an older tractor assuming you can add a loader later. Even if you find a loader for sale that will fit, your tractor may simply not have the necessary "oomph" to make it work properly.

Something else that many modern tractors have that few older ones do is four-wheel drive. This is perhaps the best reason why you might want to buy a small import instead of an older American tractor, because a four-wheel-drive tractor will do a lot more than twice the work of a two-wheel-drive, and you'll spend less time getting it unstuck or filling up holes that spinning rear wheels have dug.

Implements

A tractor without implements is little more than unacceptably slow transportation. With the proper implements, however, you can move the world (eventually). Many people simply leave their implements out in the open, but they'll last much longer and be more serviceable if kept in a shed or under a tarp. Implements should also be kept liberally lubricated with heavy grease.

When buying implements, compare several designs. Heavy plate steel on the body of a bush-hog, for example, means an implement that will last ten times longer than a design that utilizes thin sheet metal.

Here's a partial list of some of the more popular examples of what's available:

IMPLEMENTS FOR THREE-POINT HITCH

- Bush Hog: mows down grass, weeds, and heavy brush
- Finish Mower: mows your lawn very uniformly
- Turning Plow: breaks and turns sod
- Cultivator: cultivates between crop rows; breaks up clumps
- Post-Hole Auger: can dig small post holes or large holes for planting orchard trees
- Post Pounder: drives metal or wooden fence posts
- Straight Blade: ditches and grades your driveway
- Box Blade: grades and fills your driveway
- Rock Rake: grades roads and moves rocks into a windrow
- Water Pump
- Log Splitter

IMPLEMENTS FOR FRONT LOADER

- Bucket
- Grapple
- Tree Shear
- Stump Grinder
- Post-Hole Auger
- Forklift
- Bulldozer

Skid-Steer Loaders

If you need to lift, move, and place heavy items very precisely, and you don't have much use for mowers, plows, blades, and other straight-line implements, then you might be better off with a skid-steer loader. Skid-steers are very maneuverable, able to turn 360 degrees in their own length, and so precise that you can easily place heavy objects exactly where you want them to within less than an inch of variance. Their price is similar to that of tractors, and they can usually be maintained by the same people. You can examine thousands of used ones for sale at Tractorhouse.com's sister site, *www.machinerytrader.com*. If you're farming a plot of land of an acre or less, and part of your operation involves quite a bit of heavy lifting, you may find a loader to make more sense for your purposes, even if you thought your place was too small for a tractor, because of the remarkable maneuverability of a skid-steer.

One word of caution though: You can get many of the same implements for a skid-steer that you can buy for a tractor, but because they are driven by hydraulics rather than a PTO, they'll cost considerably more money. Some of this may be unavoidable. For example, a hydraulic grapple to fit a tractor's loader will cost about as much as one for a skid-steer, since they are essentially the same device, but a post-hole auger for the skid-steer will cost twice or more what the PTO-driven auger that fits on the back of a tractor will set you back.

Chainsaws

If you live anywhere where trees grow, or if you do any rough carpentry at all, you're probably going to need a chainsaw several times a year at the very least. You can buy one at a big-box store, but if the store is one of those that insists everything they sell be produced at the very lowest price possible, this is not a good idea. Buy a chainsaw from a chainsaw (small-equipment) dealer who doesn't do anything else. If you're handy mechanically, buy a used saw; if it has anything wrong with it, you can probably fix it. If you're not particularly handy, buy only a new saw or a used one from a dealer who'll be around to fix it and perhaps honor a short-term warranty.

If your chainsaw needs are very few, a handsaw is probably enough for you, but if it becomes obvious that you have more to cut than you have time or strength to saw by hand, then consider buying a little more powerful saw than the bottom-of-the-line model. A little extra power in a chainsaw will translate into more work-savings than you might suppose, and the slightly longer bar will come in handy quite often.

When they're running right, chainsaws don't cost much to operate, and their maintenance only amounts to adding more fuel and keeping the chain taut and sharp. Keep the chain tight enough that the guides on the bottom side of the chain (opposite the cutting side) stay within their groove, just barely, when you pull the chain away from the bar. If the chain becomes too loose, it will come off the bar.

There are a couple of automated ways to sharpen a chainsaw chain. Dremel (*www.dremel.com*) makes an attachment for their Moto-Saw that does a serviceable job, or you can buy a larger unit that attaches to your workbench like a vise and holds the chain in a jig, then allowing a cutting wheel to be lowered onto the chain at exactly the correct angle. This device requires that you remove the chain to sharpen it, so it isn't as much of a time-saver as you might suppose.

Frankly, these two solutions are more for city slickers than for farmers. Farmers will buy a chainsaw file, stick the pointed end into a corn-cob for a handle, set the bar of the saw in a vice (if one is handy), and file the teeth by hand. This is just about as quick as the automated solutions, and it's probably at least as accurate, plus you're much less likely to cut too deep when sharpening by hand. Just try it a few times—you'll get the hang of it.

ESSENTIAL

Whatever method you use to sharpen your chainsaw, don't forget to file down the depth gauges, which are small protrusions set between each cutting tooth on the chain. If these are too high, the chain won't cut; if they're too low, the saw will bite too deeply and be difficult to control.

If you're uncertain how to go about sharpening the chain your first time, check out the Internet. There are lots of video clips that will show you exactly how it's done.

If your saw starts to cut in a slight curve, this is caused by a dull chain or irregular chain-sharpening. If you hit a rock, or the chain gets too dull on one side, or you're just not sharpening it properly, it can cease to cut straight. A common problem is that farmers tend to add a little more pressure when sharpening one side of the chain than the other, depending on whether they're right-handed or left-handed.

Rotary Garden Tillers

The author hopes that you'll be following his advice to do all of your planting in raised beds, but admittedly, that isn't always ideal for every situation. If you're planning something that requires a small field of tilled soil not large enough for a tractor and plow to be a necessity, then the only feasible option is to use a rotary tiller. There are two choices in garden tillers, and these two machines are so far apart from one another that the difference is almost laughable.

FACT

Using a rotary tiller destroys the soil's beneficial insects, worms, and spiders and ruins the aeration and drainage of the soil. Repeated tilling leaves the soil looking pretty and smooth, but when the rains come, the water has no place to go and the soil has fewer worms to channel it.

The first type of rotary tiller is the one with front-mounted tines. The advantage of these is that they are much cheaper than those with rear tines. That is the *only* advantage that they have. Front-tine tillers are clumsy, hard to control in any but the finest soil conditions, and if there are any rocks in your garden area, you'll find out right away: When the tines hit a well-anchored stone, the machine will lurch forward a foot or two, leaving a spot untilled. Front-tine tillers don't have wheels, or if they do, the wheels are only supposed to be used when you move the machine across pavement. When working in dirt, the tines are the only connection the tiller has with the earth. When you're in smooth, even soil, the tines spin fairly smoothly, but in anything else the tines grab traction and send the machine (and the operator) rocketing forward a short distance. An afternoon of this will have you wondering if using a hoe wouldn't be easier. If you have lots of rocks, count on having lots of spots untilled. Breaking sod with a front-tine tiller is just about impossible. If your soil is rock-free and even enough for a front-tine tiller to work smoothly, then you probably don't need a tiller at all. Add to this the fact that they tend to use poorer quality engines that are relatively short-lived. Don't buy one of these things.

A rear-tine tiller, on the other hand, controls its own forward speed with driving wheels equipped with tractor-lug tires. If you have smooth, rock-free soil, you can easily control the machine with one hand. If you have rocks, or need to break sod, a small, middle-buster plow can be attached to the tiller that will hold the machine back while it ejects the rocks or chews the sod.

In contrast to the front-tine tillers, the rear-tine tillers will cost you about three times as much, are generally of much higher quality, and can last you for years if properly maintained. The proper name for these machines is actually "two-wheel tractors" because they can pull other implements, such as the plow mentioned or wings to hill up windrows for potato planting, and they can also pull small trailers.

Wood Chippers

A wood chipper is just the sort of thing you want to find very cheaply at a farm auction, because while they're quite handy for grinding up your compostable materials. A wood chipper is a real bonus to have when you clean up storm damage, and they can turn weeds and kitchen waste in high-nitrogen composting material. The only real problem with wood chippers is that they tend to cost $500 to $1,500 new and you can chop up a lot of leaves and dried manure with an old push-mower for that kind of money.

However, you may have a special need that will justify the price, such as a large compost-making project, or you may simply find a way to get one for less money. If you start attending farm sales, garage sales, and staking yourself out at your local Craigslist's site, you're likely to come up with a good one capable of shredding brush for many years to come at an affordable price.

Wood chippers are great pieces of equipment to own. Besides the self-powered ones, you can buy models that will run off of your tractor's PTO or the hydraulics of your skid-steer, but hydraulic models tend to be quite a lot more expensive than the engine-driven ones.

Trailers

As mentioned earlier, if you own equipment, it is frequently very handy if you have some way to move that equipment, either to the shop for repairs or to another property for work away from home. It is also very handy if you have the power to bring home large and clumsy articles, such as household furnishings, feed, building materials, or compostables. Even if you have a pickup truck, you don't have enough capacity to handle all of these things.

That's why you probably need a trailer. There are, of course, all kinds and sizes of trailers, but for your farm purposes, a simple flat-bed with either one or two axles will suffice. Which you need depends on what you're hauling. Anything less than 1,000 or maybe 1,500 pounds wouldn't require more than a single-axle trailer, but it's nice to have extra capacity, and if you have a tractor that weighs a ton or better, you'll feel a lot more secure on the highway pulling it on a tandem-axle trailer.

FACT

A trailer that is incorrectly loaded can begin to sway and shimmy, and this can send the towing vehicle out of control. To keep this from happening, you should always put the largest percentage of the trailer's weight in front of the axle or axles.

If you've never towed a trailer before, the most important thing is to secure your load. You want it fastened down to the trailer so that there's no slack in the restraints and no movement is possible. Anything else simply isn't safe. You can achieve this level of security one of two ways: with log chain and steel load binders, also known as "boomers," or with nylon ratchet straps. Of these two, the steel binders are quicker and more likely to cause your fingers to get pinched in the chain links, or scratch or mar whatever you're fastening to the trailer. The nylon ones are safer for your soft tissues and your paint job, but more tedious to fasten and remove.

Finally, regardless of whether you choose the single- or double-axle trailer for towing on the road, you will probably find it very handy to have an off-road trailer—a smaller, narrower one to pull behind the tractor maneuvering around home. Many times, you'll find a small two-wheel trailer to be the handiest way to move tools, trash, or materials too big to carry about your property.

CHAPTER 18

Hand Tools

There is something elegant about the simplicity of hand tools that have evolved over eons. Consider, for example, the path traveled by the first digging tool—probably a sharp stick—on its way to evolving into the long-handled shovel, the adze-mattock, or the pick. Imagine if you could transport yourself back to the Stone Age, taking with you a steel-bladed shovel with a fiberglass handle. You would be regarded as a sorcerer of the highest magnitude, but your "magic" would be largely a matter only of superior materials; the inherent designs of our tools in comparison of their Stone Age counterparts have changed very little over the ages.

The Workshop

Hand tools make our lives so much easier. You may think that using a common hammer still requires plenty of effort, but compare that with what it would be like if all you had was a rock.

ESSENTIAL

Once rust forms on a surface, it will keep corroding that surface faster and faster. Once rust has been stopped or removed, it can be kept away by keeping tools clean and storing them with toolbox drawer liners that emit a rust-inhibiting vapor good for several months.

The fact is, the simplest tools are frequently some of the most labor-saving inventions, so it behooves you to have a good selection of hand tools, as well as a place to store, use, and repair them: that is, a workshop. The farmer needs a place indoors where he can perform tasks like sharpening tools, replacing handles, and so on. The workshop doesn't need to be a large area, but in addition to the tool-storage area, you'll need a workbench large enough to accommodate whatever jobs will be brought indoors.

The small farm workshop should also have electricity, because you'll want an electric bench grinder to sharpen blades as well as a wire brush to clean the rust off of those same tools. Yes, you could use a hand file and wire brush, but while you're doing these things, you'll want plenty of light for the job, as well as for finding things in the dark corners, and while electricity isn't the only source of light indoors, it's probably the safest and most convenient. You'll need a bench vise to hold things securely in place while you're working on them, and you'll probably find that some sort of small anvil will be handy as well.

How to Build a Tool Collection on a Budget

Like so many things, quality tools are expensive. However, there are still ways to furnish your workshop with a good selection of tools without spending a great deal of money, thanks in part to the fact that hand tools are so ubiquitous. They're so commonplace in fact, that many people who own them don't see a lot of value in the ones they have. That's why it's not unusual to see the metal heads of many tools simply thrown away if the handle breaks.

Now, a double-bit ax blade doesn't seem like a particularly valuable commodity (especially when you don't need an ax), but a whole new ax will run you from $30 to $50, whereas, if you have just the ax head and a $6 hickory handle, plus the time to put the two together, you can make one that will work just as well as a new one.

ESSENTIAL

You can also make your own tool handles, but it helps to know your wood properties. Hickory is often used for striking tool handles like those on hammers and axes, but elm, ash, and oak are also popular choices, and soft, flexible woods with little tendency to splinter are often used for rakes and brooms.

You'll find that there are many perfectly good tool-heads for shovels, rakes, picks, mattocks, hammers, axes—practically anything you care to name—lying someplace completely unused and unwanted. Abandoned buildings, flea markets, and your friend's garages are all likely places where you can find tool heads for free or for next to nothing.

Another excellent source of old hand tools, either whole or in parts, is the farm auction. If you don't know, farmers leaving the country, or retiring from farming, generally divest themselves of their farming tools and equipment through auctions. You can often buy a lot containing several tools at once for a very low price at these auctions, and frequently the farmer will have a box or crate full of tool heads that you can buy, usually all in one lot, for next to nothing. In fact, after you've replaced a few handles, you may marvel that people would buy a new tool just because the handle breaks.

Multiplying Your Strength

Over the ages, some mighty impressive things have been done by men using no power source at all—just the strength of their muscles and those of their animals. They built the pyramids, paved the Appian Way, and cleared the American frontier.

FACT

Modern cranes and other lifting and pulling devices powered by electricity or internal combustion engines only surpass muscle-powered machines in the speed at which they can pull or lift. By using pulleys and levers, human-operated devices can lift as just much as mechanically operated ones, albeit more slowly.

Mostly they did these things with the power of the simplest tools, like the fulcrum, the pulley, and the lever. Farmers have been using some of these work-savers for thousands of years to turn themselves into virtual supermen. Since they're cheap and plentiful, you need to take advantage of the awesome strength that hand tools can bestow upon you. When your machinery fails you and you really need to get it out of the way, there's nothing handier than a lever; when you need to pull with the strength of five men, a pulley will help you do that. There are a few basic hand tools that belong on every farm, without which, life would be more of a struggle. You'll have your own list in time, but the following sections will give you a good selection of what to start out with.

The Ten Most Useful Hand Tools for the Backyard Farmer

The following list may be only an approximation of the one you would write after you've been farming for a while, because every farm and every farmer is different, but here is a collection of some of the most useful ways to multiply your strength and expand your capabilities. You'll develop a list of your own, of course, but chances are your list will include several of these items. Not surprisingly, most of these tools are so basic that they have been part of human existence since the dawn of time, and even in this day and age, when seemingly every task has been mechanized, they still remain as useful and essential as they were thousands of years ago.

The Pulley

The basic idea behind winches and pulleys is that of the block and tackle. Using them, you are trading weight lifted (or pulled) for the *distance* you have to pull it. For example, if you have a 100-pound weight on a rope, with a single pulley between yourself and the weight, and you want to lift it 100 feet, then you'll need to put 100 pounds of force into pulling the weight up 100 feet.

This in itself will be an improvement, because pulling down on a rope is easier than pulling up. But if you add a second pulley, the weight is distributed between the two pulleys so that the effort to lift the weight is half what it was—now 50 pounds—but in order to lift it up 100 feet, you'll need to pull 200 feet of rope. And so it goes: The more pulleys you add to the equation, the less effort that's required to lift the weight, but the farther you have to pull the rope. Early cranes were built to do extremely heavy lifting using the principle of the block and tackle to achieve mechanical advantage thousands of years before the discoveries of electricity or internal combustion.

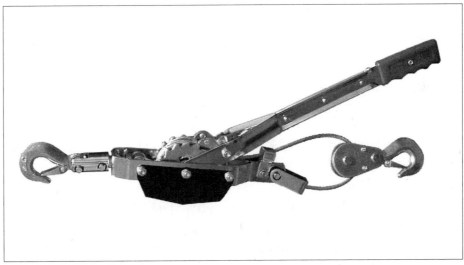

A simple come-along cable puller

You can use these principles to your own advantage whenever you need far more strength than your muscles alone can provide. You could never, for example, pull a fence wire as tightly as it needs to be pulled just with the strength of your body; with a hand winch, or come-along, it becomes a quick and easy job.

The roof design of old hay barns with the pointed overhang on one end was designed to accommodate a pulley-and-trolley system that was used to raise hay up vertically to the level of the hay loft, then move it horizontally into the back of the barn.

If you have routine heavy-lifting jobs, particularly if you do all the heavy lifting in one place, such as loading heavy items into a second-story loft, you should have a block and tackle set or a chain hoist at the ready, but any backyard farmer needs a plain old come-along (also called a cable puller) in his toolshed. There is a broad selection of such portable winches on the market with various weight ratings, and of course various price tags. The weight ratings refer to the amount of weight that the cable can support, but the weak spot is in the handle of the device. If possible, opt for tubular handles over those made of laminated steel, as the laminated handles tend to bend laterally well before the stated capacity is reached.

The Lever

Sometimes trying to get a heavy implement attached to the back of your tractor can be a big job, especially if you have an older model built before quick-hitch hardware was invented. You can't back the tractor up to it precisely enough, and every time you try, you wind up a few inches off. Unfortunately, even something as small as a five-foot bush hog can weigh several hundred pounds. Luckily, the simplest tool imaginable can save the day in this case, and you can even make one for yourself. What you need to start with is a large steel rod of an inch and a half or 2 inches in diameter by 5 or 6 feet long. Get a blacksmith to sharpen one end to a dull point and sharpen the other end to a dull blade.

A twenty-pound "persuader"

Sometimes referred to as a "spud bar," when you use this pry bar as a lever you can easily scoot the implement, an inch or so at a time, to exactly where you need it to be, and you won't even break a sweat. This is a good way to move just about anything heavy, from adjusting railroad ties in your raised bed to moving a vehicle that won't start. Depending on the thickness of the rod you choose, this device can weight 20 or 30 pounds, so it can be useful in piercing heavy materials, or as a sort of battering ram when you want to move something out of the way.

As Archimedes, the Greek mathematician, physicist, engineer, inventor, and astronomer, said, "Give me a place to stand, and I shall move the Earth." If it's the Earth you want to move, you may need something longer than 5 or 6 feet, but for the sorts of things you'll encounter around the farm, this will work perfectly. The next time you have something extremely heavy that needs to be moved, put your "persuader bar" into action. It'll knock some sense into the offending item.

Lopping Shears

When your property-management tasks move beyond simply mowing grass, your tool set needs to expand to include a strong pair of lopping shears, especially if maintaining an orchard is part of your duties. Like so many things, cheap loppers aren't cheap at all because they fail easily, and you can't buy replacement handles. Get a pair of higher-quality loppers, and they'll last you a lifetime.

Compound-action
lopping shears

Most strong sets will claim to be able to cut limbs of an inch and a half to 2 inches, but for a price you can buy models that are advertised as twice that powerful. This, of course, isn't a very scientific classification, as cutting a 2-inch pine limb is a much easier matter than bringing down a 2-inch oak bow, but you can count on the fact that long, strong handles and compound linkage will add to the lopper's capability. They're also handy for other cutting jobs, such as shortening a garden hose and clipping off overhead branches.

The High-Lift Jack

A high-lift jack is a standard item among off-road 4WD enthusiasts, who use them in a variety of ways to lift, pull, or move aside stuck vehicles in remote locations, and this is about the only jack you'll find that can pick up the axles of a tractor without having to build a tower of blocks to support it. If you turn the upper jaw to the horizontal, you can squeeze two things

A high-lift jack

together tightly or use the jack as a substitute for fence stretchers. If your truck gets stuck in mulch up to the axles, you can pick it up high and (very, very carefully) push the jack over so that the wheels land on solid, higher ground. You'll find the high-lift to be among the handiest tools you can have on the farm, because it allows you to pick over 4,500 pounds from 4½ inches off the ground up to nearly 4 feet in the air. Its basic advantage is that of the simple lever.

Always make certain that a high-lift jack is fully perpendicular when operating, and be especially mindful that you push the handle fully all the way down on each down stroke. If you don't, the handle can kick back with a tremendous force in the close vicinity of your face. The high-lift jack requires a certain amount of caution because it isn't all that stable, especially when picking something very heavy up very high. If you watch your fingers, toes, and the rest of your body and keep them clear of the device, you'll do things with this jack that you can't do with any other.

Bolt Cutters

Bolt cutters are a wonderful invention that allow you to do small miracles. Take for example, another wonderful invention of the last half-century: steel stock panels, those extremely heavy-duty portable wire fences, designed to hold cattle, hogs, and other large, destructive critters without significant damage. These are very nice for their intended use, but are also quite handy for gates, trailer racks, and trellises, provided that you have some way of *cutting* them. To do this, you could use a hacksaw, or even a file, if you don't care much about how productively you spend your time. But if you have other things to do with your life, a hefty set of bolt cutters, say about 24 inches long, will snap through those steel rods as if they were butter. Bolt cutters are the tools of choice when neutralizing a number of things: locks, chains, fences, cables, and, of course, even bolts.

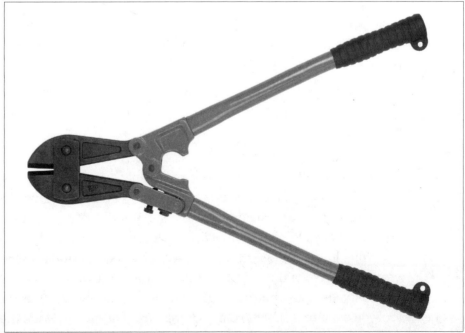

Compound-action
bolt cutters

Pole Saw

If your property contains any trees at all, you desperately need a pole saw, even though you may not know it yet. In case you've never seen a pole saw, it is exactly what it claims to be: a curved saw blade on the end of a telescoping pole. Now, it may be that you've been living on your property some while and never thought that such a saw was a necessity, or you may never have thought about one much at all, but when you begin to farm your land, you'll realize that many of your tree limbs are low enough to interfere with mowing or bush-hogging (they might be situated so that they threaten to sweep you off the tractor and into the path of the mower if you don't keep your wits about you).

A pole saw

A pole saw cures these problems semipermanently. If you have a large number of such overhanging limbs to eliminate, then you might consider renting a gas-powered version, but if you only have a few, or if you just want to keep up with the ones that grow out and develop over time, the simple pole saw is worth every cent of its low price. Not only is a pole saw cheaper than a new pair of glasses, it's cheaper than the ladder you'd need to buy in order to prune those limbs with a handsaw—and a *lot* cheaper than the hospital bill you'd get if you fell off the ladder pruning tree limbs with a handsaw.

Crowbar

The crowbar, or wrecking bar, is a major convenience for farmers (as well as cat burglars, who are more commonly associated with its use). The primary purpose of a crowbar is to pry things apart, and it certainly serves that end. The remarkable crowbar is a single tool that can be used in different ways that epitomize each of the three classes of levers.

While it may be one of the simplest of the simple tools, the uses of the crowbar are beyond a number. For example, a crowbar can be handy as a tool to make holes or furrows in the garden, it works great as the primary tool you'd use to dismantle old buildings and salvage the wood they contain without breaking any more timbers than necessary, and it's invaluable for opening stuck windows or doors. A crowbar can also be a godsend when convincing lynch pins in a tractor 3-point hitch to do your bidding, or when you just need to create a little space between two very heavy items.

The classic crowbar

Large Pipe Wrench

There are a lot of instances around the farm when you need to grasp and turn a round pipe, shaft, rod, or dowel, and in nearly every case, a pipe wrench is the best tool to use to do it. If the cylindrical object you need to rotate is small enough, you can just use a pair of pliers, but when you need to turn large pipes or shafts, such as a PTO drive or a long-rusted irrigation pipe, then a large pipe wrench is what you have to have.

"Large" is of course a relative term. Pipe wrenches come up to 5 feet long, with gaping jaws that open to bite down on pipes of up to 8 inches in diameter. Needless to say, you'll pay a small fortune for one of these giant wrenches new, and there aren't many to be found used, but a wrench of "only" 18 to 24 inches will still give you superhuman strength when it comes to turning things, and if that isn't enough, you can always employ the next item.

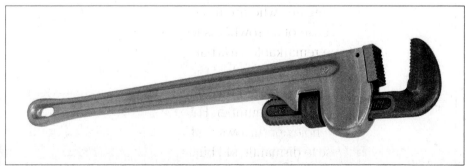

A 24-inch
pipe wrench

Cheater Bar

So let's say that you have your 60-inch pipe wrench gripping the 8-inch rusted well casing you want to turn, and even with a neighbor's help, the two of you can't seem to budge the thing a single millimeter. Are you going to give up? No; you simply "cheat."

A simple pipe to be used as a cheater, shown here applied to a large wrench.

ALERT

The use of a cheater bar can multiply your bare-handed strength so greatly that you may very well exceed the structural limits of whatever device you're working on. You may crack lug nuts, sever handles, or snap load binders by applying too much force. Be prepared to react (get out of the way) in case this occurs.

The cheater bar is simply a long steel pipe fitted over the handle of the wrench and extending the effective handle length as much as you need to achieve the leverage that's required to break loose the pipe in question. This technique can be used on just about any sort of wrench whose handle will fit inside the pipe you pick. You can boom a tractor to a trailer so securely that the tires will flatten out. You can turn the largest, most rusted nut or bolt on the farm with ease. In fact, a cheater will give you the strength of ten men, if that's what you need, and with it, the item that you want to turn will either behave the way you want it to, or break off completely.

The Adze or Mattock

You may not be familiar with either the word "adze" or the word "mattock," but you've probably seen quite a few adze-mattocks in your life. As mentioned earlier in this chapter, the earliest digging tool was probably a sharp stick or bone. The first time a human tried to improve on the sticks and bones found laying on the ground, the result was probably the first adze, the basic design of which mimics the shape of the human hand digging into soft soil.

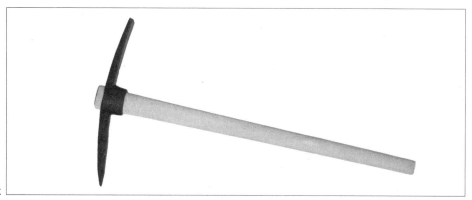

A pick mattock

The adze is a horizontal blade (as opposed to the ax, a vertical blade) on a handle. When the adze is paired with an ax on a single tool head, that tool is referred to as a "cutting mattock"; when the adze is paired with a pick, that's known as a "pick mattock."

FACT

The adze is a truly ancient tool and archeologists have discovered examples dating back to the Mesolithic period. Whereas once adzes were used in carpentry, shipbuilding, and making railroad ties, today they are used primarily in gardening and digging in hard ground and are referred to as mattocks.

Perhaps because of its very basic nature, the adze is arguably the most useful hand tool on the farm, especially as a short-handled, one-hand tool. With it, you can chop into rocky soil and thick sod with ease, perhaps easier than with your spading fork, but you can also use it in fine garden soil where the broad blade can take the place of a simple garden trowel, or if sharpened, do a bang-up job of chopping weeds to shreds. Once you've had one around for a while, you'll wonder how you got by before.

CHAPTER 19

Expand the Growing Season

One of the best and most obvious ways to boost any farm's potential is to expand the growing season, which for the purposes here means taking your gardening projects indoors either in a small way with a hotbed or in a big way with a greenhouse. Not only will you enjoy a longer income-producing season, but you will also have complete control over the growing environment, allowing you to branch out and try new products to offer to your customers.

The Cold Frame

A cold frame is a planting bed that is protected from the elements by a transparent or translucent cover. You could think of it as a micro-greenhouse. There are several handy uses for a cold frame. First, the cold frame makes an excellent place to shelter young perennial plants in transition from the greenhouse to their eventual planting spot. Second, it can be used as a spot to overwinter young cuttings you've started during the summer. The cold frame is also a good environment in which to acclimate, or "harden," young seedlings before exposing them directly to the uncertainties of early spring weather. Finally, and perhaps most commonly, many people use cold frames as a place to start seeds earlier in the spring than would be possible in the chilly open air.

Cold frames should be located on a spot where there is good drainage so that the contents don't flood during rainy weather, and of course they need an unobstructed southern exposure. The temperature inside the cold frame will generally be five or ten degrees warmer than the outside air, which protects against frost. If there is a windbreak on the north side, such as a building, hedge, or fence, so much the better, as this will help keep the temperature inside the cold frame a bit higher. In the absence of such existing windbreaks, you can place a course or two of straw or hay bales on the north side of the cold frame. If an extremely cold night is anticipated, a blanket or tarp can be laid over the glazing material.

In a typical installation, the cold frame is a rectangular box with the front (south) wall slightly lower than the back, which is covered with glass or transparent/translucent plastic as the glazing material, so that the glazing slopes slightly to allow sun into the frame and rain to run off. The dimensions are, of course, up to the builder, but if you have an old window, glass door, or sheet of rigid plastic, you'll want to size the frame to match that. The frame can be constructed of any material, including wood, masonry, or metal, but if the installation is intended to be permanent, wood should be treated with a nontoxic preservative, and if metal is used, some sort of insulation will be needed as well. Whatever material you choose, a 1-inch thickness of expanded styrene board will provide a great deal of insulation at very low cost.

During construction, don't forget that you'll want to be able to raise the glazing in order to relieve the heat during particularly warm days as the season progresses, and when you do, it's better if you can raise the side opposite the direction the wind is coming from. If your design doesn't allow for the glazing to be raised from either side, make it open against the prevailing winds in your area.

The Hotbed

A hotbed is simply a cold frame with some source of heating, so that it becomes even more of a miniature greenhouse. You can heat your hotbed with electrical cables, electric light bulbs, or manure. If you don't have and can't get electricity to your garden site, then manure is your option. Manure has the advantage that it can be used anywhere, and when it's done heating the hotbed, it can be used as compost. However, heating with manure is difficult to control precisely, if you require such precision, and it needs to be replaced regularly. Incandescent light bulbs are getting more difficult to obtain, so you may decide that electrical cables are your best choice.

You'll want to measure the amount of electrical-cable heat you apply to your hotbed in watts per square foot. An approximate application in Zone 5 would be twelve watts per square foot, so determine the number of watts your cables produce, and match that with the number of square feet in your hotbed. In order to maintain a constant temperature, you'll need some form of thermostat to regulate the heat. Some cables come with built-in thermostats, or you can add one yourself.

A Quick Cold Frame or Hotbed

A cheap, simple, and fast way to construct a cold frame or hotbed is to place straw bales directly on the ground so that they form a square or rectangular box. How big this box will be depends on how much space you need and how many panes of glass or plastic you have in what configuration. When you've positioned the straw bales in the square shape you want, then all you need to do is lay some glazing material, such as old windows, old storm doors, large transparent plastic panels, poly-film, or something of that nature, across the top of the straw-bale box. This will make a cozy compartment inside the straw where your plants will get full sunlight, yet be protected from frost at night.

Another variation is, in combination with raised beds built from timbers or railroad ties, to lay the glass directly on the sides of the raised bed so that you can let your garden be a hotbed for the first few weeks of spring. If you designed your bed with this in mind—that is, if the timbers are sufficiently higher than the soil line so there is room for growing plants under the glass—then this method is even easier than using the straw bales. Not only can you extend the season in this manner, but you can also start many seeds directly in the garden, thus avoiding the shock of transplanting them when the time comes.

The Greenhouse

Having a greenhouse gives you, as a grower, literally a whole new environment to grow in. Free from the limitations of winter, you can grow just about anything you decide you want to grow, assuming that you do things correctly. Just remember though, that the more you try to extend a greenhouse, that is, the lower the temperatures outdoors that you're battling, the more difficult it gets. You won't have any trouble simply growing cool-season plants beyond their normal growing range, but as you get deeper into winter in the more northerly climes, you may need to provide an additional heat source besides the sun, or look for ways to store the sun's radiant heat such as concrete blocks or drums of water. Depending on what you want to grow and when, it may become necessary to provide additional light sources in order to achieve the particular day-length that some flowering plants require.

Many small growers begin with a shed-roof sort of greenhouse attached to the south wall of the house or other building. Such a design can have several advantages over a free-standing unit because it makes the greenhouse more available, both to you and to electric outlets and heated walls. That shared wall will ensure that heating the greenhouse is an easier task and because the greenhouse acts as insulation, heating the house is less costly as well.

If you have a greenhouse, you can produce marketable plants and gorgeous produce year-round while at the same time commanding a higher price for what you grow.

Glazing Materials

A hundred years ago, there were very few greenhouses, and only one choice of glazing material (not counting mica). In fact, that dearth of materials was the prime reason why there were so few greenhouses compared to the profusion of hoop houses seen in the last few decades. Where once the greenhouse was but another expensive fancy of the ridiculously wealthy, today you'll see portable greenhouses springing up in grocery-store parking lots to provide customers with bedding plants and hanging baskets at the beginning of the growing season. In this regard, the materials involved have made all the difference.

ALERT

If you use glass as glazing for your greenhouse or hotbed, always use tempered glass. When common annealed glass breaks, it shatters into pointed shards that can be quite dangerous when they fall, but tempered glass only breaks into small squares, which aren't likely to hurt anyone.

Along with the transition away from glass, greenhouse owners have had to concern themselves with other aspects of the performance of glazing materials. Glass provides about 90 percent light transmission and, believe it or not, some of the plastics are superior in this regard—at least when they're newly installed; over time, hazing occurs from ultraviolet light effects, from dust, and from grime buildup. There is very little difference in the amount of light passed through "frosted" glass or plastic and clear examples of the same material, and diffused light will illuminate areas that would be shaded using clear glass, so it's superior.

Glass

The pricey greenhouses of commercial nurseries and the wealthy gentry were all glazed with real glass, and maintenance consisted of replacing the hundreds of panes when they broke. As you can imagine, a heavy hail storm could be a disaster for the unlucky gardener. Also, besides being heavy, brittle, and dangerous, glass does not diffuse light well, and your plants won't do as well under it as they will under a more translucent material that will provide a more even, shadow-less light.

FACT

Over 17 percent of the fresh tomato crop in all of North America is grown in greenhouses. As large as that number is, it is far smaller than the percentage of the tomato crop in Europe, where land is at a premium and there are fewer tillable areas with the appropriate weather.

Today, plastic has replaced glass, even in many of the old structures that were originally glazed with glass. Glass has one superior characteristic to plastic, and that is its long-term transparency, although some new plastics rival glass even in this regard.

6 Mil, 4-Year Poly Film

This soft material is treated for UV resistance to protect against degradation from the sun, and comes in widths from 16 to 50 feet. The manufacturers offer it in clear or white, and it is intended to be replaced every four years. Poly film is easy to handle and cut and is the cheapest solution for glazing a greenhouse, but of course it doesn't last as long, nor is it as durable as other materials.

Reinforced, Multilayer Poly Film

This comes in multiple layers, totaling 8 to 10 mils in thickness. It is reinforced with a fabric of cotton cord. Much stronger and somewhat longer-lasting than the 6 mil product, the clear version has 80 percent light transmission and the white version 20 percent.

Clear Vinyl

Vinyl is the clearest synthetic material available, and is recommended in applications where that is of particular importance, but is only available in widths up to 54 inches. Like the other plastics, the rated life is four years.

Polycarbonate Sheets

Sold under the trade name Lexan, among others, these are 6 mil or 8 mil corrugated semi-rigid sheets that come 4 or 6 feet wide by up to 24 feet long. They offer 80 percent light transmission in white and actually provide a degree of insulation value due to their corrugations, and the manufacturer offers a ten-year warranty. Naturally, they cost about seven times as much as 6 mil poly film.

Solexx Greenhouse Paneling

This is a double-walled polyethylene 4 feet, 1 inch wide by either 60 or 100 feet long. It provides 77 percent light transmission and a gentle, diffused light, as well as the most insulation value of all the materials listed here, although it should be noted that even this is not a great deal of insulation.

Greenhouse Heating and Cooling

While it can get pretty warm inside any greenhouse on a sunny day, even in the coldest weather that heat won't last for very long after the sun goes down. You can, of course, heat a greenhouse with any conventional means of heater, such as gas or electric, but glass and thin plastic films don't provide very much insulation to keep the heat in, so these aren't very economical solutions. Typically, greenhouse heating utilizes heaters burning low-cost fuels like wood or sawdust pellets, but the price can still be considerable. It's suggested that you include passive solar devices like black-painted concrete blocks or steel drums full of water to catch and hold heat to augment your regular heat source, as these only cost as much as the initial purchase price, if any.

When placing a new greenhouse, remember that the sun's position is quite different in the summer when you're building your greenhouse than in winter when you're growing things in it. Make sure that no part of the new greenhouse is shaded during any part of a winter day.

The greenhouse should also have enough ventilation that it can be kept from overheating during warmer times, but active cooling—refrigeration or air conditioning—isn't generally considered viable. Most commercial greenhouse owners set up large fans to keep air moving, something that plants require anyway, and to keep the temperatures inside the greenhouse down to acceptable levels.

The Conventional Greenhouse

This is the sort of greenhouse that pops into your mind when you hear the word. The conventional greenhouse is shaped like a regular house, with straight walls and a double-pitched roof, although single-pitched roofs are also used. Traditionally, all the walls and both pitches of the roof are made of glazing material. That is part of its inherent inefficiency, because the sun only comes from the south, so having a completely north-glazed wall provides you with extra cost and greater heat-loss in return for no obvious benefits. Although this was the style of the great private greenhouses of England in the nineteenth and twentieth centuries, this style is seen more often in modern times applied to small, prefabricated (and rather pricey) greenhouses intended for backyard gardeners. These aren't as large, or as efficient, as what the backyard farmer will need to have if her plan is to produce marketable produce and products.

The Hoop House

This is the design that has revolutionized private greenhouse construction and made them such a common part of everyday life. The hoop house is a transparent Quonset hut design; that is, a large half-tube as long as the job calls for, at 10 to 30 feet wide. Their construction is a series of steel, aluminum, or plastic hoops—thus the name—set upright and covered with glazing material. You can build your own, or there are many kits offered to the public.

The French word for greenhouse, "orangery," stems from the fact that the first French greenhouses were grown to protect citrus trees. Later, George Washington grew pineapples in a greenhouse at Mount Vernon that he referred to as a "pinery." Early greenhouses were often used to grow crops not only out of season, but also out of their native habitat.

Compared to the conventional structure, hoop houses are fast and low-cost to build. They are also typically built of the same materials on their north and south sides, although you sometimes see examples with insulating materials on the lower parts of the north walls, and quite often the end walls are insulated wood stud walls. The advent of the hoop house in the 1980s was the death-knell of many long-established commercial greenhouse businesses, because these interlopers can be set up anywhere—in a back yard, an empty lot, or even in a parking lot.

Like the conventional structures, hoop houses are hard to heat. Some people have experimented with passive solar heat sinks, in the form of concrete blocks or steel drums filled with water, to catch and store the sun's warmth during the day to keep the house warm overnight. The hoop house is a good design for the backyard farmer, however, because, of the three types of greenhouse, the hoop house gives him the most amount of growing area for his money.

The Below-Grade Solar Greenhouse

Here is a design that anyone can love. While it's not as quick to build as the hoop house, it can be almost as inexpensive, and it is far more efficient than either of the other designs. Construction is started with a backhoe that excavates a rectangular hole in the ground from 4 to 8 feet deep. If the hole is in level ground, then the fill material is placed on the north side of the hole to be bermed later as part of the north wall.

ESSENTIAL

Don't forget that plants need ventilation and moving air to grow healthy stems and to keep mold and mildew at bay. Commercial greenhouses install whole-house attic fans in one or both ends of their greenhouses. Smaller structures can get by with one of two box fans at each end of the room.

The excavation has a level floor except at the front (south) side, where a trench 2 or 3 feet deep is dug to act as a heat sink. Cold air will settle into this sink overnight, leaving the rest of the area warmer. The greenhouse can be accessed by a staircase cut from grade level down into one sidewall.

Depending on how much effort and expense the builder wants to go to, the walls of the excavation can be reinforced with bagged earth, wood frame construction, concrete block, or even nothing at all, although not having reinforcement will limit the life of the greenhouse, as the walls will slowly crumble to the floor.

Since there is quite a bit of condensation inside a greenhouse, the floor should be covered with screened creek gravel, wooden pallets, or any other material that won't turn to mud when wet. Also, as with any greenhouse, anything that can be done to avoid having standing water inside the building should be practiced.

The roof, which can be a wooden frame covered with glazing material, will be approximately perpendicular to the sun at winter solstice, and there may or may not be a glazed front wall, again depending on the terrain of the site. If the greenhouse is broad enough north to south that the sun will reach the lowest-placed plants and not be shaded by the south wall, then no front wall is required, and the only glazed exterior wall will be the roof. Since that roof is a flat, single plane, it can easily be glazed on both top and bottom, adding even more insulating dead-air between the two faces.

Benefits of In-Ground Design

Obviously, this design provides a significant amount of insulation from winter temperatures and if combined with passive solar heat storage, can provide warmth, even overnight, and even in very cold climates. Rolling an insulated blanket over the glazed roof overnight can extend this even further. Another advantage of the in-ground design is that the amount of glazing material is limited only to what is needed; that is, only the part where the sun comes in. This means not only that less glazing material is needed initially, but also that much less is required each time the glazing has to be replaced, and if you're using one of the four-year-warranty products, that will run into considerable savings over time. Cleaning time and shade-cloth costs are also reduced proportionally to the smaller glazed area.

Greenhouse-Specific Problems

While having a greenhouse makes it possible to grow just about any fruit or vegetable that might strike your fancy, know too that there are also some problems associated specifically with greenhouse-based propagation and cultivation.

Temperature Control

Temperatures inside a greenhouse can change rapidly, especially while on the way up. You may leave the greenhouse unattended for an hour or two when the sun may come out of the clouds, and in very short order a plant-perfect atmosphere may see its temperature rise enough to be fatal to the plants inside. To avoid this happening, automatic fans and/or roof vents can be installed and set to activate either when a particular temperature is reached or at the time of day when high temperatures can be expected to become a problem. Additionally, during the summer months, greenhouses are covered in commercial shade cloth, which comes in variations of from 40 percent to 70 percent shade, and in extreme climates, evaporative coolers are employed, although these can be expensive.

It is also worth noting that a larger greenhouse has a better ability to buffer hot and cold temperature swings due to the greater thermal mass; that is, they take longer to heat up and longer to cool down, which you may use to your advantage depending on the climate where the greenhouse is located.

Excess Humidity

When humidity inside the greenhouse gets too high, plants start to have trouble passing the oxygen and water they produce back into the atmosphere. At the same time, too-high humidity fosters the growth of fungus and diseases. Fans and venting will help this situation also, but the gardener also needs to avoid overwatering and allowing standing water to pool on the floor and on the tables inside the greenhouse.

Indoor Pests

Outdoors, an infestation of insect pests can be quite a problem, but at least some of the pests will move on to attack your neighbor's gardens. Since the greenhouse is a closed environment, any bad-news bugs you develop can only stay and reproduce, so your response has to be even swifter and more thorough than it would be were the problem outside. All the same anti-insect measures should be taken, and introducing natural insect enemies like ladybugs and praying mantises works even better, since they don't escape to other fields or farms either.

Poor Air Circulation

As discussed earlier, plants need good air circulation for healthy growth. Without it, stems become weak little noodles that can't remain upright on their own, humidity gets out of hand, and diseases thrive. Again, fans and ventilation are the answer, but it will also help if you'll leave enough space between plants for air to circulate freely.

Snow Loading

Snow Load is expressed in pounds per square foot. Specifically, it is the calculated weight, per square foot of snow. Calculated, because there is no specific weight of snow. Light, fluffly, new snow is, well, light and fluffy, but heavy slushy snow can be almost as dense as water, which weighs about 62 pounds per cubic foot. It is of the very greatest importance, if it snows where you live, that you remember that heavy snow can easily collapse your entire greenhouse in one big storm. You can find snow load information for your state on the web at *www.fs.fed.us/t-d/snow_load/states.htm* in pounds per square foot. It ranges from zero pounds per square foot in Florida to 300 pounds per square foot in Alaska. Before you spend the money on a kit or build a greenhouse yourself, make certain that it won't be lying flat on the ground after the first heavy snow by knowing what you can expect. Nearly all urban areas adopt the Uniform Building Code, or a similar modification of same, which will define the snow-load for your area and how to build to meet the challenge, but many rural areas have no building codes at all.

CHAPTER 20

Food Storage

You've planted, you've watered, you've weeded, and you've killed every bad-intentioned bug in your end of the county, or if not, you've certainly given it your best shot. Now you're starting to reap the benefits: You've got fresh food by the bucketful, but the job isn't over yet. Now it's time to take it to the bank—to put away the bounty you've created over these last few months, and enjoy a winter of plenty in which you and your family share a pantry full of the best foods you've ever had.

Saving Every Morsel

You've been living the good life since late spring, enjoying your fresh salad vegetables, your ripe berries, and your rich and delicious, home-grown fresh eggs. Plus, you've harvested enough to have a few things to sell at the farmers' market, but all that's only taken you through the summer. In order to achieve what you've set out to do, you need to be able to do more than just harvest and enjoy; you need to put away every bit of food you've grown so that nothing is wasted, and so that you have a stockpile of wholesome, organic goodies to eat and market all winter long until it's time to start picking next year's crop.

FACT

Honey may not keep forever, but it will keep close to forever. Edible honey has been found in Egyptian tombs that were 2,000 to 3,000 years old. Honey may crystallize or grow cloudy over time, but it remains safe for consumption.

Well, luckily for you, there are numerous ways for you to do this. To enhance the variety of your meals as well as to avoid putting all your eggs in one basket, so to speak, you really ought to try all of them. Some methods work better for some foods than for others, but this can often be simply a matter of taste.

One caution: storing every bit of uneaten food isn't really that difficult, but you need to be prepared to do it when the food becomes available, so read over this chapter to make absolutely certain that you have everything you need on hand to preserve your harvest the minute you need it. Preserving fresh food is much better than preserving food that's starting to get old even before it gets packed away in the cellar, freezer, or cupboard.

Frozen Storage

Freezing is one of the easiest ways to store food, and also one of the best in terms of retaining the original flavor, but unless you live at the North Pole, freezing costs money because you have to keep the freezer running 24/7 all year round. In order to freeze food, you'll need a freezer that's already been brought to the desired low temperature, and you'll need containers. Most any container will do, so long as it will keep the air out and the moisture in. Plastic containers work very well in part because they can expand as needed when their contents freeze, but metal or glass containers will work also if you'll take care to leave a little space inside to allow for the expansion of the contents. Plastic bags work nicely because they can be closed as tightly as possible to minimize the air in each package.

Vegetables

Garden and orchard produce is an excellent candidate for freezing, if the appropriate steps are taken, such as blanching. Fresh produce contains enzymes that work to destroy the flavors of your food over time, even while they're in storage. These enzymes can survive freezing, but they can't survive high heat, so you'll want to resort to blanching. In this process, the freshly-picked produce is quickly scalded with boiling water, or steamed, to kill as many of the enzymes as possible, then just as quickly cooled under cold water before being packed into the freezing containers and stored in the freezer. For the best results, freeze the produce as soon as possible after harvesting. Any vegetables that are to be cooked before eating will freeze well; those that are generally eaten raw, not so much.

Fruits

Most fruits freeze even better than vegetables because they don't need to be blanched. In fact, fruits frozen properly retain more of their flavor and nutrition than when using any other storage method. You can freeze fruit dry or in a sweet liquid. Freezing them dry is acceptable, but they will tend to retain more of their flavor, color, and texture in a light syrup. This does not have to be a sugar-syrup, which has little or no nutritional value. You can make a light syrup with 1 part mildly-flavored honey to 3 parts extremely hot water. Let the syrup cool before adding it to the fruit. You can also add pectin to the syrup, which will retard darkening of the fruit. Fruit should be thawed in its original container and served before it has fully thawed.

Milk

You can freeze milk whether whole, skimmed, pasteurized, or raw by pouring it into glass or plastic containers and allowing about two inches of space in the top for expansion. Whole milk can be kept in the freezer for four to five months, but cream shouldn't be kept for more than two or three months. When freezing cream, the butterfat tends to separate so you can't use it directly, such as on berries or in your coffee, and it may not whip well. Rather, beat it lightly before using and use it for cooking crème sauces, gravies, or custards and that sort of thing.

Eggs

Eggs will keep for up to six months in the freezer. Use only the eggs you have gathered that day. Eggs from yesterday or the day before should be eaten fresh and not stored. To freeze eggs, they will need to be shelled first and then you can freeze them whole, or freeze the whites and yolks separately. Whichever way you choose, you'll need to stabilize the yolks so that they don't become hard or thick after they're thawed. Do this by adding 1 teaspoon of salt, or of honey, for each twelve yolks and break and stir the yolks; or, if you're freezing the whole eggs, scramble them together with the salt or honey. Eggs should be thawed completely before using, and use them immediately after thawing.

Meat

Freezing is the safest and easiest way to store meat long-term. Having said that, you should not attempt to freeze processed or spiced meats, and cured or smoked meats should not be frozen for longer than two months, because they oxidize more rapidly than fresh-frozen meats. Seasonings limit the freezer life of meats, so if you want to freeze sausage, for example, freeze only the ground meat, and add the seasonings after you thaw the package out.

ALERT

When thawing frozen food, as soon as the food reaches 40°F, bacteria that may have been present before freezing starts to grow again, so avoid letting it get that warm before it is thawed. The three safe ways to thaw perishable food are: in the refrigerator, in cold water, or in a microwave.

Heavy plastic, aluminum foil, and freezer paper all work suitably to seal the moisture inside the packages. Freezer burn occurs when the meat is allowed to dry out, resulting in loss of taste and color, so it is of the utmost importance that the packages be wrapped air-tight to preserve freshness and avoid rancidity. Pork and cured meats should be wrapped in double-thickness.

Cold Storage

This is one of the oldest and easiest methods of storage, assuming you already have your storage place completed. Many vegetables and some fruits will keep very well for months in cold storage. The basic idea behind cold storage is to keep the foodstuffs you want to carry over the season in a cool, but not freezing, place that has enough moisture to keep the produce from shriveling. Traditionally, this was done in an outdoor root cellar, or if the cellar was under the farmhouse, it would have had a dirt floor that created a nice moist atmosphere, and an outlet to the outdoors to let enough cold in to keep the food cool, but not frozen.

These days, there aren't a lot of root cellars left, and basement floors tend to be paved, but if you don't have one of these storage rooms, you can improvise using containers, crates, or barrels in protected outdoor locations.

Leave Them in the Ground

The simplest way to put root crops into cold storage is to just leave them in the ground where they grew. Cover them with a mulch thick enough to keep the ground from freezing, and if there's any doubt, after the mulch has been applied, mark them so that you can find them later on in the dead of winter. Then dig them up and use them as needed.

A Straw-Bale Root Cellar

Many crops will keep well in proper cold storage, including apples, pears, grapes, squash, onions, cabbage, celery, garlic, potatoes, and even peppers and tomatoes. You can make a quick, easy, and affordable place to do your cold storage by building one from hay or straw bales. Simply place bales on the ground in a square that leaves a box inside where the produce will be kept and then cover the top with a second layer of bales, which will amount to both the ceiling, and the door of your storage space. You can place a brick or stick of wood under one or two of the top bales to provide ventilation; this should be removed when freezing temperatures prevail.

Some of your produce like onions, garlic, and winter squash will require curing, which is leaving them in the field to dry out for a couple of weeks after harvesting before you put them in storage.

ALERT

You shouldn't store apples and potatoes together. Apples produce ethylene gas as they ripen, which can cause the potatoes to sprout. As if that weren't enough reason, the potatoes will give the apples a musty flavor. You also shouldn't store onions and potatoes together because each produces gases that will cause the other to spoil.

You can also store produce in containers filled with slightly moist sand or dry newspapers to keep the individual fruits from touching one another. There are many different ways to keep fruits and vegetables in cold storage, so you will benefit by doing a little research to find out the optimum conditions for the foods you have the most of. A good general rule that applies to all of them is that you should only use your best samples for storing. Bruised or damaged fruit should be used fresh.

Canning

While canning is a bit labor intensive, it has some outstanding advantages. For example, once food has been canned, it has a long shelf life and can be kept about any place in the home, unlike freezing or cold storage, where you have a relatively small area to fill (that once filled can do no more); with canning, you can preserve foods until your home is bursting at the seams with stored food. You also don't need to make a large investment like buying a deep freezer; all that's required for canning is a pressure canner and as many canning jars as you need to do the job.

FACT

The first canned food was prepared by Nicolas Appert, a Paris chef, in response to a cash prize offered by the French military for a new method of preserving food. Appert spent fifteen years experimenting before perfecting his method of packing food in glass jars sealed with cork and sealing wax, and placing them in boiling water.

The basic concept behind canning is that you sterilize the food and the container with high heat and then pack the one inside the other. High-acid foods (pickles, tomatoes, fruits, etc.) need to be sterilized by boiling temperatures (212°F), but low-acid foods like meat, dairy, and vegetables can develop dangerous toxins if not processed at 240°F or higher, which makes the pressure canner necessary for these foods. Sealing the jars creates a vacuum that protects the color, flavor, and nutritional elements of the food inside and protects against rancidity from oxidation.

Can only the freshest foods in the best conditions, and sort out individual fruits so that each container has fruits of about the same size; this way the temperatures are more likely to remain even throughout each jar.

ESSENTIAL

When canning, if you live at a higher elevation (over 1,000 feet above sea level) you'll need to increase the water bath processing time in order to compensate for the lower temperature of boiling water at high altitudes, because the atmospheric pressure is lower the higher you go.

Before the food is even harvested, have the canning equipment clean and ready to use so as to get the canning done quickly when the produce is at its freshest state possible.

The National Center for Home Food Preservation has a website at *http://nchfp.uga.edu* that is a rich source of information on all types of food preservation, but especially canning, and there you can find detailed instructions on how to can just about any specific foods you might want to preserve.

Drying

Drying food is unquestionably the oldest method of food preservation, and one of the easiest. These days it is mostly done in a food dehydrator, a small low-priced electrical appliance that accomplishes the drying as quickly as possible. Foods that are commonly dried include fruits, fruit leathers, herbs, seeds, roots, and of course, meats.

The quicker the drying can be accomplished, the better quality the finished product will have in both taste and vitamin content. Drying can also be accomplished outdoors in a dry, sunny climate. You can also dry food directly on the racks of your kitchen oven.

A Quick, Cheap, Homemade Food Dehydrator

If you'd like to try out food drying a bit before you commit yourself to the purchase of a dehydrator, you can make a serviceable one for yourself without spending a lot of money.

To do this, you only need three common items: a window box-fan, four paper air-conditioner filters about the same size as the fan (20" × 20") and two bungee cords. If you buy the cheapest examples of these that you can find, you should be able to get the whole shebang for less than thirty bucks.

ESSENTIAL

When dehydrating food, faster is better, and a higher temperature means drying will take place faster. However, if the temperature is *too* high, the outside of the fruit or vegetable will dry out and harden faster than the inside, which may not get fully dehydrated and thus spoil in storage.

Putting your low-budget dehydrator into operation is the easiest part of the job, much easier even than slicing and preparing the food you want to dry. A very good food to start out with is marinated strips of flank steak. Simply spread out the steak strips on the air-conditioner filters, and stack the filters one on top of the other. Then fix the stack of beef-laden filters to the front (the windy side) of the box fan and turn it on. Just a few short hours later, you will have some of the tastiest beef jerky of your life.

Drying Fruits and Vegetables

Drying produce is much the same as drying jerky, only it usually doesn't take quite as long. The main caveat is that you need to be careful to slice all the pieces to a uniform thickness so they'll all dry in about the same time. As when freezing, vegetables should be blanched before drying (with some exceptions, such as mushrooms), but fruits need only to be washed, cored, peeled if you desire, and sliced, although you may want to blanch grapes and plums to crack the skins so that the pulp will dry faster.

Unlike the steak jerky, you'll want to rehydrate most vegetables and some of the fruits that you dry before you use them. To do this, pour a cup and a half of boiling water over each cup of dried food and let it stand until all the water has been absorbed back into the food. This will take a couple of hours for most vegetables, and perhaps overnight for most fruits.

Drying Herbs

This process is so simple that it doesn't require anything other than the herbs you're drying. Pick the herbs just before they blossom in order to get the leaves when they're fullest of their essential oils. Cut them in the morning as soon as the dew has dried, and try to use only clean plants so that you don't need to wash them, artificially adding to their moisture content. Letting the leaves remain on the stems, bring them indoors and hang them upside down in a warm, dry place with good air circulation and no direct light. This is the best method for drying sage, savory, oregano, basil, marjoram, mint, lemon balm, and horehound. When drying thyme, parsley, lemon verbena, rosemary, and chervil, remove the leaves from the stem and spread them in a single layer on a tray.

Herbs are at their peak flavor if they can be dried in three of four days, but that isn't always possible in many climates. If the herbs aren't perfectly dry in two weeks, put them in an oven at 100°F until they are.

Fermentation

Like drying, fermentation is one of the oldest and most natural forms of food preservation, so old that it predates humankind. The basic idea behind fermentation is that you allow food to decay in such a way that it makes a more desirable product. You're probably thinking that you've seen plenty of decayed food, and it didn't seem all that desirable. You'd be right, but just as with so many things, there's good decay and bad decay. Decay is caused by bacteria, so it's not surprising that good decay comes from what is considered to be good bacteria.

Perhaps you've never imagined that you have any relationship with bacteria, but if you've ever eaten any fermented foods, and you surely have, then you've relied on the work of certain bacteria. If you've prepared fermented food, then you've given these bacteria what they wanted, carbohydrates, and they've given you what you wanted, food-preserving acids.

In the fermentation process, the good microbes starve out the bad microbes, which cause the deterioration of food. Fermentation done the right way to the right foods can cause them to remain deliciously edible for years, but most people ferment foods more for the improvements they make to the foods than for the increased shelf-life. Bread is fermented for the tangy taste of sourdough, cocoa beans are fermented to improve the taste of chocolate, and yogurt and kefir are fermented to make them tasty and more easily digested.

In fact, fermentation is used in some of our favorite, most sophisticated tastes, such as prosciutto, blue cheese, wine, beer, pickled vegetables, and even butter.

By now, you may be growing tired of hearing how everything home-made is tastier and more nutritious than what you can buy in the store, but if you still need to be convinced, try making your own sauerkraut sometime. You may not even care for sauerkraut, but that's because all you've ever had is the dull factory version out of a can. Traditional European sauerkraut frequently has more than just cabbage in its ingredients, and in this regard is more like Kimchi, the Korean fermented cabbage dish, which also includes other vegetables. Traditional sauerkraut contains the basic ingredients of cabbage and sea salt, but may also include garlic, onion, peppers, and even apples.

Like many fermented foods, sauerkraut can be allowed to ferment for months in search of just the right flavor, but during the process of lactic acid fermentation, a wholly new food emerges that is higher in vitamins and beneficial bacteria, so much so that the increased shelf-life over fresh cabbage is all but forgotten.

It's a win-win situation.

Other Methods of Preserving Foods

Sometimes you may find that the best way to preserve particular foods can be to change them into other foods. Butter, for example, is easier to keep or freeze than cream, and cheese is easier to store than both of these. Pickling is a safe and tasty way to preserve many vegetables, and all you need is a large vessel and plenty of brine to do the job.

Smoking meat, while considerably more of an undertaking than making cheese or pickles, is a good and time-honored way to preserve meats and fish by converting them into new foods.

Be sure, though, that you thoroughly research smoking and curing before attempting them yourself, or better yet, watch and learn from an experienced hand. Meat products are extremely perishable, while nitrates and nitrites used in some curing operations can be toxic to humans in great enough amounts.

CHAPTER 21

Truck Farming— Cash from Your Crops

While some may say it is important to keep your hobbies separate from your employment, the ability to turn a profit while doing something you love tends to mean that you can continue doing what you love indefinitely—and how bad is that? For most farmers, being able to keep farming depends entirely on being able to make a profit from his efforts. Whether you can become a viable farmer doesn't depend so much on how large your farm is (large farmers go broke every day), but on how well you can manage the farm you have. You've already learned that you can produce a cornucopia of food on a very small plot of ground, so turning this surplus into cash is just a matter of managing the business end of your small farm. However, before you attempt to go about selling meat, milk, or even eggs, you should investigate the appropriate laws for such sales.

Imaginative Marketing

Farmers' markets can sometimes be discouraging. It's not enough for you to simply show up there with something to sell. In order to optimize your income, you need to do three things: first, you need to sell something people want to buy; second, you need to market it at a price customers can afford and are willing to pay; and third, you need to make what you're selling more desirable to the buyer than your competitors do. If you accomplish all of these things, then you can make some money. Do these things very well, and you can probably stay in business for a long, long while.

Learning What People Want to Buy

Years ago, *Saturday Night Live* ran a skit about a fellow who opened a new shop in a new mall. This shop only sold one thing: Scotch Tape. The results, of course, were hilariously dismal. That's not to suggest that people don't want to buy Scotch Tape; it's just that they want to buy a lot of things, preferably at the same location. When you're just starting out, this lack of diversity is one of the biggest mistakes you can make. Whether you're growing for a farmers' market, a community supported agriculture (CSA), a food co-op, or as a direct supplier to restaurants and local specialty shops, you need to have a broad selection of products to offer to new clients. The broader your selection, the more sales you will make. Period.

Later, you may learn that one or two of these items is proving to be either especially popular or especially profitable, and you may want to specialize a bit, but until you find out what your market wants, you need to offer as much diversity as you can muster.

Making What You're Selling More Desirable

Have you ever noticed how much effort the supermarkets go to in making their produce attractive? They put it under colored lights; they have automatic sprinklers to spray their veggies with a dewy sheen; they pack fruits in red mesh bags that give the impression of riper, more brightly colored fruit than the bag actually contains. If they go to that much trouble when their competitors may be on the other side of town, then imagine how much more critical it is for you to produce an attractive display when your competition is only a few steps away!

ESSENTIAL

LocalHarvest.org maintains an Internet forum with threads on CSA, farmers' markets, farms and farming, and livestock. If you want to learn from people who have been successful at backyard farming, you should join and participate in this and other similar forums. You'll not only find answers to your questions, you'll find customers for your products.

This sort of competition brings out the very best side of capitalism, because the solution to competition is to improve your offering. You should make your displays as attractive as possible. Don't sell everything you have, just sell the best, and use the rest at home. Put everything you bring to sell out in plain sight—a bulging bin of ripe plums is much more mouthwatering than two or three plums rolling around loose on a tabletop. All this is advertising, and advertising is what energizes commerce. Imagine if, instead of all the multimillion dollar advertising you see on television, you got a post card in your mailbox that said something like, "We make Ford cars. Please buy one." That might sell a few cars, but probably not too many. If you think people don't care about things like this, that they only want the lowest price, you're doing yourself and your produce a disservice.

Expanding Your Selection May Mean Educating Customers

If you've ever had any experience working in a grocery store, you may have been amazed at how little some people know about fresh produce. For example, there are a startling number of folks who don't have a clue what a common avocado is, but, rather remarkably, most of these folks are familiar with, and enjoy, guacamole. There's a lesson there: if you want to introduce people to anything new, give them a sample. In this case, a taste of guacamole on a cracker along with a recipe might create buyers where once there were none.

Offer What Others Don't

The story of free enterprise is offering what the competition doesn't. If your sales location, farmers' market, home store, or whatever is in a small rural setting, then coming up with new things to outdo the competition probably won't be that difficult. If it's in a bigger venue, then there are probably a lot of things you can learn from your fellow farmers. At any rate, if you add baked goods or homemade candies to your lineup, they're sure to be something that everyone else isn't selling. Another route to follow is, in addition to selling the most popular items, try to market less-common things that you personally enjoy. Say, for example, that in the course of your life's experience you once encountered the kiwano melon (also known as the horned melon), and were so smitten by its taste that you started growing your own kiwano melons. Now, anyone else less enthusiastic who happened to have a few melons for sale might set them aside and, if anyone asked what they were, they'd say, "Meh . . . they're kiwano melons . . . do you want one?" You, on the other hand, would have an impressive display of your best, plumpest melons, and when asked, you would reply, "Why, those are *kiwano melons*! They're the most delicious things I've ever tasted—sheer ambrosia! I grow as many as I can every summer. We practically live on the things. Here's a printout I made of all the best ways to prepare them after you've eaten all you want raw." Without question, you will sell more kiwano melons than the next guy. There is no substitute for enthusiasm, or for the knowledge that you acquire by being enthusiastic, or for offering something that your competitors don't offer.

Selling Veggies, Fruits, and Other Farm Products

If you have the attitude that you can't sell anything, your first step needs to be to search the Internet for the expression, "how to make money market-gardening." You will, of course, receive thousands of results, but of these, each one will come from someone in a situation not exactly like yours, but close enough to make their answer well worth considering. Mostly, these responses will come from forums that you should join and take part in. You'll get good ideas and good information as well as commiseration for what you're trying to do.

FACT

According to a report from the U.S. Department of Agriculture, sales of "local foods," whether they were sold through CSAs, farmers' markets, food co-ops, direct-farm sales, or through groceries or restaurants totaled $4.8 billion in 2008. This figure has doubled in the last two decades.

The second thing you need to do is to sit down and list the places where you can sell what you grow. This will include the farmers' market(s) of course, but if you have any exposure to a highway, you can set up a roadside stand on your property. An effective roadside stand will have large enough signage placed in such a way that potential customers see it before they're upon it, so that they have time to slow down, and there will also be some convenient places for them to park their cars while they browse through your merchandise.

Be sure to look into Community Supported Agriculture in your area, and advertise your farm on CSA websites and forums. CSA will get you customers who tell you what they want before you even grow it. There will be more on this later in the chapter.

ALERT

Before getting started in Community Supported Agriculture, especially before accepting any money, be absolutely certain that you can deliver what you promise. Although crop failures and natural disasters are part of the buyer's risk, no one likes to lose money, and you should do all you can to see that your client's interests are well protected.

Some of the best advice on how to sell your produce is to practice succession planting so that you have something to sell throughout the growing season and, if you have a greenhouse, even beyond the growing season.

Another good piece of advice is to give customers the best deal you can. In typical agriculture, the farmer gets 20 percent or even less of the eventual sale price. You, on the other hand, are getting 100 percent, so you have a little room to be generous. Having said that, you shouldn't be so noble that you cheapen the customer's perception of your wares. It's okay to price your produce competitively, but don't give it away. People still judge value by what something costs, whether this is an accurate measure or not.

Expand Your Repertoire

You've probably noticed that people will spend more money on things they enjoy than on things they need. If you think about it, you probably know a lot more people who own houses far exceeding what their minimum needs are. Not to mention, how many folks buy the bottom-of-the-line car when all those fancy options are available? People who buy the very minimum of what they need to get by probably don't care about fresh produce or quality food anyway—they're likely to be buying the very cheapest, sugar-laden, mass-produced food products that they can find, and you don't really want to try to compete in that market.

QUESTION

Do I need insurance to sell at a farmers' market?
The farmers' market probably doesn't make this a requirement, but if you have a space or stall, you might be prudent to carry some sort of "slip and fall" insurance. If you have a farm policy, then this might be covered already, but you should talk to your agent.

On the other hand, consider this: Bedding plants typically sell for around $1.50 for a pack of four or six. You can sell bedding plants and make a nice markup over what a few seeds and some potting soils cost you, but suppose you put those seeds and soil into a hanging basket? Then you have to pay for the basket, of course, but your other costs remain about the same, and it isn't uncommon to see hanging planters selling for ten to twenty dollars each. So don't think the only thing you can sell from your garden has to be edible. Fresh flowers are very popular, and they frequently tend to sell to folks who have more to spend than the least they can get by on.

As long as you're considering flowers, don't forget the other ornamentals: pumpkins, Indian corn, and gourds are quite popular, and bring a nice price in the late fall when you may be putting much of the garden to bed for the winter. In fact, there was a pumpkin shortage in the autumn of 2012 that was considered such a catastrophe for jack-o-lantern season that it was the subject of national news reports.

Cultivating Customers for CSA

CSA, or Community Supported Agriculture (CSA), is the small farmer's dream come true, because once you have built a clientele of reliable customers, you remove several of the great unknowns from your farming operation. These unknowns include not knowing who will buy your produce, when they will buy it, and how much you'll be paid. In this regard, CSA can give you the kind of security you get from employment without many of the frustrations.

Additionally, following the CSA model, you can concentrate your sales and promotion efforts during the winter, leaving you free to do what you do best: plant, cultivate, and harvest during the growing season. Equally important, since CSA sales are made through membership dues, or "subscriptions," the farmer gets income early in the year—many CSA farmers charge the full year's cost up front, but you can also break this into installments. Either way gives you money during times when traditional farming has little to offer.

ESSENTIAL

Farming can offer certain tax benefits that will help your backyard farm become more financially solvent. Get a copy of the Internal Revenue Service's Farmers Tax Guide, (IRS Publication 225) which will help you learn everything from what kinds of records to keep to how to claim travel expenses (available online at *www.irs.gov/publications/ p225*).

You can also make arrangements with other farmers to include some of their produce in the boxes you give to your customers and some of yours in theirs, so as to always have enough to keep the customers happy and well-supplied. As with any business arrangement, it's important that you make it clear to your customers what they can expect and what they can't.

Food Co-Ops

See if there is a food co-op operating near enough to your farm to make selling produce through or to them economically feasible. Food co-ops are basically distribution outlets designed to offer consumers an alternative to conventional grocery stores. Food co-ops typically trade in locally grown organic foods, which would make them ideal customers for small producers like you.

The National Cooperative Grocers Association (NCGA) is composed of 146 member food cooperatives. They have a website that you should investigate at *www.ncga.coop*.

Food co-ops typically put strict requirements on the foods that they will buy, but you'll probably meet most of these requirements anyway, as they tend to insist that foods they buy not contain things like artificial colors, flavors, preservatives, additives, high-fructose corn syrups, hormones, antibiotics, carcinogens, or hydrogenated oils. In other words, they want to buy exactly what you have to sell, so don't ignore this resource.

Small Specialty Stores and Restaurants

You can find a list of all the organic food stores in the United States at *www.organicstorelocator.com*, and you should look into these as potential customers. This is a particularly helpful link because they also list vegan and kosher food stores. In addition to these are ethnic specialty shops catering to clients of other ethnic and cultural backgrounds, as well as the smaller regular grocery stores in your area. Like most small businesses, these folks are always looking for reliable and reasonable suppliers of the foods that they market, so some of them are likely to be very pleased to see you. If you're going to be in the business of producing food, it is a very sensible idea to get to know as many people as possible whose business it is to market the sort of foods you produce. It just makes good sense.

FACT

Laws regarding the sale of fresh eggs differ from state to state, and you should contact your local extension office to learn about the rules in your state. However, most state laws allow ample room for small farmers selling eggs raised on the farm directly to the public.

If you live close enough to a city with gourmet restaurants, this too is an excellent market for fresh and perhaps unusual foods. The gourmet cook tries to set her establishment apart from everyday cafes and restaurants by offering fresher, higher-quality produce, and if you'll try to imagine yourself in her place, it could be something of a challenge to find reliable suppliers of the sort of high-quality fruits and vegetables that she demands. Ask if there are any items that she just can't seem to find a supplier for; you may discover a niche market for yourself. Such places also like to offer a varied and eclectic menu to their clientele, so if you happen to show up with an unusual item that they haven't found for sale locally, it can be pretty easy to get your foot in the door with the chef.

Becoming Your Own Salesperson

Nobody wants to be a salesperson. That's because to most folks, the term conjures up pushy used-car salesmen or door-to-door peddlers trying to intimidate people into buying junk that they don't really want. Admit it: You've had those feelings, too.

However, the fact is that we're all salespeople. Even if you have a low-paying, get-no-respect, dead-end job, you had to sell yourself to get the job, and to a degree you have to sell yourself every day in order to keep it. Remember also that, in most companies, the sales staff may not be the most educated or the highest-ranking employees, but they probably make as much money as anyone there.

FACT

Even though most consumers say that they agree with the government's *Dietary Guidelines for Americans (2010)*, which call for eating a more plant-based diet, only one-third of those surveyed believed themselves to be knowledgeable about how to do that. Many consumers would benefit from information about how to prepare and serve fruits and vegetables.

Successful salespeople aren't men or women who talk other people into buying things they don't want or don't need, because successful salespeople want to do business with the same people over and over for as long as possible. Successful salespeople are the folks who help you to get what you want, and who doesn't want to be helpful?

Successful salespeople also tend to get what they want. In your case, what you want is a steady and profitable income, and what your customers want just happens to be the fruits, vegetables, eggs, flowers, and all the other things you produce. You've probably already noticed that hardly anyone ever knocks on your door and asks you if you have any fresh food to sell. That means that in order to have the things you want, you are going to need to talk to a few people and guide them in the process of getting the things that they want. You may not find this as enjoyable as tending a garden or nurturing a flock of hens, but most people would agree that just talking to people every so often is generally much easier and more enjoyable than spending eight hours a day, five days a week working for someone else. In fact, people can actually be quite interesting and fun, and you can learn quite a lot from them.

So if all you have to do is put on clean clothes and ask the local small grocer, the food co-op representative, or someone interested in subscribing to your CSA if there's anything that you can do to help them, and in return, many of them agree to give you money that will keep your farm and your dreams alive—well, most people would consider that a small price to pay.

So . . . Do You Think You're a Farmer Yet?

When the news anchor on TV tells you what the unemployment rate is and how much worse it would be if they counted all the people that have stopped looking for work, do you ever wonder how that works? Do you ever ask yourself how people suddenly decide one day that looking for work is just too much trouble with too little hope of success, so they just quit? Don't you wonder, if they have an option of not having a job, why they ever looked for one in the first place? Well, you're not alone. There are a number of people for whom the idea of giving up on trying to make a living just isn't an option, and chances are, you're one of them.

The mere fact that you've read this book suggests that the idea of becoming a backyard farmer and working for yourself—striving toward goals that you set for yourself and not what some employer demands of you—appeals to you.

You need to know that you can do that; that you can achieve that dream. The idea of being the master of your own destiny, of spending your time in nature dealing with the seasons, and living things, and the Earth itself—you can have that. You can have that if you decide you'd rather risk the whims of nature than the whims of your boss.

You can have that if you decide that this is what you're going to do, and if every morning when you wake up, you work on making that goal a reality. You can have that if you never let yourself become convinced that you can't have it.

All you need to do is to keep that single goal in mind as you work to make gains every day, so that first you're supplementing your diet with food you've grown yourself, and then you're supplementing your income with money you've made for yourself without the help of someone else's company. Then one day, you reach the point where you ask yourself why you need food that you can't recognize as food, and why you need to spend time working a job that doesn't give you the satisfaction you can get by working for yourself.

You can have that.

Untold millions have had those things since humans planted the first seeds and domesticated the first animals, and you can have that, too.

If only you don't give up and stop trying.

Good luck to you, Backyard Farmer, and good farming!

APPENDIX A

Glossary

Arable

Tillable and capable of producing crops

Air drainage

The downhill flow of cold air relative to warmer air, which rises

Apiary

A place where a colony or colonies of bees are kept

Berry

The botanical term for a simple fruit with embedded seeds, such as the grape, blueberry, strawberry, and tomato, or, in grains, a single kernel

Blanching

To scald briefly, then drain

Broody

Said of a hen during a stage when she is inclined to sit on eggs

Capon

A cockerel castrated to improve the flesh for use as food

Castration

The removal of the testes

Chicken tractor

A movable pen open to the turf; designed for pasture rotation

Clay

A heavy soil that is plastic when wet, but which dries to a solid

Cold frame

Also hotbed. A small glazed enclosure in which to acclimate plants to the outdoors

Come-along
A hand-operated winch

Compost
Fertilizer made from decayed organic substances

Cria
A baby vicuna, llama, guanaco, or alpaca

CSA
Community Supported Agriculture; a system in which people purchase a share or subscribe to a farm program to receive food and other farm products from the farmer

Cultivar
A variety of plant that originated under cultivation

Dry-laid
A stone fence or wall built without mortar

Espalier
Training the trunk or branches of a plant, typically a fruit tree, to grow in a single plane

Free-range
Permitting livestock or poultry to forage freely as opposed to being confined in a feedlot, cage, or house

Friable
Said of rock or soil that is loose and easily crumbled

Front loader
A hydraulically activated scoop or forks mounted on a tractor or other heavy equipment

Frost pocket

A low-lying area where cold air congregates, and where frost is most likely to form

Frost line

The lower limit of where the ground will freeze

Green manure

Growing plants plowed under to provide decaying material to fertilize the soil

Green sawdust

New, unrotted sawdust that will draw the nitrogen from soil to which it is added

GVWR

Gross Vehicle Weight Rating—the maximum operating weight of a vehicle and its load, but excluding any trailer

GCWR

Gross Combined Weight Rating—the maximum operating weight of a vehicle and its load including any trailers and cargo

Hair sheep

As opposed to a wool sheep; any variety of sheep growing hair instead of wool

Hardpan

A subterranean layer of hard, impenetrable soil or clay found anywhere from a few inches to several feet beneath the surface

Hardwood

One of many broad-leaved dicotyledonous trees, including most nut trees. As opposed to a softwood or conifer

Humus
The dark organic material in soil produced by the decomposition of vegetable or animal matter, which is essential to the fertility of the Earth

Implements
The heavy tools carried, and perhaps powered, by a farm tractor, such as mowers, plows, combines, etc.

Insecticidal soap
Any of the potassium fatty-acid soaps used to control plant pests

Keet
A young or hatchling guinea fowl

Laying hedge
The traditional practice of making a hedge more dense and impenetrable by training it to grow horizontally

Legume
A family of plants that fixes nitrogen in the soil; that is, when the plant dies, its nitrogen is released back into the soil. Legumes include beans, peas, locust, clover, and peanuts

Loam
A rich, friable soil containing a relatively equal mixture of sand and silt and a somewhat smaller proportion of clay

Locavore
A person who attempts to eat only foods produced in the local area

Manure tea
Manure steeped in water to be used as a plant fertilizer

Molting
The process of shedding feathers, skin, or fur that will be replaced by new growth

Mulch

A soil covering placed around plants to retard evaporation and weed growth, frequently made from compost, straw, grass clippings, newspapers, or plastic

N-P-K

Nitrogen, phosphorus and potassium (from the periodic table) the three most important elements to plant growth

Organic

Derived from living tissue; known in agricultural and horticultural circles to be the opposite of "chemical"

Polled

Born without horns naturally

PTO

Power Take-Off, a rotating shaft in the rear of a tractor that transfers power from the tractor's engine to rotating implements such as mowers, augurs, etc.

R value

A measure of the resistance of insulation to heat flow

Skid-steer loader

A piece of heavy equipment distinguished by braking one side or the other to steer the machine rather than by turning the steering wheel in the desired direction

Solstice

The two times of the year when the sun reaches its northernmost and southernmost positions in the sky

Soluble grit

Or flint grit; the type of grit that chickens ingest to aid in their digestion, as opposed to oyster-shell grit, which they ingest to aid in making eggshells

Southern exposure

Said of a location with an open view to the southern sky, ergo full sun

Snow load

The calculated weight of snow expected in a given area, for purposes of roof design.

Truck farm

Or market farm; a small farm producing fruit, vegetables, and other food-stuffs, plus flowers for sale directly to the public

Wattle

A fence woven from posts and sticks or bark; also the fleshy appendage hanging down from the throat of chickens and turkeys

Wether

A castrated ram

Withers

The highest part of the back at the base of the neck of a horse, cow, sheep, or other livestock

Recommended Websites

Due to the breadth of the topic of backyard farming, you may want to continue learning about specific subjects. The list below is a collection of several of these websites that should prove the most useful in this quest.

Homestead.org—The Homesteader's Free Library

Hundreds of topics on raising small livestock, gardening, and rural living in general. Maintains an active discussion forum for members.

www.homestead.org

LocalHarvest.com—Real food, Real farmers, Real community

Information on family farms and Community Supported Agriculture. Maintains an active discussion forum for members.

www.localharvest.org

The Urban Homestead—A City Farm Since 1985

The owners produce over 6,000 pounds of organic food annually on one-tenth of an acre on a city lot.

Urbanhomestead.org

The International Miniature Cattle Breeders Society and Registry

The definitive source for information on all breeds of miniature cattle.

Minicattle.com

The Alpaca Owners and Breeders Association

Everything you need to know about alpacas, fiber, and fashion.

Alpacainfo.com

Sheep 201

A beginner's guide to raising sheep.

Sheep101.info

Backyard Chickens

The basics of raising chickens

Backyardchickens.com

Bee Culture Magazine

The definitive source on American beekeeping

www.beeculture.com

The National Center for Home Food Preservation

Information on preserving food at home. Funded by the U.S. Department of Agriculture

Nchfp.uga.edu

The National Cooperative Grocers Association
News and information on food co-ops across America
www.ncga.coop

Organic Gardening
The website of the popular magazine covers all aspects of organic gardening. Free newsletter.
Organicgardening.com

TractorHouse.com
New and used farm equipment for sale. A good place to learn typical prices.
www.tractorhouse.com/default.aspx

Index

Y

Z